Two Treatises of Government. In the Former the False Principles and Foundation of Sir Robert Filmer and his Followers are Detected and Overthrown. The Latter is an Essay Concerning the True Original Extent and end of Civil Government. By John Locke

T W O
T R E A T I S E S
O F
GOVERNMENT.

IN THE FORMER

The Falſe Principles and Foundation of Sir
ROBERT FILMER and his Followers
are detected and overthrown.

THE LATTER IS

AN ESSAY

CONCERNING

The TRUE ORIGINAL EXTENT and END
of CIVIL GOVERNMENT.

By JOHN LOCKE.

Salus populi ſuprema lex eſto.

DUBLIN:

Printed by and for SARAH COTTER; and J SHEPPARD,
Bookſellers, in *Skinner-Row,*
MDCCLXVI.

The prefent Edition of this Book has not only been collated with the firft three Editions, which were publifhed during the Author's Life, but alfo has the Advantage of his laft Corrections and Improvements, from a Copy delivered by him to Mr. PETER COSTE, communicated to the Editor, and now lodged in Chrift College, Cambridge.

PREFACE.

READER,

THOU haſt here the beginning and end of a diſcourſe concerning government, what fate has otherwiſe diſpoſed of the papers that ſhould have filled up the middle, and were more than all the reſt, it is not worth while to tell thee. Theſe, which remain, I hope are ſufficient to eſtabliſh the throne of our great reſtorer, our preſent King William; to make good his title, in the conſent of the people, which being the only one of all lawful governments, he has more fully and clearly, than any prince in Chriſtendom; and to juſtify to the world the people of England, whoſe love of their juſt and natural rights, with their reſolution to preſerve them, ſaved the nation when it was on the very brink of ſlavery and ruin If theſe papers have that evidence, I flatter myſelf is to be found in them, there will be no great miſs of thoſe which are loſt, and my reader may be ſatisfied without them : for I imagine, I ſhall have neither the time, nor inclination to repeat my pains, and fill up the wanting part of my anſwer, by tracing Sir Robert again, through all the windings and obſcurities, which are to be met with in the ſeveral branches of his wonderful ſyſtem. The king, and body of the nation, have ſince ſo thoroughly confuted his Hy-

pothefis

pothefis, that I fuppofe no body hereafter will have either the confidence to appear againft our common fafety, and be again an advocate for flavery; or the weaknefs to be deceived with contradictions dreffed up in a popular ftile, and well-turned periods · for if any one will be at the pains, himfelf, in thofe parts, which are here untouched, to ftrip Sir Robert's difcourfes of the flourifh of doubtful expreffions, and endeavour to reduce his words to direct, pofitive, intelligible propofitions, and then compare them one with another, he will quickly be fatisfied, there was never fo much glib nonfenfe put together in well-founding Englifh. If he think it not worth while to examine his works all thro', let him make an experiment in that part, where he treats of ufurpation, and let him try, whether he can, with all his fkill, make Sir Robert intelligible, and confiftent with himfelf, or common fenfe I fhould not fpeak fo plainly of a gentleman, long fince paft anfwering, had not the pulpit, of late years, publicly owned his doctrine, and made it the current divinity of the times It is neceffary thofe men, who taking on them to be teachers, have fo dangeroufly mifled others, fhould be openly fhewed of what authority this their Patriarch is, whom they have fo blindly followed, that fo they may either retract what upon fo ill grounds they have vented, and cannot be maintained; or elfe juftify thofe principles which they preached up for gofpel, though they had no better an author than an Englifh courtier. for I fhould not have writ againft Sir Robert, or taken the pains to fhew his miftakes, inconfiftencies, and want of (what he fo much boafts of, and pretends wholly to build on) fcripture-proofs, were there not men amongft us, who, by crying up his books, and

espoufing

efpoufing his doctrine, fave me from the reproach of writing againft a dead adverfary. They have been fo zealous in this point, that, if I have done him any wrong, I cannot hope they fhould fpare me I wifh, where they have done the truth and the public wrong, they would be as ready to redrefs it, and allow its' juft weight to this reflection, viz that there cannot be done a greater mifchief to prince and people, than the propagating wrong notions concerning government, that fo at laft all times might not have reafon to complain of the Drum Ecclefiaftic If any one, concerned really for truth, undertake the confutation of my Hypothefis, I promife him either to recant my miftake, upon fair conviction, or to anfwer his difficulties But he muft remember two things.

First, That cavilling here and there, at fome expreffion, or little incidents of my difcourfe, is not an anfwer to my book

Secondly, That I fhall not take railing for arguments, nor think either of thefe worth my notice, though I fhall always look on myfelf as bound to give fatisfaction to any one, who fhall appear to be confcientioufly fcrupulous in the point, and fhall fhew any juft grounds for his fcruples

I have nothing more, but to advertife the reader, that Obfervations ftands for Obfervations on Hobbs, Milton, &c and that a bare quotation of pages always means pages of his Patriarcha, Edition 1680.

CONTENTS.

CONTENTS OF BOOK I.

CONTENTS OF BOOK II

OF

OF

GOVERNMENT.

BOOK I.

CHAP. I.

§ 1 SLAVERY is so vile and miserable an estate of man, and so directly opposite to the generous temper and courage of our nation; that it is hardly to be conceived, that an *Englishman*, much less a gentleman, should plead for it. And truly I should have taken Sir *Robert Filmer's Patriarcha*, as any other treatise, which would persuade all men, that they are slaves, and ought to be so, for such another exercise of wit, as was his who writ the encomium of *Nero*, rather than for a serious discourse meant in earnest, had not the gravity of the title and epistle, the picture in the front of the book, and the applause that followed it, required me to believe, that the author and publisher were both in earnest. I therefore took it into my hands, with all the expectation, and read it through with all the attention due to a treatise that made such a noise at its coming abroad, and cannot but confess my self mightily surprised, that in a book, which was to provide chains for all mankind, I should find nothing but a rope of sand, useful perhaps to such, whose skill and business it is to raise a dust, and would blind the people, the better to mislead them, but

B 17

in truth is not of any force to draw those into bondage, who have their eyes open, and so much sense about them, as to consider, that chains are but an ill wearing, how much care soever hath been taken to file and polish them.

§ 2 If any one think I take too much liberty in speaking so freely of a man, who is the great champion of absolute power, and the idol of those who worship it, I beseech him to make this small allowance for once, to one, who, even after the reading of Sir *Robert*'s book, cannot but think himself, as the laws allow him, a freeman and I know no fault it is to do so, unless any one better skilled in the fate of it, than I, should have it revealed to him, that this treatise, which has lain dormant so long, was, when it appeared in the world, to carry, by strength of its arguments, all liberty out of it; and that from thenceforth our author's short model was to be the pattern in the mount, and the perfect standard of politics for the future His system lies in a little compass, it is no more but this,

That all government is absolute monarchy.
And the ground he builds on, is this,
That no man is born free.

§ 3 In this last age a generation of men has sprung up amongst us, that would flatter princes with an opinion, that they have a divine right to absolute power, let the laws by which they are constituted, and are to govern, and the conditions under which they enter upon their authority, be what they will, and their engagements to observe them never so well ratified by solemn oaths and promises To make way for this doctrine, they have denied mankind a right to natural freedom, whereby they have not only, as much as in them lies, exposed all subjects to the utmost misery

misery of tyranny and oppression, but have also unsettled the titles, and shaken the thrones of princes (for they too, by these mens system, except only one, are all born slaves, and by divine right are subjects to *Adam*'s right heir,) as if they had designed to make war upon all government, and subvert the very foundations of human society, to serve their present turn.

§ 4. However we must believe them upon their own bare words, when they tell us, we are all born slaves, and we must continue so, there is no remedy for it, life and thraldom we enter'd into together, and can never be quit of the one, till we part with the other. Scripture or reason I am sure do not any where say so, notwithstanding the noise of divine right, as if divine authority hath subjected us to the unlimited will of another. An admirable state of mankind, and that which they have not had wit enough to find out till this latter age. For, however Sir *Robert Filmer* seems to condemn the novelty of the contrary opinion, *Patr.* p 3. yet I believe it will be hard for him to find any other age, or country of the world, but this, which has asserted monarchy to be *jure divino.* And he confesses, *Patr.* p 4. That *Heyward, Blackwood, Barclay, and others, that have bravely vindicated the right of kings in most points,* never thought of this, *but with one consent admitted the natural liberty and equality of mankind.*

§ 5 By whom this doctrine came at first to be broached, and brought in fashion amongst us, and what sad effects it gave rise to, I leave to historians to relate, or to the memory of those, who were contemporaries with *Sibthorp* and *Manwering,* to recollect. My business at present is only to consider what Sir *Robert Filmer,* who is

B 2   allowed

allowed to have carried this argument farthest,
and is supposed to have brought it to perfection,
has said in it; for from him every one, who
would be as fashionable as *French* was at court,
has learned, and runs away with this short system
of politics, viz. *Men are not born free, and there-*
fore could never have the liberty to choose either go-
vernors, or forms of government Princes have
their power absolute, and by divine right; for
slaves could never have a right to compact or
consent *Adam* was an absolute monarch, and so
are all princes ever since.

CHAP II.

Of Paternal and Regal Power

§ 6. SIR *Robert Filmer's* great position is,
that *men are not naturally free* This is
the foundation on which his absolute monarchy
stands, and from which it erects itself to an height,
that its power is above every power, *caput inter*
nubila, so high above all earthly and human things,
that thought can scarce reach it; that promises
and oaths, which tye the infinite Deity, cannot
confine it But if this foundation fails, all his
fabric falls with it, and governments must be left
again to the old way of being made by contrivance, and the consent of men ('Ανθρωπινη κτίσις)
making use of their reason to unite together into
society To prove this grand position of his, he
tells us, p 12 *Men are born in subjection to their*
parents, and therefore cannot be free. And this
authority of parents, he calls *royal authority,* p
12, 14. *Fatherly authority, right of fatherhood,*
p. 12, 20. One would have thought he would,

in

in the beginning of such a work as this, on which was to depend the authority of princes, and the obedience of subjects, have told us exprefly, what that fatherly authority is, have defined it, though not limited it, because in some other treatises of his he tells us, it is unlimited, and * unlimitable ; he should at least have given us such an account of it, that we might have had an entire notion of this *fatherhood*, or *fatherly authority*, whenever it came in our way in his writings this I expected to have found in the first chapter of his *Patriarcha* But instead thereof, having, 1 *en paffant*, made his obeysance to the *arcana imperii*, p 5 2. made his compliment to the *rights and liberties of this, or any other nation*, p. 6. which he is going presently to null and destroy; and 3. made his leg to those learned men, who did not see so far into the matter as himself, p 7 he comes to fall on *Bellarmine*, p 8. and, by a victory over him, establishes his *fatherly authority* beyond any question. *Bellarmine* being routed by his own confession, p. 11 the day is clear got, and there is no more need of any forces: for having done that, I observe not that he states the question, or rallies up any arguments to make good his opinion, but rather tells us the story, as he thinks fit, of this strange kind of domineering phantom, called the *fatherhood*, which whoever could catch, presently got

B 3 empire,

---

* In grants and gifts that have their original from God or nature, as the power of the father hath, no inferior power of man can limit, nor make any law of prescription against them *Observations*, 158

The scripture teaches, that supreme power was originally the father, without any limitation *Observations*, 245.

empire, and unlimited absolute power   He affures us how this *fatherhood* began in *Adam*, continued its courfe, and kept the world in order all the time of the *patriarchs* till the flood, got out of the ark with *Noah* and his fons, made and fupported all the kings of the earth till the captivity of the *Ifraelites* in *Egypt*, and then the poor *fatherhood* was under hatches, till *God, by giving the* Ifraelites *kings, re-eftablifhed the ancient and prime right of the lineal fucceffion in paternal government*   This is his bufinefs from p 12 to 19.   And then obviating an objection, and clearing a difficulty or two with one half reafon, p. 23 *to confirm the natural right of regal power,* he ends the firft chapter   I hope it is no injury to call an half quotation an half reafon, for God fays, *Honour thy father and mother* , but our author contents himfelf with half, leaves out *thy mother* quite, as little ferviceable to his purpofe. But of that more in another place

§ 7 I do not think our author fo little fkilled in the way of writing difcourfes of this nature, nor fo carelefs of the point in hand, that he by over-fight commits the fault, that he himfelf, in his *Anarchy of a mixed Monarchy*, p 239, objects to Mr Hunton in thefe words : *Where firft I charge the author, that he hath not given us any definition, or defcription of monarchy in general ; for by the rules of method he fhould have firft defined*   And by the like rule of method Sir *Robert* fhould have told us, what his *fatherhood* or *fatherly authority* is, before he had told us, in whom it was to be found, and talked fo much of it   But perhaps Sir *Robert* found, that this *fatherly authority*, this power of fathers, and of kings, for he makes them both the fame, p. 24 would make a very odd and frightful figure, and very
dif-

difagreeing, with what either children imagine of their parents, or fubjects of their kings, if he fhou'd have given us the whole draught together in that gigantic form, he had painted it in his own fancy, and therefore, like a wary phyfician, when he would have his patient fwallow fome harfh or *corrofive liquor*, he mingles it with a large quantity of that which may dilute it, that the fcattered parts may go down with lefs feeling, and caufe lefs averfion

§ 8 Let us then endeavour to find what account he gives us of this *fatherly authority*, as it lies fcattered in the feveral parts of his writing And firft, as it was vefted in *him*, he fays, *Not only* Adam, *but the fucceeding patriar be, bad, by right of fatherhood, royal authority over their children,* p 12 *This lordfhip which* Adam *by command had over the whole world, and by right defcending from him the patriarchs did enjoy, was as large and ample as the abfolute dominion of any monarch, which hath been fince the creation,* p 13 *Dominion of life and death, making war, and concluding peace,* p 13 Adam *and the patriarchs had abfolute power of life and death,* p 35 *Kings, in the right of parents, fucceed to the exercife of fupreme jurifdiction,* p 19 *As kingly power is by the law of God, fo it hath no inferior law to limit it;* Adam *was lord of all,* p 40 .*The father of a family governs by no other law, than by his own will,* p 78 *The fuperiority of princes is above laws,* p 79 *The unlimited jurifdiction of kings, is fo amply defcribed by* Samuel, p 80 *Kings are above the laws,* p 93 And to this purpofe fee a great deal more which our author delivers in *Bodin's* words. *It is certain, that all laws, privileges, and grants of princes, have no force, but during their life, if they be not ratified by the exprefs*

B 4 *confent,*

consent, or by sufferance of the prince following, especially privileges, Observations, p 279. The reason why laws have been also made by kings, was this, when kings were either busied with wars, or distracted with public cares, so that every private man could not have access to their persons, to learn their wills and pleasure, then were laws of necessity invented, that so every particular subject might find his prince's pleasure decyphered unto him in the tables of his laws, p 92 In a monarchy, the king must by necessity be above the laws, p 100 A perfect kingdom is that, wherein the king rules all things according to his own will, p 100. Neither common nor statute laws are, or can be, any diminution of that general power, which kings have over their people by right of fatherhood, p 115 Adam was the father, king, and lord over his family, a son, a subject, and a servant or slave, were one and the same thing at first The father had power to dispose or sell his children or servants; whence we find, that the first reckoning up of goods in scripture, the man-servant and the maid-servant, are numbered among the possessions and substance of the owner, as other goods were, Observations, Pref God also hath given to the father a right or liberty, to alien his power over his children to any other, whence we find the sale and gift of children to have much been in use in the beginning of the world, when men had their servants for a possession and an inheritance, as well as other goods, whereupon we find the power of castrating and making eunuchs much in use in old times, Observations, p. 155. Law is nothing else but the will of him that hath the power of the supreme father, Observations, p. 223 It was God's ordinance that the supremacy should be unlimited in Adam, and as large as all the acts of his will, and as in him so in all

others

others that have supreme power, Obfervations, p. 245.

§ 9 I have been fain to trouble my reader with thefe feveral quotations in our author's own words, that in them might be feen his own defcription of his *fatherly authority*, as it lies fcattered up and down in his writings, which he fuppofes was firft vefted in *Adam*, and by right belongs to all princes ever fince. This *fatherly authority* then, or *right of fatherhood*, in our author's fenfe, is a divine unalterable right of fovereignty, whereby a father or a prince hath an abfolute, arbitrary, unlimited, and unlimitable power over the lives, liberties, and eftates of his children and fubjects; fo that he may take or alienate their eftates, fell, caftrate, or ufe their perfons as he pleafes, they being all his flaves, and he lord or proprietor of every thing, and his unbounded will their law.

§ 10. Our author having placed fuch a mighty power in *Adam*, and upon that fuppofition founded all government, and all power of princes, it is reafonable to expect, that he fhould have proved this with arguments clear and evident, fuitable to the weightinefs of the caufe, that fince men had nothing elfe left them, they might in flavery have fuch undeniable proofs of its neceffity, that their confciences might be convinced, and oblige them to fubmit peaceably to that abfolute dominion, which their governors had a right to exercife over them Without this, what good could our author do, or pretend to do, by erecting fuch an unlimited power, but flatter the natural vanity and ambition of men, too apt of itfelf to grow and encreafe with the poffeffion of any power? and by perfuading thofe, who, by the confent of their fellow-men, are advanced

great, but limited degrees of it, that by that
part which is given them, they have a right to
all, that was not fo, and therefore may do what
they pleafe, becaufe they have authority to do
more than others, and fo tempt them to do what
is neither for their own, nor the good of thofe
under their care, whereby great mifchiefs cannot but follow.

§ 11 The fovereignty of *Adam*, being that on
which, as a fure bafis, our author builds his
mighty abfolute monarchy, I expected, that in
his *Patriarcha*, this his main fuppofition would
have been proved, and eftablifhed with all that
evidence of arguments, that fuch a fundamental
tenet required, and that this, on which the great
ftrefs of the bufinefs depends, would have been
made out with reafons fufficient to juftify the
confidence with which it was affumed   But in
all that treatife, I could find very little tending
that way, the thing is there fo taken for granted,
without proof, that I could fcarce believe myfelf,
when, upon attentive reading that treatife, I
found there fo mighty a ftructure raifed upon the
bare fuppofition of this foundation   for it is fcarce
credible, that in a difcourfe, where he pretends
to confute the *erroneous principle* of man's *natural
freedom*, he fhould do it by a bare fuppofition of
Adam's authority, without offering any proof for
that authority.   Indeed he confidently fays, that
Adam had royal authority, p 12, and 13   *Abfolute lordfhip and dominion of life and death*, p. 13.
An univerfal monarchy, p 33   *Abfolute power of
life and death*, p 35   He is very frequent in
fuch affertions, but, what is ftrange, in all his
whole *Patriarcha* I find not one pretence of a
reafon to eftablifh this his great foundation of
government, not any thing that looks like an
argument,

argument, but these words   *To confirm this na-*
tural right of regal power, we find in the Decalogue,
that the law which enjoyns obedience to kings is de-
livered in the terms, Honour thy father, *as if all*
power were originally in the father   And why
may I not add as well, that in the *Decalogue*, the
law that enjoyns obedience to queens, is delivered
in the terms of *Honour thy mother*, as if all power were originally in the mother ?   The argument,
as Sir *Robert* puts it, will hold as well for one as
the other   but of this, more in its due place

§ 12 All that I take notice of here, is, that
this is all our author says in this first, or any of
the following chapters, to prove the *absolute power of Adam*, which is his great principle and yet,
as if he had there settled it upon sure demonstration, he begins his second chapter with these
words, *By conferring these proofs and reasons,*
drawn from the authority of the scripture   Where
those proofs and reasons for *Adam*'s sovereignty
are, bating that of *Honour thy father*, above
mentioned, I confess, I cannot find, unless what
he says, p 11 *In these words we have an evident*
confession, viz. of Bellarmine, *that creation made*
man prince of his posterity, must be taken for
proofs and reasons drawn from scripture, or for
any sort of proof at all. though from thence by
a new way of inference, in the words immediately following, he concludes, *the royal authority of*
Adam sufficiently settled in him.

§ 13 If he has in that chapter, or any where
in the whole treatise, given any other proofs of
Adam's royal authority, other than by often re-
peating it, which, among some men, goes for
argument, I desire any body for him to shew me
the place and page, that I may be convinced of
my mistake, and acknowledge my oversight. It
no

no fuch arguments are to be found, I befeech thofe men, who have fo much cried up this book, to confider, whether they do not give the world caufe to fufpect, that it is not the force of reafon and argument, that makes them for abfolute monarchy, but fome other by intereft, and therefore are refolved to applaud any author, that writes in favour of this doctrine, whether he fupport it with reafon or no But I hope they do not expect, that rational and indifferent men fhould be brought over to their opinion, becaufe this their great doctor of it, in a difcourfe made on purpofe, to fet up the *abfolute monarchical power of Adam*, in oppofition to the *natural freedom* of mankind, has faid fo little to prove it, from whence it is rather naturally to be concluded, that there is little to be faid.

§ 14 But that I might omit no care to inform myfelf in cur author's full fenfe, I confulted his *Obfervations on Ariftotle, Hobbes, &c.* to fee whether in difputing with others he made ufe of any arguments for this his darling tenet of *Adam's fovereignty*; fince in his treatife of the *Natural Power of Kings*, he hath been fo fparing of them. In his Obfervations on Mr *Hobbes's Lev athan*, I think he he has put, in fhort, all thofe arguments for it together, which in his writings I find him any where to make ufe of his words are thefe: *If God created only Adam, and of a piece of him made the woman, and if by generation from them two, as parts of them, all mankind be propagated · if alfo God gave to Adam not only the dominion over the woman and the children that fhould iffue from them, but alfo over all the earth to fubdue it, and over all the creatures on it, fo that as long as Adam lived, no man could claim or enjoy any thing but by donation, affignation or permiffion from him, I won-*
der

der, &c. Obfervations, 165 Here we have the
fum of all his arguments, for *Adam's fovereignty*,
and againft *natural freedom*, which I find up and
down in his other treatifes · and they are thefe
following , *God's creation of Adam*, the *dominion*
he gave him *over Eve*, and the *dominion* he had as
father over his children : all which I fhall particularly confider.

C H A P. III

Of Adam's Title to Sovereignty by Creation.

§ 15 SIR *Robert*, in his preface to his Obfervations on *Ariftotle's* politics, tells us, *A
natural freedom of mankind cannot be fuppofed
without the denial of the creation of* Adam · but
how *Adam's* being created, which was nothing
but his receiving a being immediately from omni-
potence and the hand of God, gave *Adam* a *fovereignty* over any thing, I cannot fee, nor confequently underftand, how a *fuppofition of natural
freedom is a denial of* Adam's *creation*, and would
be glad any body elfe (fince our author did not
vouchfafe us the favour) would make it out for
him : for I find no difficulty to fuppofe the *freedom of mankind*, though I have always believed
the *creation of Adam* He was created, or began
to exift, by God's immediate power, without the
intervention of parents or the pre-exiftence of
any of the fame fpecies to beget him, when it
pleafed God he fhould ; and fo did the lion, the
king of beafts, before him, by the fame creating
power of God : and if bare exiftence by that
power, and in that way, will give dominion,
without any more ado, our author, by this argument,

ment, will make the lion have as good a title to
it, as he, and certainly the antienter   No ! for
Adam had his title *by the appointment of God,* says
our author in another place.   Then bare *creation*
gave him not dominion, and one might have *sup-
pos'd mankind free* without *the denying the creation
of Adam,* since it was God's *appointment* made
him monarch

§ 16 But let us see, how he puts his *creation*
and this *appointment* together   *By the appointment
of God,* says Sir *Robert, as soon as* Adam *was
created, he was monarch of the world, though he
had no subjects , for though there could not be actual
government till there were subjects, yet by the right
of nature it was due to* Adam *to be governor of
his posterity · though not in act, yet at least in habit* Adam *was a king from his creation*   I wish he
had told us here, what he meant *by God's appointment* for whatsoever providence orders, or
the law of nature directs, or positive revelation
declares, may be said to be *by God's appointment :*
but I suppose it cannot be meant here in the first
sense, *i e* by providence , because that would be
to say no more, but that *as soon as* Adam *was
created* he was *de facto* monarch, because *by right
of nature it was due to* Adam, *to be governor of
his posterity*   But he could not *de facto* be by
providence constituted the governor of the world,
at a time when there was actually no government,
no subjects to be governed, which our author here
confesses   *Monarch of the world* is also differently
used by our author , for sometimes he means by
it a proprietor of all the world exclusive of the
rest of mankind, and thus he does in the same
page of his preface before cited   *Adam,* says he,
*being commanded to multiply and people the earth,
and to subdue it, and having dominion given him*
                                                    over

over all creatures, was thereby the monarch of the whole world, none of his posterity had any right to possess any thing but by his grant or permission, or by succession from him. 2. Let us understand then by *monarch* proprietor *of the world,* and by *appointment* God's actual donation, and revealed positive grant made to *Adam,* 1 Gen 28 as we see Sir *Robert* himself does in this parallel place, and then his argument will stand thus, *by the positive grant of God: as soon as* Adam was *created, he was proprietor of the world, because by the right of nature it was due to* Adam *to be governor of his posterity* In which way of arguing there are two manifest falshoods *First,* It is false that God made that grant to *Adam,* as soon as he was created, since, tho' it stands in the text immediately after his creation, yet it is plain it could not be spoken to *Adam,* till after *Eve* was made and brought to him and how then could he be *monarch by appointment as soon as created,* especially since he calls, if I mistake not, that which God says to *Eve,* III. Gen 16, *the original grant of government,* which not being till after the fall, when *Adam* was somewhat, at least in time, and very much distant in condition, from his *creation,* I cannot see, how our author can say in this sense, that *by God's appointment, as soon as* Adam *was created, he was monarch of the world* *Secondly,* were it true that God's actual donation *appointed* Adam *monarch of the world as soon as he was created,* yet the reason here given for it would not prove it, but it would always be a false inference, that God, by a positive donation, *appointed* Adam *monarch of the world, because by right of nature it was due to* Adam *to be governor of his posterity* for having given him the right of government by nature, there was no need of a positive donation;

nation; at least it will never be a proof of such a donation.

§ 17 On the other side the matter will not be much mended, if we understand *by God's appointment* the law of nature (though it be a pretty harsh expression for it in this place) and *by monarch of the world,* sovereign ruler of mankind for then the sentence under consideration must run thus *By the law of nature, as soon as* Adam *was created he was governor of mankind, for by right of nature it was due to* Adam *to be governor of his posterity ;* which amounts to this, he was *governor by right of nature,* because he was *governor by right of nature* but supposing we should grant, that a man is *by nature governor* of his children, *Adam* could not hereby *be monarch as soon as created* for this right of nature being founded in his being their father, how *Adam* could have a natural right to be governor, before he was a father, when by being a father only he had that *right,* is, methinks, hard to conceive, unless he will have him to be a father before he was a father, and to have a title before he had it.

§ 18 To this foreseen objection, our author answers very logically, *he was governor in habit, and not in act* a very pretty way of being a governor without government, a father without children, and a king without subjects And thus Sir *Robert* was an author before he writ his book; not *in act* it is true, but in *habit,* for when he had once published it, it was due to him *by the right of nature,* to be an author, as much as it was *to* Adam *to be governor of his children,* when he had begot them . and if to be such a *monarch of the world,* an absolute monarch *in habit, but not in act,* will serve the turn, I should not much envy it to any of Sir *Robert's* friends, that he
thought

thought fit gracioufly to beftow it upon, though even this of *act* and *habit*, if it fignified any thing but our author's fkill in diftinctions, be not to his purpofe in this place. For the queftion is not here about *Adam's* actual exercife of government, but actually having a title to be governor. Government, fays our author, was *due* to Adam *by the right of nature* what is this right of nature? A right fathers have over their children by begetting them, *generatione jus acquiritur parentibus in liberos*, fays our author out of *Grotius, Obfervations*, 223. The right then follows the begetting as arifing from it, fo that, according to this way of reafoning or diftinguifhing of our author, *Adam*, as foon as he was created, had a title *only in habit, and not in act*, which in plain *Englifh* is, he had actually no title at all

§ 19. To fpeak lefs learnedly, and more intelligibly, one may fay of *Adam*, he was in a poffibility of being *governor*, fince it was poffible he might beget children, and thereby acquire that right of nature, be it what it will, to govern them, that accrues from thence but what connection has this with *Adam's creation*, to make him fay, that *as foon as he was created, he was monarch of the world?* for it may be as well faid of *Noah*, that as foon as he was born, he was monarch of the world, fince he was in poffibility (which in our author's fenfe is enough to make a monarch, *a monarch in habit*,) to outlive all mankind, but his own pofterity. What fuch neceffary connection there is betwixt *Adam's creation* and his *right to government*, fo that a *natural freedom of mankind cannot be fuppofed without the denial of the creation of* Adam, I confefs for my part I do not fee, nor how thofe words, *by the appointment, &c.* Obfervations, 254 how ever explained,

explained, can be put together, to make any tolerable fenfe, at leaft to eftablifh this pofition, with which they end, *viz Adam was a king from his creation*, a king, fays our author, *not in act, but in habit*, ɪ e actually no king at all

§ 20 I fear I have tired my reader's patience, by dwelling longer on this paffage, than the weightinefs of any argument in it feems to require but I have unavoidably been engaged in it by our author's way of writing, who, hudling feveral fuppofitions together, and that in doubtful and general terms, makes fuch a medley and confufion, that it is impoffible to fhew his miftakes, without examining the feveral fenfes wherein his words may be taken, and without feeing how, in any of thefe various meanings, they will confift together, and have any truth in them : for in this prefent paffage before us, how can any one argue againft this pofition of his, that *Adam was a king from his creation*, unlefs one examine, whether the words, *from his creation*, be to be taken, as they may, for the time of the commencement of his government, as the foregoing words import, *as foon as he was created he was monarch* ; or, for the caufe of it, as he fays, p. 11 *creation made man prince of his pofterity?* how farther can one judge of the truth of his being thus king, till one has examined whether king be to be taken, as the words in the beginning of this paffage would perfuade, on fuppofition of his *private dominion,* which was, by God's pofitive grant, *monarch of the world by appointment* ; or *king* on fuppofition of his *fatherly power* over his off-fpring, which was by nature, *due by the right of nature* , whether, I fay, king be to be taken in both, or one only of thefe two fenfes, or in neither of them, but only this, that

that creation made him prince, in a way different
from both the other? For though this assertion,
that *Adam was king from his creation*, be true in
no sense, yet it stands here as an evident conclusion drawn from the preceding words, though in
truth it be but a bare assertion joined to other
assertions of the same kind, which confidently
put together in words of undetermined and du-
bious meaning, look like a sort of arguing, when
there is indeed neither proof nor connection. a
way very familiar with our author. of which
having given the reader a taste here, I shall, as
much as the argument will permit me, avoid
touching on hereafter, and should not have done
it here, were it not to let the world see, how in-
coherences in matter, and suppositions without
proofs put handsomely together in good words and
a plausible stile, are apt to pass for strong reason
and good sense, till they come to be looked into
with attention.

C H A P. IV.

Of Adam's *title to Sovereignty by Donation,* Gen.
i. 28

§ 21. **H**AVING at last got through the foregoing passage, where we have been
so long detained, not by the force of arguments
and opposition, but the intricacy of the words,
and the doubtfulness of the meaning, let us go
on to his next argument, for *Adam's* sovereignty
Our author tells us in the words of Mr *Selden,*
that *Adam by donation from God,* Gen i 28. *was
made the general lord of all things, not without
such a private dominion to himself, as without his*
                                                    grant

grant did exclude his children   *This determination of Mr* Selden says our author, *is confonant to the hiftory of the* Bible, *and natural reafon,* Obfervations, 210   And in his Pref to his Obfervations on *Ariftotle,* he fays thus, *The firft government in the world was monarchical in the father of all flefh,* Adam *being commanded to multiply and people the earth, and to fubdue it, and having dominion given him over all creatures, was thereby the monarch of the whole world · none of his pofterity had any right to poffefs any thing, but by his grant or permiffion, or by fucceffion from him*   *The earth, faith the* Pfalmift, *hath he given to the children of men, which fhew the title comes from fatherhood.*

§ 22 Before I examine this argument, and the text on which it is founded, it is neceffary to defire the reader to obferve, that our author, according to his ufual method, begins in one fenfe, and concludes in another; he begins here with *Adam*'s propriety, or *private dominion, by donation*; and his conclufion is, *which fhew the title comes from fatherhood*

§. 23 But let us fee the argument. The words of the text are thefe, *and God bleffed them, and God faid unto them, be fruitful and multiply, and replenifh the earth and fubdue it, and have dominion over the fifh of the fea, and over the fowl of the air, and over every living thing that moveth upon the earth,* 1 Gen 28 from whence our author concludes, *that* Adam, *having here dominion given him over all creatures, was thereby the monarch of the whole world* whereby muft be meant, that either this grant of God gave *Adam* property, or as our author calls it, *private dominion* over the earth, and all inferior or irrational creatures, and fo confequently that he was thereby *monarch,* or 2dly, that it gave him rule and dominion over
         all

all earthly creatures whatfoever, and thereby over his children; and fo he was *monarch* · for, as Mr *Selden* has properly worded it, *Adam was made general lord of all things,* one may very clearly underftand him, that he means nothing to be granted to *Adam* here but property, and therefore he fays not one word of *Adam's mo-narchy* But our author fays, *Adam was hereby monarch of the world,* which, properly fpeaking, fignifies fovereign ruler of all the men in the world, and fo *Adam,* by this grant, muft be con-ftituted fuch a ruler. If our author means other-wife, he might with much cleainefs have faid, that *Adam was hereby proprietor of the whole world.* But he begs your pardon in that point: clear diftinct fpeaking not ferving every where to his purpofe, you muft not expect it in him, as in Mr *Selden,* or other fuch writers.

§ 24. In oppofition therefore to our author's doctrine, that *Adam was monarch of the whole world,* founded on this place, I fhall fhew,

1 That by this grant, 1 *Gen* 28 God gave no immediate power to *Adam* over men, over his children, over thofe of his own fpecies, and fo he was not made ruler, or *monarch,* by this charter.

2 That by this grant God gave him not *private dominion* over the inferior creatures, but right in common with all mankind, fo neither was he *monarch,* upon the account of the property here given him.

§ 25. 1. That this donation, 1. *Gen.* 28. gave *Adam* no power over men, will appear if we con-fider the words of it for fince all pofitive grants convey no more than the exprefs words they are made in will carry, let us fee which of them here will comprehend mankind, or *Adam's* pofterity; and thofe, I imagine, if any, muft be thefe,
thefe

every living thing that moveth · the words in *He-brew* are, חיה הרמשת ı e *Beſtiam Reptantem*, of which words the ſcripture itſelf is the beſt in-terpreter · God having created the fiſhes and fowls the 5*th* day, the beginning of the 6*th*, he creates the irrational inhabitants of the dry land, which, *v* 24. are deſcribed in theſe words, *let the earth bring forth the living creature after his kind ; cattle and creeping things, and beaſts of the earth, af-ter his kind, and* v 2 *and God made the beaſts of the earth after his kind, and cattle after their kind, and every thing that creepeth on the earth after his kind·* here, in the creation of the brute inhabitants of the earth, he firſt ſpeaks of them all under one general name, of *living creatures*, and then afterwards di-vides them into three ranks, ı *Cattle*, or ſuch crea-tures as were or might be tame, and ſo be the pri-vate poſſeſſion of particular men , 2 חיה which, *ver* 24, and 25, in our Bible, is tranſlated beaſts, and by the *Septuagint* θηρία, *wild beaſts*, and is the ſame word, that here in our text, *ver* 28 where we have this great charter to *Adam*, is tranſlated *living thing*, and is alſo the ſame word uſed, *Gen* ıx 2. where this grant is renewed to *Noah*, and there'like-wiſe tranſlated *beaſt*. 3. The third rank were the creeping animals, which *ver* 24, and 25, are com-prized under the word, הרמשת, the ſame that is uſed here, *ver* 28 and is tranſlated *moving*, but in the former verſes *creeping*, and by the *Septuagint* in all theſe places, ἑρπετά, or reptils , from whence it appears, that the words which we tranſlate here in God's donation, *ver* 28 *living creatures moving*, are the ſame, which in the hiſtory of the creation, *ver* 24, 25, ſignify two ranks of terreſtrial crea-tures, *viz wild beaſts* and *reptils*, and are ſo un-derſtood by the *Septuagint*

§ 26. When God had made the irrational ani-

mals

mals of the world, divided into three kinds, from the places of their habitation, *viz fishes of the sea, fowls of the air*, and living creatures of the earth, and these again into *cattle, wild beasts*, and *reptils*, he considers of making man, and the dominion he should have over the terrestrial world, *ver 26*, and then he reckons up the inhabitants of these three kingdoms, but in the terrestrial leaves out the second rank חיה or wild beasts. but here, *ver 28* where he actually exercises this design, and gives him this dominion, the text mentions *the fishes of the sea, and fowls of the air*, and the *terrestrial creatures* in the words that signify the *wild beasts* and *reptils*, though translated *living thing that moveth*, leaving out cattle. In both which places, though the word that signifies *wild beasts* be omitted in one, and that which signifies *cattle* in the other, yet, since God certainly executed in one place, what he declares he designed in the other, we cannot but understand the same in both places, and have here only an account, how the terrestrial irrational animals, which were already created and reckoned up at their creation, in three distinct ranks *of cattle, wild beasts*, and *reptils*, were here, *ver 28*, actually put under the dominion of man, as they were designed, *ver 26* nor do these words contain in them the least appearance of any thing that can be wrested to signify God's giving to one man dominion over another, to *Adam* over his posterity

§ 27. And this further appears from *Gen* ix 2 where God renewing this charter to *Noah* and his sons, he gives them dominion over the *fowls of the air, and the fishes of the sea, and the terrestrial creatures*, expressed by חיה and דרמש wild beasts and reptils, the same words that in the text

text before us, 1. *Gen.* 28. are tranflated *every moving thing, that moveth on the earth,* which by no means can comprehend man, the grant being made to *Noah* and his fons, all the men then living, and not to one part of men over another: which is yet more evident from the very next words, *ver.* 3 where God gives every שרמ *every moving thing,* the very words ufed *ch* 1. 28 to them for food. By all which it is plain that God's donation to *Adam,* *ch* 1 28. and his defignation *ver.* 26 and his grant again to *Noah* and his fons, refer to and contain in them, neither more nor lefs than the works of the creation the 5th day, and the beginning of the 6th, as they are fet down from the 20th to the 26th *ver.* inclufively of the 1ft *ch.* and fo comprehend all the fpecies of irrational animals of the *terraqueous globe,* tho' all the words, whereby they are expreffed in the hiftory of their creation, are no where ufed in any of the following grants, but fome of them omitted in one, and fome in another.   From whence I think it is paft all doubt, that man cannot be comprehended in this grant, nor any dominion over thofe of his own fpecies be conveyed to *Adam*   All the terreftrial irrational creatures are enumerated at their creation, *ver* 25. under the names *beafts of the earth, cattle and creeping things,* but man, being not then created, was not contained under any of thofe names; and therefore, whether we underftand the *Hebrew* words right or no, they cannot be fuppofed to comprehend man, in the very fame hiftory, and the very next verfes following, efpecially fince that *Hebrew* word שרמ which, if any in this donation to *Adam, ch.* 1 28. muft comprehend man, is fo plainly ufed in contradiftinction to him, as *Gen* vi 20 vii. 14, 21, 23 *Gen.* viii 17, 19. And if God made all
mankind

mankind flaves to *Adam* and his heirs by giving
Adam dominion over *every living thing that moveth
on the earth*, ch 1 28 as our author would have
it, methinks Sir *Robert* fhould have carried his
monarchical power one ftep higher, and fatisfied
the world, that princes might eat their fubjects
too, fince God gave as full power to *Noah* and
his heirs, *ch* ix 2 to eat *every living th ng that
moveth*, as he did to *Adam* to have dominion over
them, the *Hebrew* words in both places being the
fame

§ 28 *David*, who might be fuppofed to underftand the donation of God in this text, and
the right of kings too, as well as our author in
his comment on this place, as the learned and
judicious *Ainfworth* calls it, in the 8th *Pfalm*,
finds here no fuch charter of monarchical power,
his words are, *Thou haft made him*, i e man, the
Son of man, *a little lower than the angels; thou
madeft him to have dominion over the works of thy
hands; thou haft put all things under his feet, all
fheep and oxen, and the beafts of the field, and the
fowls of the air, and fifh of the fea, and whatfoever paffeth thro' the paths of the fea* In which
words, if any one can find out, that there is meant
any monarchical power of one man over another,
but only the dominion of the whole fpecies of
mankind, over the inferior fpecies of creatures,
he may, for aught I know, deferve to be one of
Sir *Robert's monarchs in habit*, for the rarenefs of
the difcovery And by this time, I hope it is
evident, that he that gave *dominion over every
living thing that moveth on the earth*, gave *Adam*
no monarchical power over thofe of his own
fpecies, which will yet appear more fully in the
next thing I am to fhew

C   §. 29.

§ 29. 2 Whatever God gave by the words of this grant, 1 *Gen* 28. it was not to *Adam* in particular, exclusive of all other men · whatever *dominion* he had thereby, it was not a *private dominion*, but a dominion in common with the rest of mankind   That this donation was not made in particular to *Adam*, appears evidently from the words of the text, it being made to more than one, for it was spoken in the plural number, God blessed *them*, and said unto *them*, Have dominion.   God says unto *Adam* and *Eve*, Have dominion ; *thereby*, says our author, *Adam was monarch of the world*   but the grant being to them, i. e spoke to *Eve* also, as many interpreters think with reason, that these words were not spoken till *Adam* had his wife, must not she thereby be lady, as well as he lord of the world ? If it be said, that *Eve* was subjected to *Adam*, it seems she was not so subjected to him, as to hinder her *dominion* over the creatures, or *property* in them : for shall we say that God ever made a joint grant to two, and one only was to have the benefit of it ?

§. 30. But perhaps it will be said, *Eve* was not made till afterward . grant it so, what advantage will our author get by it ? The text will be only the more directly against him, and shew that God, in this donation, gave the world to mankind in common, and not to *Adam* in particular   The word *them* in the text must include the species of man, for it is certain *them* can by no means signify *Adam* alone   In the 26th verse, where God declares his intention to give this dominion, it is plain he meant, that he would make a species of creatures, that should have dominion over the other species of this terrestrial globe . the words are, *And God said, Let us make*
                                                              man

man in our image, after our likeness, and let them have dominion over the fish, &c. They then were to have dominion. Who? even those who were to have the image of God, the individuals of that species of man, that he was going to make; for that them should signify Adam singly, exclusive of the rest that should be in the world with him, is against both scripture and all reason: and it cannot possibly be made sense, if man in the former part of the verse do not signify the same with them in the latter; only man there, as is usual, is taken for the species, and them the individuals of that species and we have a reason in the very text. God makes him in his own image, after his own likeness; makes him an intellectual creature, and so capable of dominion: for wherein soever else the image of God consisted, the intellectual nature was certainly a part of it, and belonged to the whole species, and enabled them to have dominion over the inferior creatures; and therefore David says in the 8th Psalm above cited, Thou hast made him little lower than the angels, thou hast made him to have dominion. It is not of Adam king David speaks here, for verse 4 it is plain, it is of man, and the son of man, of the species of mankind.

§ 31 And that this grant spoken to Adam was made to him, and the whole species of man, is clear from our author's own proof out of the Psalmist The earth, saith the Psalmist, hath he given to the children of men; which shews the title comes from fatherhood These are Sir Robert's words in the preface before cited, and a strange inference it is he makes; God hath given the earth to the children of men, ergo the title comes from fatherhood It is pity the propriety of the Hebrew tongue had not used fathers of men, in-

stead

stead of *children of men*, to exprefs mankind :
then indeed our author might have had the coun-
tenance of the found of the words, to have placed
the *title* in the *fatherhood*   But to conclude, that
the *fatherhood* had the right to the earth, becaufe
God gave it *to the children of men*, is a way of
arguing peculiar to our author   and a man muft
have a great mind to go contrary to the found
as well as fenfe of the words, before he could
light on it   But the fenfe is yet harder, and
more remote from our author's purpofe   for as
it ftands in his preface, it is to prove *Adam*'s being monarch, and his reafoning is thus, *God gave
the earth to the children of men*, ergo *Adam was
monarch of the world.*   I defy any man to make
a more pleafant conclufion than this, which cannot be excufed from the moft obvious abfurdity,
till it can be fhewn, that *by children of men*, he
who had no father, *Adam* alone is fignified , but
whatever our author does, the fcripture fpeaks
not nonfenfe.

   § 32 To maintain this *property and private
dominion of* Adam, our author labours in the
following page to deftroy the community granted
to *Noah* and his fons, in that parallel place, ix
Gen. 1, 2, 3 and he endeavours to do it two
ways

   1. Sir *Robert* would perfuade us againft the
exprefs words of the fcripture, that what was
here granted to *Noah*, was not granted to his fons
in common with him.   His words are, *As for the
general community between* Noah *and his fons,
which Mr* Selden *will have to be granted to them,*
ix Gen 2 *the text doth not warrant it*   What
warrant our author would have, when the plain
exprefs words of fcripture, not capable of another
meaning, will not fatisfy him, who pretends to
                                                    build

build wholly on fcripture, is not eafy to imagine. The text fays, *God bleffed* Noah *and his fons, and faid unto them,* i e as our author would have it, *unto him* for, faith he, *although the fons are there mentioned with* Noah *in the bleffing, yet it may beft be underftood, with a fubordination or benediction in fucceffion,* Obfervations, 211. That indeed is *beft,* for our author to be underftood, which beft ferves to his purpofe, but that truly *may beft be underftood* by any body elfe, which beft agrees with the plain conftruction of the words, and arifes from the obvious meaning of the place, and then with *fubordination* and *in fucceffion,* will not *be beft underftood,* in a grant of God, where he himfelf puts them not, nor mentions any fuch limitation But yet, our author has reafons, why it *may beft be underftood fo* *The bleffing,* fays he in the following words, *might truly be fulfilled, if the fons, either under or after their father, enjoyed a private dominion,* Obfervations, 211. which is to fay, that a grant, whofe exprefs words give a joint title in prefent (for the text fays, into your hands they are delivered) *may beft be underftood with a fubordination* or *in fucceffion,* becaufe it is poffible, that in *fubordination,* or *in fucceffion,* it may be enjoyed. Which is all one as to fay, that a grant of any thing in prefent poffeffion *may beft be underftood* of reverfion, becaufe it is poffible one may live to enjoy it in reverfion If the grant be indeed to a father and to his fons after him, who is fo kind as to let his children enjoy it prefently in common with him, one may truly fay, as to the event one will be as good as the other, but it can never be true, that what the exprefs words grant in poffeffion, and in common, *may beft be underftood,* to be in reverfion. The fum of all his reafoning amounts to this: God

C 3   did

did not give to the fons of *Noah* the world in
common with their father, becaufe it was poffible
they might enjoy it under, or after him   A very
good fort of argument againft an exprefs text of
fcripture : but God muft not be believed, though
he fpeaks it himfelf, when he fays he does any
thing, which will not confift with Sir *Robert's*
hypothefis.

§ 33 For it is plain, however he would exclude them, that part of this *benediction*, as he
would have it in *fucceffion*, muft needs be meant
to the fons, and not to *Noah* himfelf at all   *Be
fruitful, and multiply, and replenifh the earth,* fays
God, in this bleffing. This part of the benediction, as appears by the fequel, concerned not
Noah himfelf at all, for we read not of any
children he had after the flood, and in the following chapter, where his pofterity is reckoned
up, there is no mention of any, and fo this
benediction in fucceffion was not to take place till
350 years after: and to fave our author's imaginary *monarchy*, the peopling of the world muft
be deferred 350 years, for this part of the benediction cannot be underftood with *fubordination,*
unlefs our author will fay, that they muft afk
leave of their father *Noah* to lie with their wives.
But in this one point our author is conftant to
himfelf in all his difcourfes, he takes great care
there fhould be monarchs in the world, but very
little that there fhould be people ; and indeed his
way of government is not the way to people the
world · for how much abfolute monarchy helps
to fulfil this great and primary bleffing of God
Almighty, *Be fruitful, and multiply, and replenifh
the earth,* which contains in it the improvement
too of arts and fciences, and the conveniences of
life, may be feen in thofe large and rich countries
                                        which

which are happy under the *Turkish* government,
where are not now to be found one third, nay in
many, if not moft parts of them one thirtieth,
perhaps I might fay not one hundredth of the
people, that were formerly, as will eafily appear
to any one, who will compare the accounts we
have of it at this time, with antient hiftory But
this by the by.

§ 34 The other parts of this *benediction*, or
grant, are fo expreffed, that they muft needs be
underftood to belong equally to them all; as
much to *Noah*'s fons as to *Noah* himfelf, and not
to his fons *with a fubordination*, or *in fucceffion*.
The fear of you, and the dread of you, fays God,
fhall be upon every beaft, &c. Will any body but
our author fay, that the creatures feared and ftood
in awe of *Noah* only, and not of his fons without
his leave, or till after his death? And the following words, *into your hands they are delivered*,
are they to be underftood as our author fays, if
your father pleafe, or they fhall be delivered into
your hands hereafter? If this be to argue from
fcripture, I know not what may not be proved
by it; and I can fcarce fee how much this differs
from that *fiction and fanfie*, or how much a furer
foundation it will prove, than the opinions of
philofophers and poets, which our author fo much
condemns in his preface

§ 35. But our author goes on to prove, that
*it may beft be underftood with a fubordination, or
a benediction in fucceffion*; *for*, fays he, *it is not
probable that the private dominion which God gave
to* Adam, *and by his donation, affignation, or ceffion,
to his children, was abrogated, and a community
of all things inftituted between* Noah *and his fons*
———*Noah was left the fole heir of the world;
why fhould it be thought that God would difinherit*

C 4 *him*

him of his birth-right, and make him of all men in the world the only tenant in common with his children? Observations, 211

§ 36 The prejudices of our own ill-grounded opinions, however by us called *probable,* cannot author fe us to understand scripture contrary to the direct and plain meaning of the words. I grant, it is not probable, that *Adam's private dominion* was here *abrogated*   because it is more than improbable, (for it will never be proved) that ever *Adam* had any such *private dominion ·* and since parallel places of scripture are most probable to make us know how they *may be best understood,* there needs but the comparing this blessing here to *Noah* and his sons after the flood, with that to *Adam* after the creation, 1 *Gen* 28 to assure any one that God gave *Adam* no such *private dominion* It is *probable,* I confess, that *Noah* should have the same title, the same property and dominion after the flood, that *Adam* had before it · but since *private dominion* cannot consist with the blessing and grant God gave to him and his sons in common, it is a sufficient reason to conclude, that *Adam* had none, especially since in the donation made to him, there are no words that express it, or do in the least favour it, and then let my reader judge whether *it may best be understood,* when in the one place there is not one word for it, not to say what has been above proved, that the text itself proves the contrary ; and in the other, the words and sense are directly against it.

§. 37 But our author says, Noah *was the sole heir of the world ; why should it be thought that God would disinherit him of his birth-right ? Heir* indeed, in *England,* signifies the eldest son, who is by the law of *England* to have all his father's
land ;

land, but where God ever appointed any such *heir of the world*, our author would have done well to have shewed us; and how *God disinherited him of his birth-right*, or what harm was done him if God gave his sons a right to make use of a part of the earth for the support of themselves and families, when the whole was not only more than *Noah* himself, but infinitely more than they all could make use of, and the possessions of one could not at all prejudice, or, as to any use, streighten that of the other

§ 38 Our author probably foreseeing he might not be very successful in persuading people out of their senses, and, say what he could, men would be apt to believe the plain words of scripture, and think, as they saw, that the grant was spoken to *Noah* and his sons jointly, he endeavours to insinuate, as if this grant to *Noah* conveyed no property, no dominion, because *subduing the earth and dominion over the creatures are therein omitted, nor the earth once named* And therefore, says he, *there is a considerable difference between these two texts, the first blessing gave* Adam *a dominion over the earth and all creatures; the latter allows* Noah *liberty to use the living creatures for food here is no alteration or diminishing of his title to a property of all things, but an enlargement only of his commons,* Observations, 211. So that in our author's sense, all that was said here to *Noah* and his sons, gave them no dominion, no property, but only *enlarged* the *commons*, *their commons,* I should say, since God says, *to you are they given,* though our author says *his,* for as for *Noah*'s sons, they, it seems, by Sir *Robert*'s appointment, during their father's life-time, were to keep fasting days

C 5   § 39 And

§. 39 Any one but our author would be mightily
fufpected to be blinded with prejudice, that in all
this bleffing to *Noah* and his fons, could fee nothing but *only* an enlargement of commons : for
as to *dominion,* which our author thinks omitted,
the fear of you, and the dread of you, fays God,
fhall be upon every beaft, which I fuppofe expreffes
the *dominion,* or fuperiority was defigned man
over the living creatures, as fully as may be;
for in that fear and dread feems chiefly to confift what was given to *Adam* over the inferior animals; who, as abfolute a monarch as he was,
could not make bold with a fark or rabbet
to fatisfy his hunger, and had the herbs but in
common with the beafts, as is plain from 1 *Gen.*
2, 9, and 30. In the next place, it is manifeft
that in this bleffing to *Noah* and his fons, property is not only given in clear words, but in a
larger extent than it was to *Adam Into your hands
they are given,* fays God to *Noah* and his fons ;
which words, if they give not property, nay,
property in poffeffion, it will be hard to find
words that can , fince there is not a way to exprefs a man's being poffeffed of any thing more
natural, nor more certain, than to fay, *it is delivered into his hands And ver. 3.* to fhew, that
they had then given them the utmoft property
man is capable of, which is to have a right to
deftroy any thing by ufing it , *Every moving thing
that liveth,* faith God, *fhall be meat for you ;*
which was not allowed to *Adam* in his charter.
This our author calls, *a liberty of ufing them for
food, and only an enlargement of commons, but no
alteration of property,* Obfervations, 211 What
other property man can have in the creatures,
but the *liberty of ufing them,* is hard to be underftood : fo that if the firft bleffing, as our author
says,

says, gave Adam *dominion over the creatures*, and the blessing to *Noah* and his sons, gave them *such a liberty to use them*, as *Adam* had not, it must needs give them something that *Adam* with all his sovereignty wanted, something that one would be apt to take for a greater property; for certainly he has no absolute dominion over even the brutal part of the creatures, and the property he has in them is very narrow and scanty, who cannot make that use of them, which is permitted to another. Should any one who is absolute lord of a country, have bidden our author *subdue the earth*, and given him dominion over the creatures in it, but not have permitted him to have taken a kid or a lamb out of the flock, to satisfy his hunger, I guess, he would scarce have thought himself lord or proprietor of that land, or the cattle on it, but would have found the difference between *having dominion*, which a shepherd may have, and having full property as an owner. So that, had it been his own *case*, Sir *Robert*, I believe, would have thought here was an *alteration*, nay, an enlarging of *property*, and that *Noah* and his children had by this grant, not only property given them, but such a property given them in the creatures, as *Adam* had not. For however, in respect of one another, men may be allowed to have propriety in their distinct portions of the creatures; yet in respect of God the maker of heaven and earth, who is sole lord and proprietor of the whole world, man's propriety in the creatures is nothing but that *liberty to use them*, which God has permitted, and so man's property may be altered and enlarged, as we see it was here, after the flood, when other uses of them are allowed, which before were not. From all which I suppose it is clear, that neither *Adam*, nor *Noah*,

had

had any *private dominion*, any property in the creatures, exclusive of his posterity, as they should succeffively grow up into need of them, and come to be able to make use of them.

§ 40 Thus we have examined our author's argument for *Adam's monarchy*, founded on the blessing pronounced, 1 *Gen.* 28. Wherein I think it is impossible for any sober reader, to find any other but the setting of mankind above the other kinds of creatures, in this habitable earth of ours. It is nothing but the giving to man, the whole species of man, as the chief inhabitant, who is the image of his Maker, the dominion over the other creatures This lies so obvious in the plain words, that any one, but our author, would have thought it necessary to have shewn, how these words, that seemed to say the quite contrary, gave *Adam monarchical absolute power* over other men, or the *sole property* in all the creatures; and methinks in a business of this moment, and that whereon he builds all that follows, he should have done something more than barely cite, words which apparently make against him; for I confess, I cannot see any thing in them, tending to *Adam's monarchy*, or *private dominion*, but quite the contrary And I the less deplore the dulness of my apprehension herein, since I find the apostle seems to have as little notion of any such *private dominion of Adam* as I, when he says, God *gives us all things richly to enjoy*, which he could not do, if it were all given away already, to Monarch *Adam*, and the monarchs his heirs and successors To conclude, this text is so far from proving *Adam* sole proprietor, that on the contrary, it is a confirmation of the original community of all things amongst the sons of men, which appearing from this donation

nation of God, as well as other places of fcripture, the fovereignty of *Adam*, built upon his
private dominion, muft fall, not having any foundation to fupport it.

§ 41. But yet, if after all, any one will
needs have it fo, that by this donation of God,
Adam was made fole proprietor of the whole
earth, what will this be to his fovereignty ? and
how will it appear, that *propriety* in land gives
a man power over the life of another ? c how
will the poffeffion even of the whole earth give
any one a fovereign arbitrary authority, over the
perfons of men ? The moft fpecious thing to be
faid, is, that he that is proprietor of the whole
world, may deny all the reft of mankind food,
and fo at his pleafure ftarve them, if they will not
acknowledge his fovereignty, and obey his will.
If this were true, it would be a good argument
to prove, that there never was any fuch *property*,
that God never gave any fuch *private dominion*;
fince it is more reafonable to think, that God
who bid mankind increafe and multiply, fhould
rather himfelf give them all a right to make ufe
of the food and raiment, and other conveniences
of life, the materials whereof he had fo plentifully provided for them ; than to make them depend upon the will of a man for their fubfiftence,
who fhould have power to deftroy them all when
he pleafed, and who, being no better than other
men, was in fucceffion likelier, by want and the
dependence of a fcanty fortune, to tie them to
hard fervice, than by liberal allowance of the
conveniences of life to promote the great defign
of God, *increafe* and *multiply* he that doubts
this, let him look into the abfolute monarchies
of the world, and fee what becomes of the conveniences of life, and the multitudes of people.

§ 42.

§. 42. But we know God hath not left one man fo to the mercy of another, that he may ftarve him if he pleafe. God the Lord and Father of all has given no one of his children fuch a property in his peculiar portion of the things of this world, but that he has given his needy brother a right to the furplufage of his goods; fo that it cannot juftly be denied him, when his preffing wants call for it and therefore no man could ever have a juft power over the life of another by right of property in land or poffeffions; fince it would always be a fin, in any man of eftate, to let his brother perifh for want of affording him relief out of his plenty. As *juftice* gives every man a title to the product of his honeft induftry, and the fair acquifitions of his anceftors defcended to him; fo *charity* gives every man a title to fo much out of another's plenty, as will keep him from extreme want, where he has no means to fubfift otherwife and a man can no more juftly make ufe of another's neceffity, to force him to become his vaffal, by witholding that relief, God requires him to afford to the wants of his brother, than he that has more ftrength can feize upon a weaker, mafter him to his obedience, and with a dagger at his throat offer him death or flavery

§. 43 Should any one make fo perverfe an ufe of God's bleffings poured on him with a liberal hand, fhould any one be cruel and uncharitable to that extremity, yet all this would not prove that propriety in land, even in this cafe, gave any authority over the perfons of men, but only that compact might, fince the authority of the rich proprietor, and the fubjection of the needy, beggar, began not from the poffeffion of the Lord, but the confent of the poor man, who
preferred

preferred being his subject to starving. And the man he thus submits to, can pretend to no more power over him, than he has consented to, upon compact. Upon this ground a man's having his stores filled in a time of scarcity, having money in his pocket, being in a vessel at sea, being able to swim, &c. may as well be the foundation of rule and dominion, as being possessor of all the land in the world ; any of these being sufficient to enable me to save a man's life, who would perish if such assistance were denied him ; and any thing, by this rule, that may be an occasion of working upon another's necessity, to save his life, or any thing dear to him, at the rate of his freedom, may be made a foundation of sovereignty, as well as property. From all which it is clear, that though God should have given *Adam private dominion*, yet that *private dominion* could give him no *sovereignty*, but we have already sufficiently proved, that God gave him no *no private dominion*

CHAP V.

Of Adam's *Title to Sovereignty by the Subjection of* Eve.

§ 44. THE next place of scripture we find our author builds his monarchy of *Adam* on, is in *Gen* 26 *And thy desire shall be to thy husband, and he shall rule over thee Here we have* (says he) *the original grant of government,* from whence he concludes, in the following part of the page, Observations, 244 *That the supreme power is settled in the fatherhood, and limited to one kind of government, that is, to monarchy.* For let his premises be what they

will

will, this is always the conclusion, let *rule,* in any text, be but once named, and presently *absolute monarchy* is by divine right established. If any one will but carefully read our author's own reasoning from these words, *Observations,* 244. and consider, among other things, *the line and posterity of* Adam, as he there brings them in, he will find some difficulty to make sense of what he says, but we will allow this at present to his peculiar way of writing, and consider the force of the text in hand. The words are the curse of God upon the woman, for having been the first and forwardest in the disobedience, and if we will consider the occasion of what God says here to our first parents, that he was denouncing judgment, and declaring his wrath against them both, for their disobedience, we cannot suppose that this was the time, wherein God was granting *Adam* prerogatives and privileges, investing him with dignity and authority, elevating him to dominion and monarchy. for though, as a helper in the temptation, *Eve* was laid below him, and so he had accidentally a superiority over her, for her greater punishment, yet he too had his share in the fall, as well as the sin, and was laid lower, as may be seen in the following verses ; and it would be hard to imagine, that God, in the same breath, should make him universal *monarch* over all mankind, and a day-labourer for his life ; turn him out of *paradise to till the ground, ver* 23 and at the same time advance him to a throne, and all the privileges and ease of absolute power.

§ 45 This was not a time, when *Adam* could expect any favours, any grant of privileges, from his offended Maker If this be *the original grant of government,* as our author tells us, and *Adam* was now made monarch, whatever Sir *Robert* would

would have him, it is plain, God made him but a very poor monarch, such an one, as our author himself would have counted it no great privilege to be God sets him to work for his living, and seems rather to give him a spade into his hand, to subdue the earth, than a sceptre to rule over its inhabitants. *In the sweat of thy face thou shalt eat thy bread*, says God to him, *ver* 19. This was unavoidable, may it perhaps be answered, because he was yet without subjects, and had nobody to work for him, but afterwards, long as he did above 900 years, he might have people enough, whom he might command, to work for him, no, says God, not only whilst thou art without other help, save thy wife, but as long as thou livest, shalt thou live by thy labour, *In the sweat of thy face, shalt thou eat thy bread, till thou return unto the ground, for out of it wast thou taken, for dust thou art, and unto dust shalt thou return, v* 19 It will perhaps be answered again in favour of our author, that these words are not spoken personally to *Adam*, but in him, as their representative, to all mankind, this being a curse upon mankind, because of the fall.

§ 46 God, I believe, speaks differently from men, because he speaks with more truth, more certainty, but when he vouchsafes to speak to men, I do not think he speaks differently from them, in crossing the rules of language in use amongst them this would not be to condescend to their capacities, when he humbles himself to speak to them, but to lose his design in speaking what, thus spoken, they could not understand And yet thus must we think of God, if the interpretations of scripture, necessary to maintain our author's doctrine, must be received for good for by the ordinary rules of language, it will be very

hard

hard to underſtand what God ſays, if what he
ſpeaks here, in the ſingular number, to *Adam*,
muſt be underſtood to be ſpoken to all mankind,
and what he ſays in the plural number, 1. *Gen.*
26, and 28 muſt be underſtood of *Adam* alone,
excluſive of all others, and what he ſays to *Noah*
and his ſons jointly, muſt be underſtood to be
meant to *Noah* alone, *Gen* ix.

§ 47. Farther it is to be noted, that theſe
words here of iii *Gen* 16 which our author calls
the original grant of government, were not ſpoken
to *Adam*, neither indeed was there any grant in
them made to *Adam*, but a puniſhment laid upon
Eve: and if we will take them as they were directed in particular to her, or in her, as their repreſentative, to all other women, they will at
moſt concern the female ſex only, and import no
more, but that ſubjection they ſhould ordinarily be
in to their huſbands: but there is here no more
law to oblige a woman to ſuch a ſubjection, if
the circumſtances either of her condition, or contract with her huſband, ſhould exempt her from
it, than there is, that ſhe ſhould bring forth her
children in ſorrow and pain, if there could be
found a remedy for it, which is alſo a part of the
ſame curſe upon her: for the whole verſe runs
thus, *Unto the woman he ſaid, I will greatly
multiply thy ſorrow and thy conception ; in ſorrow
thou ſhalt bring forth children, and thy deſire ſhall
be to thy huſband, and he ſhall rule over thee.* It
would, I think have been a hard matter for any
body, but our author, to have found out a grant
of *monarchical government to Adam* in theſe words,
which were neither ſpoke to, nor of him ; neither will any one, I ſuppoſe, by theſe words,
think the weaker ſex, as by a law, ſo ſubjected to
the curſe contained in them, that it is their du-

ty

ty not to endeavour to avoid it And will any one ſay, that *Eve,* or any other woman, ſinned, if ſhe were brought to bed without thoſe multiplied pains God threatens her here with ? or that either of our queens, *Mary* or *Elizabeth,* had they married any of their ſubjects, had been by this text put into a political ſubjection to him ? or that he thereby ſhould have had *monarchical rule over her ,* God in this text, gives not, that I ſee, any authority to *Adam* over *Eve,* or to men over their wives, but only foretels what ſhould be the woman's lot, how by his providence he would order it ſo, that ſhe ſhould be ſubject to her huſband, as we ſee that generally the laws of mankind and cuſtoms of nations have ordered it ſo ; and there is, I grant, a foundation in nature for it.

§ 48 Thus when God ſays of *Jacob* and *Eſau,* that *the elder ſhould ſerve the younger,* xxv. *Gen.* 23. no body ſuppoſes that God hereby made *Jacob Eſau's* ſovereign, but foretold what ſhould *de facto* come to paſs

But if theſe words here ſpoke to *Eve* muſt needs be underſtood as a law to bind her and all other women to ſubjection, it can be no other ſubjection than what every wife owes her huſband; and then if this be the *original grant of government* and the *foundation of monarchical power,* there will be as many monarchs as there are huſbands : if therefore theſe words give any power to *Adam,* it can be only a conjugal power, not political , the power that every huſband hath to order the things of private concernment in his family, as proprietor of the goods and land there, and to have his will take place before that of his wife in all things of their common concernment; but not a political power of life and death over her much, leſs over any body elſe.

§. 49.

§ 49 This I am sure if our author will have this text to be a *grant, the original grant of government*, political government, he ought to have proved it by some better arguments than by barely saying, that *thy desire shall be unto thy husband*, was a law whereby *Eve*, and *all that should come of her*, were subjected to the absolute monarchical power of *Adam* and his heirs *Thy desire shall be to thy husband*, is too doubtful an expression, of whose signification interpreters are not agreed, to build so confidently on, and in a matter of such moment, and so great and general concernment but our author, according to his way of writing, having once named the text, concludes presently without any more ado, that the meaning is as he would have it Let the words *rule* and *subject* be but found in the text or margent, and it immediately signifies the duty of a subject to his prince ; the relation is changed, and though God says *husband*, Sir *Robert* will have it *king*, *Adam* has presently *absolute monarchical power* over *Eve*, and not only over *Eve*, but *all that should come of her*, though the scripture says not a word of it, nor our author a word to prove it But *Adam* must for all that be an absolute monarch, and so down to the end of the chapter. And here I leave my reader to consider, whether my bare saying, without offering any reasons to evince it, that this text gave not *Adam* that *absolute monarchical power*, our author supposes, be not as sufficient to destroy that power, as his bare assertion is to establish it, since the text mentions neither *prince* nor *people*, speaks nothing of *absolute* or *monarchical power*, but the subjection of *Eve* to *Adam*, a wife to her husband. And he that would trace our author so all through, would make a short and sufficient answer to the greatest part

of

of the grounds he proceeds on, and abundantly confute them by barely denying, it being a sufficient answer to assertions without proof, to deny them without giving a reason. And therefore should I have said nothing but barely denied, that by this text *the supreme power was settled and founded by God himself, in the fatherhood, limited to monarchy, and that to* Adam's *person and heirs,* all which our author notably concludes from these words, as may be seen in the same page, *Observations,* 244 it had been a sufficient answer: should I have desired any sober man only to have read the text, and considered to whom, and on what occasion it was spoken, he would no doubt have wondered how our author found out *monarchical absolute power in it,* had he not had an exceeding good faculty to find it himself, where he could not shew it others. And thus we have examined the two places of scripture, all that I remember our author brings to prove *Adam's* sovereignty, that supremacy, which he says, *it was God's ordinance should be unlimited in* Adam, *and as large as all the acts of his will,* Observations, 254. viz 1 *Gen.* 28. and iii. *Gen* 16. one whereof signifies only the subjection of the inferior ranks of creatures to mankind, and the other the subjection that is due from a wife to her husband, both far enough from that which subjects owe the governors of political societies.

CHAP. VI.

Of Adam's *Title to Sovereignty by Fatherhood.*

§. 50. THERE is one thing more, and then
I think I have given you all that our
author brings for proof of *Adam*'s sovereignty,
and that is a suppofition of a natural right of dominion over his children, by being their father:
and this title of *fatherhood* he is fo pleafed with,
that you will find it brought in almoft in every
page, particularly he fays, *not only* Adam, *but
the fucceeding patriarchs had by right of fatherhood
royal authority over their children,* p 12   And in
the fame page, *this fubjection of children being the
fountain of all regal authority,* &c.   This being,
as one would think by his fo frequent mentioning
it, the main bafis of all his frame, we may well
expect clear and evident reafon for it, fince he
lays it down as a pofition neceffary to his purpofe,
that *every man that is born is fo far from being
free, that by his very birth he becomes a fubject of
him that begets him,* Obfervations, 156 fo that
Adam being the only man created, and all ever
fince being begotten, no body has been born free.
If we afk how *Adam* comes by this power over
his children, he tells us here it is by begetting
them · and fo again, *Obfervations,* 223 *this natural dominion of* Adam, fays he, *may be proved
out of* Grotius *himfelf, who teacheth, that generatione jus acquiritur parentibus in liberos*   And indeed the act of begetting being that which makes
a man a father, his right of a father over his
children can naturally arife from nothing elfe

§ 51.

§ 51. *Grotius* tells us not here how far this *jus in liberos*, this power of parents over their children extends; but our author, always very clear in the point, assures us, it is *supreme power*, and like that of absolute monarchs over their flaves, absolute power of life and death. He that should demand of him, how, or for what reason it is, that begetting a child gives the father such an absolute power over him, will find him answer nothing. we are to take his word for this, as well as several other things; and by that the laws of nature and the constitutions of government must stand or fall. Had he been an absolute monarch, this way of talking might have suited well enough; *pro ratione voluntas* might have been of force in his mouth, but in the way of proof or argument is very unbecoming, and will little advantage his plea for absolute monarchy Sir *Robert* has too much leffened a subject's authority to leave himself the hopes of establishing any thing by his bare saying it; one flave's opinion without proof is not of weight enough to dispose of the liberty and fortunes of all mankind. If all men are not, as I think they are, naturally equal, I am sure all flaves are; and then I may without presumption oppose my single opinion to his, and be confident that my saying, *that begetting of children makes them not flaves to their fathers, as certainly* sets all mankind free, as his affirming the contrary makes them all flaves But that this position, which is the foundation of all their doctrine, who would have monarchy to be *jure divino*, may have all fair play, let us hear what reasons others give for it, since our author offers none.

§ 52. The argument, I have heard others make use of, to prove that fathers, by begetting them, come by an abfolute power over their children, is this; that *fathers have a power over the lives of their children, becaufe they give them life and being,* which is the only proof it is capable of fince there can be no reafon, why naturally one man fhould have any claim or pretence of right over that in another, which was never his, which he beftowed not, but was received from the bounty of another   1 I anfwer, that every one who gives another any thing, has not always thereby a right to take it away again. But, 2 They who fay the *father* gives life to his children, are fo dazzled with the thoughts of monarchy, that they do not, as they ought, remember God, who is *the author and giver of life · it is in him alone we live, move, and have our being.* How can he be thought to give life to another, that knows not wherein his own life confifts? Philofophers are at a lofs about it after their moft diligent enquiries, and anatomifts, after their whole lives and ftudies fpent in diffections, and diligent examining the bodies of men, confefs their ignorance in the ftructure and ufe of many parts of man's body, and in that operation wherein life confifts in the whole   And doth the rude plough-man, or the more ignorant voluptuary, frame or fafhion fuch an admirable engine as this is, and then put life and fenfe into it ? Can any man fay, he formed the parts that are neceffary to the life of his child? or can he fuppofe himfelf to give the life, and yet not know what fubject is fit to receive it, noi what actions or organs are neceffary for its reception or prefervation ?

§ 53 To give life to that which has yet no being, is to frame and make a living creature, fafhion the parts, and mould and fuit them to their ufes, and having proportioned and fitted them

them together, to put into them a living foul. He that could do this, might indeed have fome pretence to deftroy his own workmanfhip But is there any one fo bold, that dares thus far arrogate to himfelf the incomprehenfible works of the almighty? Who alone did at firft, and continues ftill to make a living foul, he alone can breathe in the breath of life If any one thinks himfelf an artift at this, let him number up the parts of his child's body which he hath made, tell me their ufes and operations, and when the living and rational foul began to inhabit this curious ftructure, when fenfe began, and how this engine, which he has framed, thinks and reafons: if he made it, let him, when it is out of order, mend it, at leaft tell wherein the defects lie. *Shall he that made the eye not fee?* fays the Pfalmift, *Pfalm* xciv 9. See thefe men's vanities! the ftructure of that one part is fufficient to convince us of an all-wife contriver, and he has fo vifible a claim to us as his workmanfhip, that one of the ordinary appellations of God in fcripture is, *God our Maker, and the Lord our Maker* And therefore though our author, for the magnifying his *fatherhood,* be pleafed to fay, *Obfervations,* 159 *That even the power which God himfelf exercifeth over mankind is by right of fatherhood,* yet this fatherhood is fuch an one as utterly excludes all pretence of title in earthly parents, for he is *king,* becaufe he is indeed maker of us all, which no parents can pretend to be of their children

§ 54 But had men fkill and power to make their children, it is not fo flight a piece of workmanfhip, that it can be imagined, they could make them without defigning it What father of a thoufand, when he begets a child, thinks farther than the fatisfying his prefent appetite?

D   God

God in his infinite wisdom has put strong desires of copulation into the constitution of men, thereby to continue the race of mankind, which he doth most commonly without the intention, and often against the consent and will of the begetter. And indeed those who desire and design children, are but the occasions of their being, and when they design and wish to beget them, do little more towards their making, than *Deucalion* and his wife in the fable did towards the making of mankind, by throwing pebbles over their heads.

§ 55 But grant that the parents made their children, gave them life and being, and that hence there followed an absolute power This would give the *father* but a joint dominion with the mother over them for no body can deny but that the woman hath an equal share, if not the greater, as nourishing the child a long time in her own body out of her own substance there it is fashioned, and from her it receives the materials and principles of its constitution and it is so hard to imagine the rational soul should presently inhabit the yet unformed embrio, as soon as the father has done his part in the act of generation, that if it must be supposed to derive any thing from the parents, it must certainly owe most to the mother But be that as it will, the mother cannot be denied an equal share in begetting of the child, and so the absolute authority of the *father* will not arise from hence Our author indeed is of another mind, for he says, *We know that God at the creation gave the sovereignty to the man over the woman, as being the nobler and principal agent in generation,* Observations, 172 I remember not this in my Bible, and when the place is brought where God at the creation gave the sovereignty to man over the woman,

man, and that for this reason, because *he is the nobler and principal agent in generation*, it will be time enough to consider, and answer it But it is no new th ng for our author to tell us his own fancies for certain and divine tru hs, tho' there be often a great deal of d fference between his and divine revelations, for God in the scripture says, *his father and his mother that begot him*

§ 56 They who alledge the practice of mankind, for *exposing or selling* their children, as a proof of their power over them, are with Sir *Robert* happy arguers, and cannot but recommend their opinion, by founding it on the most shameful action, and most unnatural murder, human nature is capable of The dens of lions and nurseries of wolves know no such cruelty as this · these savage inhabitants of the desert obey God and nature in being tender and careful of their off-spring they will hunt, watch, fight, and almost starve for the preservation of their young; never part with them, never forsake them, till they are able to shift for themselves And is it the privilege of man alone to act more contrary to nature than the wild and most untamed part of the creation ? doth God forbid us under the severest penalty, that of death, to take away the life of any man, a stranger, and upon provocation ? and does he permit us to destroy those, he has given us the charge and care of ; and by the dictates of nature and reason, as well as his revealed command, requires us to preserve ? He has in all the parts of the creation taken a peculiar care to propagate and continue the several species of creatures, and makes the individuals act so strongly to this end, that they sometimes neglect their own private good for it, and seem to forget that general rule, which nature teaches all things,

D 2

of self-preservation; and the preservation of their young, as the strongest principle in them, over-rules the constitution of their particular natures Thus we see, when their young stand in need of it, the timorous become valiant, the fierce and savage kind, and the ravenous tender and liberal

§ 57 But if the example of what hath been done, be the rule of what ought to be, history would have furnished our author with instances of this *absolute fatherly power* in its height and perfection, and he might have shewed us in *Peru*, people that begot children on purpose to fatten and eat them   The story is so remarkable, that I cannot but set it down in the author's words   " In some provinces, *says he*, they were " so liquorish after man's flesh, that they would " not have the patience to stay till the breath " was out of the body, but would suck the blood " as it ran from the wounds of the dying man, " they had public shambles of man's flesh, and " their madness herein was to that degree, that " they spared not their own children, which they " had begot on strangers taken in war · for they " made their captives their mistresses, and choice- " ly nourished the children they had by them, " till about thirteen years old they butchered " and eat them, and they served the mothers " after the same fashion, when they grew past " child bearing, and ceased to bring them any " more roasters," *Garcilasso de la Vega hist des Yncas de Peru*, l i c 12

§. 58. Thus far can the busy mind of man carry him to a brutality below the level of beasts, when he quits his reason, which places him almost equal to angels   Nor can it be otherwise in a creature, whose thoughts are more than the sands,
and

and wider than the ocean, where fancy and passion
must needs run him into strange courses, if reason,
which is his only star and compass, be not that
he steers by. The imagination is always restless,
and suggests variety of thoughts, and the will,
reason being laid aside, is ready for every extra-
vagant project, and in this state, he that goes
farthest out of the way, is thought fittest to lead,
and is sure of most followers: and when fashion
hath once established what folly or craft began,
custom makes it sacred, and it will be thought
impudence, or madness, to contradict or question
it He that will impartially survey the nations of
the world, will find so much of their religions,
governments and manners, brought in and continued amongst them by these means, that he will
have but little reverence for the practices which
are in use and credit amongst men, and will have
reason to think, that the woods and forests, where
the irrational untaught inhabitants keep right by
following nature, are fitter to give us rules, than
cities and palaces, where those that call themselves
civil and rational, go out of their way, by the
authority of example If precedents are sufficient
to establish a rule in this case, our author might
have found in holy writ children sacrificed by
their parents, and this amongst the people of
God themselves the *Psalmist* tells us, *Psal* cvi.
38 *They shed innocent blood, even the blood of their
sons and of their daughters, whom they sacrificed
unto the idols of Canaan* But God judged not
of this by our authors rule, nor allowed of the
authority of practice against his righteous law;
but as it follows there, *the land was polluted with
blood, therefore was the wrath of the Lord kindled
against his people, insomuch that he abhorred his
own inheritance.* The killing of their children,

though

though it wer efafhionable, was charged on them
as *innocent blood*, a d to had in the account of
God the guilt of m rder, as the offering them to
idols had the guil t idolatry

§ 59 Let t l n, as Sir Su *Robert* fays, that
*anci ntly it v as u ual for men to fell a d caflrate
thr cildren*, Obiervation , 155 Let it be,
th they expofed them, adu to it, f you pl ate,
for this is full greater power, that they begat
them for their tables, to fat and eat them: if
this proves a right to do fo, we may, by the fame
argument, juftify adultery, inceft and fedomy,
for there are examples of thefe too, both ancient
and modern, fins, which I fuppofe have their
principal aggravation from this, that they crofs
the main intention of nature, which willeth the
increafe of mankind, and the continuation of the
fpecies in the higheft perfection, and the diftinction of families, with the fecurity of the marriage bed, as neceffary thereunto

§ 60 In confirmation of this natural authority
of the father, our author brings a lame proof
from the pofitive command of God in fcripture ·
his words are, *To confirm the natural right of regal power, we find in the Decalogue, that the law
which enjoins obedience to kings, is delivered in the
terms, Honour thy father,* p 23 *Whereas many
confefs, that government only in the abftract, is the
ordinance of God, they are not able to prove any
fuch ordinance in the fcripture, but only in the fatherly power, and therefore we find the commandment, that enjoins obedience to fuperiors, given in
the terms, Honour thy father ; fo that not only the
power and right of government, but the form of
the power governing, and the perfon having the
power, are all the ordinances of God. The firft
father had not only fimply power, but power monarchical,*

chical, as he was father immediately from God, Observations, 254   To the same purpose, the same law is cited by our author in several other places, and just after the same fashion; that is, *and mother*, as apochryphal words, are always left out, a great argument of our author's ingenuity, and the goodness of his cause, which required in its defender zeal to a degree of warmth, able to warp the sacred rule of the word of God, to make it comply with his present occasion; a way of proceeding not unusual to those, who embrace not truths because reason and revelation offer them, but espouse tenets and parties for ends different from truth, and then resolve at any rate to defend them, and so do with the words and sense of authors, they would fit to their purpose, just as *Procrustes* did with his guests, lop or stretch them, as may best fit them to the size of their notions   and they always prove like those so served, deformed, lame, and useless.

§ 61 For had our author set down this command without garbling, as God gave it, and joined *mother* to father, every reader would have seen, that it had made directly against him; and that it was so far from establishing the *monarchical power of the father*, that it set up the *mother* equal with him, and enjoined nothing but what was due in common, to both father and mother   for that is the constant tenor of the scripture, *Honour thy father and thy mother*, Exod. xx *He that smiteth his father or mother, shall surely be put to death*, xxi 15. *He that curseth his father or mother, shall surely be put to death*, ver 17 Repeated *Lev* xx 9 and by our Saviour, *Matth* xv 4 *Ye shall fear every man his mother and his father*, Lev xix 3 *If a man have a rebellious son, which will not obey the voice*

D 4   *of*

*of his father, or the voice of his mother , then shall
his father and his mother lay hold on him, and say,
This our son is stubborn and rebellious, he will not
obey our voice,* Deut xxi 18, 19, 20, 21. *Cursed
be he that setteth light by his father or his mother,*
xxvii 16 *My son, hear the instructions of thy
father, and forsake not the law of thy mother,* are
the words of *Solomon,* a king who was not igno‑
rant of what belonged to him as a father or a
king, and yet he joins *father* and *mother* together,
in all the instructions he gives children quite thro'
his book of *Proverbs Woe unto him, that sayeth
unto his father, What begettest thou, or to the wo‑
man, What hast thou brought forth ?* Isa xi ver
10 *In this have they set light by father or mother,*
Ezek xxviii 2 *And it shall come to pass, that
when any shall yet prophecy, then his father and
his mother that begat him, shall say unto him, Thou
shalt not live, and his father and his mother that
begat him, shall thrust him through when he pro‑
phesieth,* Zech. xiii 3. Here not the father only,
but the father and mother jointly, had power in
this case of life and death   Thus ran the law of
the Old Testament, and in the New they are
likewise joined, in the obedience of their chil‑
dren, *Eph* vi 1. The rule is, *Children, obey
your parents ,* and I do not remember, that I any
where read, *Children, obey your father,* and no
more   the scripture joins *mother* too in that ho‑
mage, which is due from children , and had there
been any text, where the honour or obedience of
children had been directed to the *father* alone, it
is not likely that our author, who pretends to
build all upon scripture, would have omitted it
nay, the scripture makes the authority of *father
and mother,* in respect of those they have begot,
so equal, that in some places it neglects even the
priority

priority of order, which is thought due to the father, and the *mother* is put first, as *Lev* xix 3. from which so constantly joining father and mother together, as is found quite through the scripture, we may conclude that the honour they have a title to from their children, is one common right belonging so equally to them both, that neither can claim it wholly, neither can be excluded

§ 62 One would wonder then how our author infers from the 5th commandment, that all *power was originally in the father*, how he finds *monarchical power of government settled and fixed by the commandment, Honour thy father and thy mother.* If all the honour due by the commandment, be it what it will, be the only right of the *father*, because he, as our author says, *has the sovereignty over the woman, as being the nobler and principler agent in generation*, why did God afterwards all along join the *mother* with him to share in his honour ? can the father, by this sovereignty of his, discharge the child from paying this honour to his *mother* ? The scripture gave no such licence to the *Jews*, and yet there were often breaches wide enough betwixt husband and wife, even to divorce and separation and, I think, no body will say a child may with-hold honour from his mother, or, as the scripture terms it, *set light by her*, though his father should command him to do so, no more than the mother could dispense with him for neglecting to honour his father : whereby it is plain, that this command of God gives the father no sovereignty, no supremacy.

§ 63 I agree with our author that the title to this *honour* is vested in the parents by nature, and is a right which accrues to them by their having begotten their children, and God by many positive

decla-

declarations has confirmed it to them. I also allow our author's rule, *that in grants and gifts, that have their original from God and nature, as the power of the father,* (let me add *and mother,* for whom God hath joined together, let no man put asunder) *no inferior power of men can limit, nor make any law of prescription against them,* Observations, 158 so that the mother having by this law of God, a right to honour from her children, which is not subject to the will of her husband, we see this *absolute monarchical power of the father* can neither be founded on it, nor consist with it, and he has a power very far from *monarchical,* very far from that absoluteness our author contends for, when another has over his subjects the same power he hath, and by the same title · and therefore he cannot forbear saying himself that *he cannot see how any man's children can be free from subjection to their parents,* p 12. which, in common speech, I think, signifies *mother* as well as *father,* or if *parents* here signifies only *father,* it is the first time I ever yet knew it to do so, and by such an use of words one may say any thing

§ 64. By our author's doctrine, the father having absolute jurisdiction over his children, has also the same over their issue, and the consequence is good, were it true, that the father had such a power and yet I ask our author whether the grandfather, by his sovereignty, could discharge the grandchild from paying to his father the honour due to him by the 5th commandment. If the grandfather hath, by *right of fatherhood,* sole sovereign power in him, and that obedience which is due to the supreme magistrate, be commanded in these word, *Honour thy father,* it is certain the grandfather might dispense with the grandson's

grandfon's honouring his father, which finee it is
evident in common fenfe he cannot, it follows
from hence, that *Honour thy father and mother,*
cannot mean an abfolute fubjection to a fovereign
power, but fomething elfe   The right therefore
which parents have by nature, and which is confirmed to them by the 5th commandment, cannot
be that political dominion,, which our author
would derive from it : for that being in every civil fociety fupreme fomewhere, can difcharge any
fubject from any political obedience to any one of
his fellow fubjects But what law of the magiftrate
can give a child liberty, not to *honour his father
and mother ?* It is an eternal law, annexed purely
to the relation of parents and children, and fo contains nothing of the magiftrate's power in it, nor
is fubjected to it.

§ 65 Our author fays, *God hath given to a father a right or liberty to alien his power over his
children to any other,* Obfervations, 155 I doubt
whether he can *alien* wholly the right of *honour*
that is due from them . but be that as it will, this
I am fure, he cannot *alien,* and retain the fame
power If therefore the magiftrate's fovereignty
be, as our author would have it, *nothing but the authority of a fupreme father,* p 23 it is unavoidable, that if the magiftrate hath all this paternal
right, as he muft have if *fatherhood* be the fountain of all authority , then the fubjects, though
fathers, can have no power over their children,
no right to honour from them for it cannot be
all in another's hands, and a part remain with
the parent So that, according to our author's
own doctrine, *Honour thy father and mother,* cannot poffibly be underftood of political fubjection
and obedience ; fince the laws both in the Old
and New Teftament, that commanded children

to *honour and obey their parents,* were given to
such, whose fathers were under civil government,
and fellow subjects with them in political societies, and to have bid them *honour and obey their
parents,* in our author's sense, had been to bid
them be subjects to those who had no title to it;
the right to obedience from subjects, being all
vested in another, and instead of teaching obedience, this had been to foment sedition, by setting
up powers that were not   If therefore this command, *Honour thy father and mother,* concern political dominion, it directly overthrows our author's monarchy, since it being to be paid by
every child to his father, even in society, every
father must necessarily have political dominion,
and there will be as as many sovereigns as there
are fathers besides that the mother too hath her
title, which destroys the sovereignty of one supreme monarch   But if *Honour thy father and
mother* mean something distinct from political
power, as necessarily it must, it is besides our author's business, and serves nothing to his purpose.

§ 66 *The law that enjoins obedience to kings
is delivered,* says our author, *in the terms, Honour thy father, as if all power were originally
in the father,* Observations, 254 . and that law
is also delivered, say I, in the terms, *Honour thy
mother,* as if all power were originally in the mother   I appeal whether the argument be not as
good on one side as the other, *father and mother*
being joined all along in the Old and New Testament where-ever honour or obedience is in-
joined children   Again our author tells us, Observations, 253 *that this command, Honour thy father, gives the right to govern, and makes the form
of government monarchical*   To which I answer,
that if by *Honour thy father* be meant obedience
to the political power of the magistrate, it concerns

cerns not any duty we owe to our natural fathers, who are subjects, because they, by our author's doctrine, are divested of all that power, it being placed wholly in the prince, and so being equally subjects and flaves with their children, can have no right, by that title, to any such *honour or obedience*, as contains in it political subjection. if *Honour thy father and mother* signifies the duty we owe our natural parents, as by our Saviour's interpretation, *Matth* xv 4 and all the other mentioned places, it is plain it does, then it cannot concern political obedience, but a duty that is owing to persons, who have no title to sovereignty, nor any political authority as magistrates over subjects For the person of a private father, and a title to obedience, due to the supreme magistrate, are things inconsistent, and therefore this command, which must necessarily comprehend the persons of our natural fathers, must mean a duty we owe them distinct from our obedience to the magistrate, and from which the most absolute power of princes cannot absolve us. What this duty is, we shall in its due place examine.

§ 67 And thus we have at last got thro' all, that in our author looks like an argument for that *absolute unlimited sovereignty* described, sect 8 which he supposes in *Adam* ; so that mankind ever since have been all born *flaves*, without any title to freedom But if *creation*, which gave nothing but a being, made not *Adam prince of his posterity* if *Adam, Gen* 1. 28 was not constituted lord of mankind, nor had a *private dominion* given him exclusive of his children, but only a right and power over the earth, and inferiour creatures in common with the children of men, if also *Gen* iii 16. God gave not any political power to *Adam* over his wife and children, but only subjected

jected *Eve* to *Adam*, as a punishment, or foretold
the subjection of the weaker sex, in the ordering
the common concernments of their families, but
gave not thereby to *Adam*, as to the husband,
power of life and death, which necessarily belongs
to the magistrate: if fathers by begetting their
children acquire no such power over them, and
if the command, *Honour thy father and mother,*
give it not, but only enjoins a duty owing to
parents equally, whether subjects or not, and to
the *mother* as well as the *father*; if all this be so,
as I think, by what has been said, is very evident.
then man has a *natural freedom,* notwithstanding
all our author confidently says to the contrary,
since all that share in the same common nature;
faculties and powers, are in nature equal, and
ought to partake in the same common rights and
privileges, till the manifest appointment of God,
who is *Lord over all, blessed for ever,* can be produced to shew any particular person's supremacy,
or a man's own consent subjects him to a superior   This is so plain, that our author confesses,
that Sir *John Hayward, Blackwood* and *Barclay,*
the great vindicators of the right of kings, could
not deny it, *but admit with one consent the natural*
liberty and equality of mankind, for a truth unques-
tionable   And our author hath been so far from
producing any thing, that may make good his
great position, *that Adam was absolute monarch,*
and so men are are not naturally free, that even his
own proofs make against him, so that to use his
own way of arguing, *the first erroneous principle*
failing, the whole fabric of this vast engine of absolute power *and tyranny drops down of itself,*
and there needs no more to be said in answer to
all that he builds upon so false and frail a foundation.

§. 68.

§ 68. But to save others the pains, were there any need, he is not sparing himself to shew, by his own contradictions, the weakness of his own doctrine *Adam*'s absolute and sole dominion is that, which he is every where full of, and all along builds on, and yet he tells us, p 12 *that as* Adam *was lord of his children, so his children under him had a command and power over their own children* The unlimited and undivided sovereignty of *Adam's fatherhood*, by our author's computation, stood but a little while, only during the first generation, but as soon as he had grand-children, Sir *Robert* could give but a very ill account of it *Adam, as father of his children,* saith he, *hath an absolute, unlimited royal power over them, and by virtue thereof over those that they begot, and so to all generations* , and yet *his children*, Cain, viz and *Seth,* have a paternal power over their children at the same time , so that they are at the same time *absolute lords,* and yet *vassals* and *slaves* , *Adam* has all the authority, as *grand-father of the people,* and they have a part of it as fathers of a part of them : he is absolute over them and their posterity, by having begotten them, and yet they are absolute over their children by the same title So, says our author, *Adam's children under him had power over their own children, but still with subordination to the first parent*. A good distinction that sounds well, and it is pity it signifies nothing, nor can be reconciled with our author's words. I readily grant, that supposing *Adam's absolute power* over his posterity, any of his children might have from him a delegated, and so a subordinate power over a part, or all the rest but that cannot be the power our author speaks of here , it is not a power by grant and commission, but the natural paternal power he supposes a father
ther

ther to have over his children. For 1. he says, *As Adam was lord of his children, so his children under him had a power over their own children*. they were then lords over their own children after the same manner, and by the same title, that *Adam* was, *i e* by right of generation, by right of *fatherhood* 2 It is plain he means the natural power of fathers, because he limits it to be only *over their own children*, a delegated power has no such limitation, as only over their own children, it might be over others, as well as their own children 3 If it were a delegated power, it must appear in scripture, but there is no ground in scripture to affirm, that *Adam*'s children had any other power over theirs, than what they naturally had as fathers

§. 69 But that he means here paternal power, and no other, is past doubt, from the inference he makes in these words immediately following, *I see not then how the children of* Adam, *or of any man else, can be free from subjection to their parents.* Whereby it appears that the *power* on one side, and the *subjection* on the other, our author here speaks of, is that *natural power* and *subjection* between parents and children for that which every man's children owed, could be no other, and that our author always affirms to be absolute and unlimited This natural *power* of parents over their children, *Adam* had over his posterity, says our author, and this *power* of parents over their children, his children had over theirs in his lifetime says our author also, so that *Adam*, by a natural right of father, had an absolute unlimited power over all his posterity, and at the same time his children had by the same right absolute unlimited power over theirs Here then are two absolute unlimited powers existing together,

which

which I would have any body reconcile one to
another, or to common sense For the *salvo* he
has put in of *subordination*, makes it more absurd :
to have one *absolute, unlimited,* nay *unlimitable
power* in subordination to another, is so manifest
a contradiction, that nothing can be more Adam
*is absolute prince with the unlimited authority of fa-
therhood over all his posterity* , all his posterity are
then absolutely his subjects , and, as our author
says, his slaves, children, and grand-children, are
equally in this state of subjection and slavery ;
and yet, says our author, *the children of* Adam
have paternal, i e *absolute unlimited power over
their own children*. Which in plain *English* is,
they are slaves and absolute princes at the same
time, and in the same government , and one part
of the subjects have an absolute unlimited power
over the other by the natural right of parentage.

§ 70 If any one will suppose, in favour of our
author, that he here meant, that parents, who
are in subjection themselves to the absolute authority of their father, have yet some power over
their children ; I confess he is something nearer
the truth · but he will not at all hereby help our
author : for he no where speaking of the paternal
power, but as an absolute unlimited authority,
cannot be supposed to understand any thing else
here, unless he himself had limited it, and shewed
how far it reached And that he means here paternal authority in that large extent, is plain
from the immediate following words , *This subjection of children being,* says he, *the foundation of
all regal authority,* p 12 *the subjection* then that
in the former line, he says, *every man is in to his
parents,* and consequently what *Adam*'s grand-
children were in to their parents, was that which
was the fountain of all *regal authority,* i e according

cording to our author, *absolute unlimitable authority*   And thus *Adam's* children had *regal authority over their children*, whilst they themselves
were subjects to their father, and fellow-subjects
with their children   But let him mean as he
pleases, it is plain he allows *Adam's children to
have paternal power*, p 12 as also all other fathers
to have *paternal power over their children*, Obfervations, 156   From whence one of thefe two
things will necessarily follow, that either *Adam's*
children, even in his life-time, had, and so all
other fathers have, as he phrafes it, p 12. *by
right of fatherhood, royal authority over their children*, or elfe, that *Adam, by right of fatherhood,
had not royal authority*   For it cannot be but that
paternal power does, or does not, give *royal authority* to them that have have it   if it does not,
then *Adam* could not be fovereign by this title,
nor any body elfe , and then there is an end of
all our author's politics at once   if it does give
royal authority, then every one that has *paternal
power* has *royal authority* , and then, by our author's patriarchal government, there will be as
many kings as there are fathers.

§ 71 And thus what a monarchy he hath set
up, let him and his difciples confider   Princes
certainly will have great reafon to thank him for
thefe new politics, which fet up as many abfolute
kings in every country as there are fathers of
children   And yet who can blame our author for
it, it lying unavoidably in the way of one dif-
courfing upon our author's principles ? For having placed an *abfolute power* in *fathers by right
of begetting*, he could not eafily refolve how
much of this power belonged to a fon over the
children he had begotten , and fo it fell out to
be a very hard matter to give all the power, as
                                                    he

he does, to *Adam*, and yet allow a part in his
life-time to his children, when they were parents,
and which he knew not well how to deny them.
This makes him so doubtful in his expressions,
and so uncertain where to place this absolute natural power, which he calls *fatherhood*   Sometimes *Adam* alone has it all, as p 13   *Observations*, 244, 245 *& Pref.*

Sometimes *parents* have it, which word scarce
signifies the father alone, p 12, 19

Sometimes *children* during their fathers life-
time, as p 12

Sometimes *fathers* of *families*, as p 78, and 79.

Sometimes *fathers* indefinitely, *Observations*,
155

Sometime *the heir to Adam*, Observations 253.

Sometimes *the posterity of Adam*, 244, 246.

Sometimes *prime fathers, all sons or grand-children of* Noah, *Observations*, 244

Sometimes the *eldest parents*, p. 12

Sometimes all *kings*, p 19

Sometimes all that have supreme power, *Observations*, 245.

Sometimes *heirs to those first progenitors, who
were at first the natural parents of the whole people*, p 19

Sometimes an elective king, p. 23.

Sometimes those, whether a few or a multitude,
that govern the *common-wealth*, p 23

Sometimes he that can catch it, an *usurper*,
p 23 Observations, 155.

§ 72. Thus this *new nothing*, that is to carry
with it all power, authority, and government;
this fatherhood, which is to design the person,
and establish the throne of monarchs, whom the
people are to obey, may, according to Sir *Robert*,
come into any hands, any how, and so by his
politics

politics give to democracy royal authority, and
make an usurper a lawful prince. And if it will
do all these fine feats, much good do our author and all his followers with their omnipotent
fatherhood, which can serve for nothing but to
unsettle and destroy all the lawful governments
in the world, and to establish in their room disorder, tyranny, and usurpation.

CHAP. VII.

Of Fatherhood and Property considered together as Fountains of Sovereignty

§ 73 IN the foregoing chapters we have seen
what *Adam*'s monarchy was, in our author's opinion, and upon what titles he founded it.
The foundations which he lays the chief stress on,
as those from which he thinks he may best derive
monarchical power to future princes, are two,
viz Fatherhood and property and therefore the
way he proposes to *remove the absurdities and inconveniencies of the doctrine of natural freedom*, is,
to maintain the natural and private dominion of
Adam, *Observations* 222. Conformable hereunto,
he tells us, the *grounds and principles of government necessarily depend upon the original of property*,
Observations, 108 *The subjection of children to
their parents is the fountain of all regal authority*,
p. 12 *And all power on earth is either derived or
usurped from the fatherly power, there being no
other original to be found of any power whatsoever*,
Observations, 158 I will not stand here to examine how it can be said without a contradiction,
that the *first grounds and principles of government
necessarily depend upon the original of property*, and
yet, *that there is no other original of any power*
whatsoever,

whatsoever, but that of the father it being hard to understand how there can be *no other original but fatherhood,* and yet that the *grounds and principles of government depend upon the original of property, property and fatherhood* being as far different as lord of a manor and father of children. Nor do I see how they will either of them agree with what our author says, *Observations,* 244 of Go 's sentence against *Eve,* Gen iii 16 *That is the original grant of government·* so that if that were the *original,* government had not its *original,* by our author's own confession, either from *property* or *fatherhood,* and this text, which he brings as a proof of *Adam*'s power over *Eve,* necessarily contradicts what he says of the *fatherhood,* that it is the *sole fountain of all power* for if *Adam* had any such regal power over *Eve,* as our author contends for, it must be by some other title than that of begetting

§ 74 But I leave him to reconcile these contradictions, as well as many others, which may plentifully be found in him by any one, who will but read him with a little attention, and shall come now to confider, how these two originals of government, *Adam's natural and private dominion,* will confist, and ferve to make out and establish the titles of fucceeding monarchs, who, as our author obliges them, must all derive their power from these *fountains* Let us then fuppofe *Adam* made, *by God's donation,* lord and fole proprietor of the whole earth, in as large and ample a manner as Sir *Robert* could wifh, let us fuppofe him alfo, *by right of fatherhood,* abfolute ruler over his children with an unlimited fupremacy, I afk then, upon *Adam*'s death what becomes of both his *natural* and *private dominion?* And I doubt not it will be anfwered, that they defcended

fcended to his next heir, as our author tells us in
feveral places. But this way, it is plain, cannot
poffibly convey both his *natural* and *private dominion* to the fame perfon: for fhould we
allow, that all the property, all the eftate of
the fa her, ought to defcend to the eldeft fon,
(which will need fome proof to eftablifh it) and fo
he has by that title all the *private dominion* of the
father, yet the father's *natural dominion*, the paternal power cannot defcend to him by inheritance . for it being a right that accrues to a man
only by begetting, no man can have this natural
dominion over any one he does not *beget* , urlefs
it can be fuppofed, that a man can have a right
to any thing, without doing that upon which
that right is folely founded · for if a father by
begetting, and no other title, has *natural dominion*
over his children, he that does not beget them
cannot have this *natural dominion* over them , and
therefore be it true or falfe, that our author fays,
Obfervations, 156 That *every man that is born,*
by his very birth becomes a fubject to him that be
gets him, this neceffarily follows, *viz.* That a
man by his birth cannot become a fubject to his
brother,* who did not beget him ; unlefs it can
be fuppofed that a man by the very fame title
can come to be under the *natural and abfolute do*
minion of two different men at once , or it be
fenfe to fay, that a man by birth is under the na-
tural dominion of his father, only becaufe he begat him, and a man by birth alfo is under the
natural dominion of his eldeft brother, though he
did not beget him

§ 75 If then the *private dominion of Adam*, i e
his property in the creatures, defcended at his
death all entirely to his eldeft fon, his heir,
(for, if it did not, there is prefently an end of all
Su

Sir *Robert's* monarchy) and his *natural dominion*,
the dominion a father has over his children by begetting them, belonged immediately upon *Adam's*
deceafe, equally to all his ions who had children,
by the fame title their father had it, the fovereignty founded upon *property*, and the fovereignty founded upon *fatherhood*, come to be divided;
fince *Cain*, as heir, had that of *property* alone;
Seth, and the other fons, that of *fatherhood* equally with him. This is the beft can be made of
our author's doctrine, and of the two titles of fovereignty he fets up in *Adam* one of them will either
fignify nothing; or, if they both muft ftand, they
can ferve only to confound the rights of princes,
and diforder government in his pofterity for by
building upon two titles to dominion, which cannot defcend together, and which he allows may
be feparated, (for he yields that *Adam's children
had their diftinct territories by right of private dominion*, Obfervations, 210 p 40) he makes it
perpetually a doubt upon his principles where the
fovereignty is, or to whom we owe our obedience,
fince *fatherhood* and *property* are diftinct titles, and
began prefently upon *Adam's* death to be in diftinct perfons. And which then was to give way
to the other?

§ 76 Let us take the account of it, as he himfelf gives it us. He tells us out of *Grotius*, 'That
*Adam's children by donation, affignation, or fome
kind of ceffion before he was dead, had their diftinct
territories by right of private dominion*, Abel *had
his flocks and paftures for them* · Cain *had his fields
for corn, and the land of* Nod, *where he built him
a city*, Obfervations, 210. Here it is obvious to
demand, which of thefe two after *Adam's* death
was fovereign? *Cain*, fays our author, p 19 By
what title? *As* heir; *for heirs to progenitors, who*
                                                    were

*were natural parents of their people, are not only
lords of their own children, but also of their brethren,* fays our author, p 19   What was *Cain*
heir to ? Not the entire poffeffions, not all that
which *Adam* had *private dominion* in ; for our
author allows that *Abel*, by a title derived from
his father, had *his diftinct territory for pafture by
right of private dominion*   What then *Abel* had
by *private dominion*, was exempt from *Cain*'s dominion · for he could not have *private dominion* o-
ver that that which was under the private *dominion* of another , and therefore his fovereignty
over his brother is gone with his *private dominion*,
and fo there are prefently two fovereigns, and his
imaginary title of *father hood* is out of doors, and
Cain is no prince over his brother or elfe, if *Cain*
retain his fovereignty over *Abel*, notwithftanding
his *private dominion*, it will follow, that the *firft
grounds and principles of government* have nothing
to do with *property*, whatever our author fays to
the contrary   It is true, *Abel* did not outlive
his father *Adam* ; but that makes nothing to the
argument, which will hold good againft Sir *Robert* in *Abel*'s iffue, or in *Seth*, or in any of the
pofterity of *Adam*, not defcended from *Cain*.

§ 77. The fame inconvenience he runs into
about *the three fons of Noah*, who, as he fays, p
13 *had the whole world divided amongft them by
their father*   I afk then, in which of the three
fhall we find *the eftablifhment of regal power* after
Noah's death ? If in all three, as our author there
feems to fay , then it will follow, that regal power is founded in property of land, and follows
private dominion, and not in *paternal power*, or
natural dominion , and fo there is an end of paternal power as the fountain of regal authority,
and the fo-much-magnified *fatherhood* quite va-
                                                          nifhed

rifhes If the regal power defcended to *Shem* as
eldeft, and heir to his father, then *Noah's divifion of the world by lot to his fons, or his ten years
failing about the Mediterranean to appoint each fon
his part*, which our author tells of, p 15 was labour loft , his divifion of the world to them, was
to ill, or to no purpofe for his grant to *Cham*
and *Japhet* was little worth, if *Shem*, notwithftanding this grant, as foon as *Noah* was dead,
was to be lord over them Or, if this grant of
private dominion to them, over their affigned territories, were good, here were fet up two diftinct
forts of power, not fubordinate one to the other,
with all thofe inconveniences which he mufters
up againft the *power of the people*, Obfervations,
158 which I fhall fet down in his own words, only
changing *property* for *people* *All power on earth
is either derived or ufurped from the fatherly power,
there being no other original to be found of any
power whatfoever for if there fhould be granted
two forts of power, without any fubordination of one
to the other, they would be in perpetual ftrife which
fhould be fupreme, for two fupremes cannot agree :
if the fatherly power be fupreme, then the power
grounded on private dominion muft be fubordinate,
and depend on it , and if the power grounded on
property be fupreme, then the fatherly power muft
fubmit to it, and cannot be exercifed without the licence of the proprietors, which muft quite deftroy
the frame and courfe of nature* This is his own
arguing againft two diftinct independent powers,
which I have fet down in his own words, only
putting power rifing from property, for *power of
the people*, and when he has anfwered what he
himfelf has urged here againft two diftinct powers, we fhall be better able to fee how, with any
tolerable fenfe, he can derive all regal authority

E   *from*

from the natural and private dominion of Adam, from *fatherhood and property* together, which are diftinct titles, that do not always meet in the fame perfon ; and it is plain, by his own confeſſion, preſently feparated as foon both as *Adam's* and *Noah's* death made way for fucceſſion though our author frequently in his writings jumbles them together, and omits not to make uſe of either, where he thinks it will found beſt to his purpoſe.   But the abſurdities of this will more fully appear in the next chapter, where we fhall examine the ways of conveyance of the fovereignty of *Adam*, to princes that were to reign after him

---

CHAP. VIII

Of the Conveyance of Adam's ſovereign Monarchical Power.

§. 78 SIR *Robert*, having not been very happy in any proof he brings for the fovereignty of *Adam*, is not much more fortunate in conveying it to future princes, who, if his politics be true, muſt all derive their titles from that firſt monarch. The ways he has aſſigned, as they lie fcattered up and down in his writings, I will fet down in his own words · in his preface he tells us, That *Adam being monarch of the whole world, none of his poſterity had any right to poſſeſs any thing, but by his grant or permiſſion, or by ſucceſſion from him.* Here he makes two ways of conveyance of any thing *Adam* ſtood poſſeſſed of; and thoſe are *grants* or *ſucceſſion* Again he fays, *All kings either are, or are to be reputed, the next heirs to thoſe firſt progenitors, who were at firſt the natural parents of the whole people,* p 19 *There cannot be any multitude of men whatſoever, but that in it,*
conſidered

considered by itself, there is one man amongst them, that in nature hath a right to be the king of all the rest, as being the next heir to Adam, *Observations,* 253. Here in these places *inheritance* is the only way he allows of conveying monarchical power to princes In other places he tells us, *Observations,* 155 *All power on earth is either derived or usurped from the fatherly power,* Observations, 158. *All kings that now are, or ever were, are or were either fathers of their people, or heirs of such fathers, or usurpers of the right of such fathers,* Observations, 253. And here he makes *inheritance* or *usurpation* the only ways whereby kings come by this original *power* but yet he tells us, *This fatherly empire, as it was of itself hereditary, so it was alienable by patent, and seizable by an usurper,* Observations, 190 So then here inheritance, grant, or usurpation, will convey it. And last of all, which is most admirable, he tells us, p 100 *It skills not which way kings come by their power, whether by election, donation, succession, or by any other means, for it is still the manner of the government by supreme power, that makes them properly kings, and not the means of obtaining their crowns* Which I think is a full answer to all his whole *hypothesis* and discourse about *Adam's* royal authority, as the fountain from which all princes were to derive theirs and he might have spared the trouble of speaking so much as he does, up and down, of heirs and inheritance, if to make any one *properly a king,* needs no more but *governing by supreme power, and it matters not by what means he came by it*

§. 79 By this notable way, our author may make *Oliver* as *properly king,* as any one else he could think of and had he had the happiness to live under *Massanello's* government, he could

not

not by this his own rule have forborn to have done homage to him, with *O king live for ever,* since the manner of his government by supreme power, made him *properly* king, who was but the day before *properly* a fisherman   And if *Don Quixote* had taught his 'squire to govern with supreme authority, our author no doubt could have made a most loyal subject in *Sancho Pancha's Island,* and he must needs have deserved some preferment in such governments, since I think he is the first politician, who, pretending to settle government upon its true basis, and to establish the thrones of lawful princes, ever told the world, *'That he was properly a king, whose manner of government was by supreme power, by what means soever he obtained it,* which in plain *English* is to say, that regal and supreme power is properly and truly his, who can by any means seize upon it; and if this be to be *properly a king,* I wonder how he came to think of, or where he will find, an *usurper*

§ 80 This is so strange a doctrine, that the surprise of it hath made me pass by, without their due reflection, the contradictions he runs into, by making sometimes *inheritance* alone, sometimes only *grant or inheritance,* sometimes only *inheritance or usurpation,* sometimes all these three, and at last *election,* or *any other means,* added to them. the ways whereby *Adam's* royal authority, that is, his right to supreme rule, could be conveyed down to future kings and governors. so as to give them a title to the obedience and subjection of the people   But these contradictions lie so open, that the very reading of our author's own words will discover them to any ordinary understanding and though what I have quoted out of him (with abundance more of the same strain and
coherence

coherence, which might be found in him) might
well excufe me from any farther trouble in this
argument, yet having propofed to myfelf, to examine the main parts of his doctrine, I fhall a
little more particularly confider how *inhei itance*,
grant, *ufurpation* or *election*, can any way make
out government in the world upon his principles,
or derive to any one a right of empire, from this
regal authority of *Adam* had it been never fo well
proved, that he had been abfolute monarch, and
lord of the whole world

CHAP IX.

Of Monarchy, by Inheritance from Adam

§ 81 **THOUGH** it be never fo plain, that
there ought to be government in the
world, nay, fhould all men be of our author's
mind, that divine appointment had ordained it to
be *monarchical*, yet, fince men cannot obey any
thing, that cannot command; and ideas of government in the fancy, though never fo perfect,
though never fo right, cannot give laws, nor
prefcribe rules to the actions of men; it would
be of no behoof for the fettling of order, and
eftablifhment of government in its exercife and
ufe amongft men, unlefs there were a way alfo
taught how to know the perfon to whom it belonged to have this power, and exercife this dominion over others   It is in vain then to talk of
fubjection and obedience without telling us whom
we are to obey for were I never fo fully perfuaded that there ought to be magiftracy and rule in
the world, yet I am never the lefs at liberty ftill,
till it appears who is the perfon that hath right

to my obedience, since, if there be no marks to
know him by, and distinguish him that hath
right to rule from other men, it may be myself,
as well as any other   And therefore, though
submission to government be every one's duty, yet
since that signifies nothing but submitting to the
direction and laws of such men as have authority
to command, it is not enough to make a man a
subject, to convince him that there is *regal power*
in the world, but there must be ways of design-
ing, and knowing the person to whom this *regal
power* of right belongs   and a man can never
be obliged in conscience to submit to any power,
unless he can be satisfied who is the person who
has a right to exercise that power over him   If
this were not so, there would be no distinction
between pirates and lawful princes, he that has
force is without any more ado to be obeyed, and
crowns and scepters would become the inheritance
only of violence and rapine   Men too might as
often and as innocently change their governors,
as they do their physicians, if the person cannot
be known who has a right to direct me, and
whose prescriptions I am bound to follow   To
settle therefore men's consciences, under an obligation to obedience, it is necessary that they
know not only, that there is a power somewhere
in the world, but the person who by right is vested with this power over them

§ 82 How successful our author has been in
his attempts, to set up a *monarchical absolute power* in *Adam*, the reader may judge by what has
been already said, but were that *absolute monarchy* as clear as our author would desire it, as I
presume it is the contrary, yet it could be of no
use to the government of mankind now in the
world, unless he also make out these two things.

First,

First, That this *power of Adam* was not to end with him, but was upon his deceafe conveyed intire to fome other perfon, and fo on to pofterity.

Secondly, That the princes and rulers now on earth are poffeffed of this *power of Adam*, by a right way of conveyance derived to them

§ 83 If the firft of thefe fail, the *power of Adam*, were it never fo great, never fo certain, will fignify nothing to the prefent government and focieties in the world, but we muft feek out fome other original of power for the goveinment of politys than this of *Adam*, or elfe there will be none at all in the world If the latter fail, it will deftroy the authority of the prefent governors, and abfolve the people fiom fubjection to them, fince they, having no better a claim than others to that power, which is alone the fountain of all authority, can have no title to rule over them.

§ 84 Our author, having fancied an abfolute fovereignty in *Adam*, mentions feveral ways of its conveyance to princes, that were to be his fucceffors; but that which he chiefly infifts on, is that of *inheritance*, which occurs fo often in his feveral difcourfes; and I having in the foregoing chapter quoted feveral of thefe paffages, I fhall not need here again to repeat them. This fovereignty he erects, as has been faid, upon a double foundation, *viz.* that of *property*, and that of *fatherhood*. One was the right he was fuppofed to have in all creatures, a right to poffefs the earth with the beafts, and other inferior ranks of things in it, for his private ufe, exclufive of all other men The other was the right he was fuppofed to have, to rule and govern men, all the reft of mankind.

E 4 § 85. In

§ 85. In both thefe rights, there being fup-poſed an excluſion of all other men, it muſt be upon fome reaſon peculiar to *Adam*, that they muſt both be founded

That of his *property* our author fuppofes to ariſe from God's immediate *donation*, *Gen* 1 28 and that of *fatherhood* from the act of *begetting* now in all inheritance, if the heir fucceed not to the reaſon upon which his father's right was founded, he cannot fucceed to the right which followeth from it For example, *Adam* had a right of property in the creatures upon the *donation* and *grant* of God almighty, who was lord and proprietor of them all. let this be fo as our author tells us, yet upon his death his heir can have no title to them, no fuch right of pro-perty in them, unlefs the fame reaſon, *viz* God's *donation*, vefted a right in the *heir* too : for if *Adam* could have had no property in, nor uſe

f the creatures, without this pofitive *donation* from God, and this *donation* were only perſonally to *Adam*, his *heir* could have no right by it , but upon his death it muſt revert to God, the lord and owner again ; for pofitive grants give no title farther than the exprefs words convey it, and by which only it is held And thus, if as our author himfelf contends, that *donation*, *Gen* 1 28 were made only to *Adam* perſonally, his heir could not fucceed to his property in the creatures; and if it were a donation to any but *Adam*, let it be fhewn, that it was to his heir in our author's fenfe, *i e* to one of his children, exclufive of all the reſt

§ 86 But not to follow our author too far out of the way, the plain of the caſe is this God having made man, and planted in him, as in all other animals, a ſtrong defire of felf-prefervation, and

and furnished the world with things fit for food and raiment, and other neceffaries of life, fubfervient to his defign, that man should live and abide for fome time upon the face of the earth, and not that fo curious and wonderful a piece of workmanfhip, by his own negligence, or want of neceffaries, should perish again, prefently after a few moments continuance, God, I fay, having made man and the world thus, fpoke to him, (that is, directed him by his fenfes and reafon, as he did the inferior animals by their fenfe and inftinct, which were ferviceable for his fubfiftence, and given him as the means of his *prefervation* And therefore I doubt not, but before thefe words were pronounced, *Gen* 28, 29 (if they muft be underftood literally to have been fpoken) and without any fuch verbal *donation*, man had a right to an ufe of the creatures, by the will and grant of God for the defire, ftrong defire of preferving his life and being, having been planted in him as a principle of action by God himfelf, reafon, *which was the voice of God in him*, could not but teach him and affure him, that purfuing that natural inclination he had to preferve his being, he followed the will of his maker, and therefore had a right to make ufe of thefe creatures, which by his reafon or fenfes he could difcover would be ferviceable thereunto And thus man's *property* in the creatures was founded upon the right he had to make ufe of thofe things that were neceffary or ufeful to his being

§ 8, This being the reafon and foundation of *Adam's property*, gave the fame title, on the fame ground, to all his children, not only after his death, but in his life time fo that here was no privilege of his *heir* above his other children,

L 5   which

which could exclude them from an equal right
to the use of the inferior creatures, for the comfortable prefervation of their beings, which is all
the *property* man hath in them, and fo *Adam*'s
fovereignty built on *property*, or, as our author
calls it, *private dominion*, comes to nothing Every
man had a right to the creatures, by the fame
title *Adam* had, *viz.* by the right every one had
to take care of, and provide for their fubfiftence.
and thus men had a right in common, *Adam*'s
children in common with him   But if any one
had begun, and made himfelf a property in any
particular thing, (which how he, or any one elfe
could do, fhall be fhewn in another place) that
thing, that poffeffion, if he difpofed not otherwife
of it by his pofitive grant, defcerded naturally
to his children, and they had a right to fucceed
to it, and poffefs it.

§. 88 It might reafonably be afked here, how
come children by this right of poffeffing, before
any other, the properties of their parents upon
their deceafe ? for it being perfonally the parents,
when they die, without actually transferring their
right to another, why does it not return again to
the common flock of mankind ? It will perhaps
be anfwered, that common confent hath difpofed
of it to their children   Common practice, we
fee indeed, does fo difpofe of it; but we cannot
fay, that it is the common confent of mankind,
for that hath never been afked, nor actually
given, and if common tacit confent hath
eftablifhed it, it would make but a pofitive, and
not a natural right of children to inherit the
goods of their parents but where the practice
is univerfal, it is reaf nable to think the caufe is
natural The ground hen I think to be this
The firft and ftrongeft defire God planted in
men,

men, and wrought into the very principles of their nature, being that of self-preservation, that is the foundation of a right to the creatures for the particular support and use of each individual person himself. But, next to this, God planted in men a strong desire also of propagating their kind, and continuing themselves in their posterity; and this gives children a title to share in the *property* of their parents, and a right to inherit their possessions. Men are not proprietors of what they have, meerly for themselves, their children have a title to part of it, and have their kind of right joined with their parents, in the possession which comes to be wholly their's, when death, having put an end to their parents use of it, hath taken them from their possessions, and this we call inheritance. men being by a like obligation bound to preserve what they have begotten, as to preserve themselves, their issue come to have a right in the goods they are possessed of. That children have such a right, is plain from the laws of God, and that men are convinced that children have such a right, is evident from the law of the land, both which laws require parents to provide for their children.

§ 89. For children being by the course of nature, born weak, and unable to provide for themselves, they have by the appointment of God himself, who hath thus ordered the course of nature, a right to be nourished and maintained by their parents; nay, a right not only to a bare subsistence, but to the conveniencies and comforts of life, as far as the conditions of their parents can afford it. Hence it comes, that when their parents leave the world, and so the care due to their children ceases, the effects of it are to extend as far as possibly they can, and the provisions they

they have made in their life-time, are underftood
to be intended, as nature requires they fhould,
for their children, whom, after themfelves, they
are bound to provide for though the dying parents, by exprefs words, declare nothing about
them, nature appoints the defcent of their property to their children, who thus come to have
a title, and natural right of inheritance to their
fathers goods, which the reft of mankind cannot
pretend to

§ 90 Were it not for this right of being
nourifhed and maintained by their parents, which
God and nature has given to children, and obliged
parents to as a duty, it would be reafonable, that
the father fhould inherit the eftate of his fon, and
be preferred in the inheritance before his grandchild for to the grand father there is due a long
fcore of care and expences laid out upon the
breeding and education of his fon, which one
would think in juftice ought to be paid But
that having been done in obedierce to the fame
law, whereby he received nourifhment and education from his own parents; this fcore of education, received from a man's father, is paid by
taking care, and providing for his own children,
is paid, I fay, as much as is required of payment
by alteration of property, unlefs prefent receffi-
ty of the parents require a return of goods
for their neceffary fupport and fubfiftence for
we are not now fpeaking of that reverence, ac-
knowledgment, refpect and honour, that is always due from children to their parents, but of
poffeffions and commodities of life valuable by
money But though it be incumbent on parents
to bring up and provide for their children, yet
this debt to their children does not quite cancel
the fcore due to their parents, but only is made
by

by nature preferable to it   for the debt a man
owes his father takes place, and gives the father
a right to inherit the fon's goods, where, for
want of iffue, the right of children doth not exclude that title, and therefore a man having a
right to be maintained by his children, where he
needs it, and to enjoy alfo the comforts of life
from them, when the neceffary provifion due to
them and their children will afford it, if his fon
die without iffue, the father has a right in nature
to poffefs his goods, and inherit his eftate, (whatever the municifal laws of fome countries may
abfurdly direct otherwife,) and fo again his children and their iffue from him, or, for want of
fuch, his father and his iffue But where no
fuch are to be found, i e no kindred, there we
fee the poffeffions of a private man revert to the
community, and fo in politic focieties come into
the hands of the public magiftrate, but in the
ftate of nature become again perfectly common,
no body having a right to inherit them. nor can
any one have a property in them, otherwife than
in other things common by nature, of which I
fh 'll fpeak in its due place

    § 91 I have been the larger, in fhewing upon
what ground children have a right to fucceed to
the p ffeffion of their fathers properties, not only
becaufe by it, it will appear, that if *Adam* had a
property (a titular, irfignificant, ufelefs property,
for it could be no better, for he was bound to
nourifh and maintain his children and pofterity
out of it) in the whole earth and its product, yet
all his children coming to have, by the law of
nature, and right of inheritance, a joint title, and
r 't of property in it after his death, it could
convey no right of fovereignty to any one of his
pofterity over the reft fince every one having a
                                          right

right of inheritance to his portion, they might
enjoy their inheritance, or any part of it in common, or fhare it, or fome parts of it, by divifion,
as it beft liked them But no one could pretend
to the whole in eritance, or any fovereignty fuppofed to accompany it, fince a right of inheritance gave eve y one of the reft, as well as any
one, a title to fhare in the goods of his father.
Not only upon this account, I fay, have I been
fo particular in examining the reafon of children's
inheriting the property of their fathers, but alfo
becaufe it will give us farthei l ght in the inheritance of *rule* and *power*, which in countries
where their particular municipal laws give the
whole poffeffion of land entirely to the firft-born,
and defcent of power has gone fo to men by this
cuftom, fome have been apt to be deceived into
an opinion that there was a natural or divine
right of primogeniture, to both *eftate* and *power*,
and that the inheritance of both *rule* over men,
and *property* in things, fprang from the fame
original, and were to defcend by the fame
rules

§ 92 Property, whofe original is from the
right a man ha to ufe any of the inferior creatures, for the fubfiftence and comfort of his life,
is for the benefit and f le advantage of the proprietor, fo that he may even deftroy the th ng, that he
has property in by his ufe of it, where need requires but government being for the prefervation
of every man's right and property, by preferving him from the violence or injury of others, is
for the good of the fovereid for the magiftrate's
fword being for a *terror to evil doers*, and by that
terror to inforce men to obferve the pofitive laws
of the fociety, made conformable to the laws of
nature, for the public good, *i. e.* the good of
every

every particular member of that fociety, as far as
by common rules it can be provided for, the
fword is not given the magiftrate for his own
good alone

§ 93. Children therefore, as has been fhewed,
by the dependance they have on their parents for
fubfiftence, have a right of inheritance to their
fathers property, as that which belongs to them,
for their proper good and behoof, and therefore
are fitly termed goods, wherein the firft-born has
not a fole or peculiar right by any law of God
and nature, the younger children having an equal
title with him, founded on that right they all
have to maintenance, fupport, and comfort from
their parents, and on nothing elfe But government being for the benefit of the governed, and
not the fole advantage of the governors, (but only
for their's with the reft, as they make a part of
that politic body, each of whofe parts and members are taken care of, and directed in its peculiar
functions for the good of the whole, by the laws
of fociety) cannot be inherited by the fame title,
that children have to the goods of their father.
The right a fon has to be maintained and provided with the neceffaries and conveniences of
life out of his father's ftock, gives him a right to
fucceed to his father's *property* for his own good,
but this can give him no right* to fucceed alfo
to the *rule*, which his father had over other men.
All that a child has right to claim from his father
is nourifhment and education, and the things nature furnifhes for the fupport of life · but he has
no right to demand *rule* or *dominion* from him ·
he can fubfift and receive from him the portion
of good things, and advantages of education naturally due to him, without *empire* and *dominion*.
That (if his father hath any) was vefted in him,
for

for the good and behoof of others : and therefore the son can ot claim or inherit it by a title,
which is founded wholly on his own private good
ard advantage

§ 94 We must know how the first ruler,
from whom any one claims, came by his authority, upon what ground any one has *empire*, what
his title is to it, before we can know who has a
right to succeed him in it, and inherit it from
him if the agreement ard consent of men first
gave a scepter into any one's hand, or put a
crown on his head, that also must direct its descent and conveyance, for the same authority,
that made the first a lawful *ruler*, must make the
second too, and to give right of succession in
this case inheritance, or primogeniture, can in its
self have no right, no pretence to it, any farther
than that consent, which established the form of the
government, hath so settled the succession And
this we see, the succession of crowns, in several
countries, places it on different heads, and he
comes by right of succession to be a prince in one
place, who would be a subject in another

§ 95 If God, by his positive grant and revealed declaration, first gave *rule* and *dominion* to
any man, he that will claim by that title, must
have the same positive grant of God for his successor for if that was not directed the course of
its descent and conveyance down to others, no
body can succeed to this title of the first ruler
Children have no right of inheritance to this and
primogeniture can lay no claim to it, unless God,
the author of this constitution, hath so ordained
it This we see, the pretensions of *Saul's* family, who received his crown from the immediate
appointment of God, ended with his reign, and
David, by the same title that *Saul* reigned, for
God'

God's appointment, fucceeded in his throne, to the exclufion of *Jonathan*, and all pretenfions of paternal inheritance. and if *Solomon* had a right to fucceed his father, it muft be by fome other title, than that of primogeniture A *cadet*, or fifter's fon, muft have the preference in fucceffion, if he has the fame title the firft lawful prince had and in dominion that has its foundation only in the pofitive appointment of God himfelf, *Benjamin*, the youngeft, muft have the inheritance of the crown, it God fo direct, as well as one of that tribe had the firft poffeffion.

§ 96 If *paternal right*, the act of *begetting*, give a man *rule* and *dominion*, inheritance or primogeniture can give no title for he that cannot fucceed to his father's title, which was *begetting*, cannot fucceed to that power over his brethren, which his father had by paternal right over them. But of this I fhall have occafion to fay more in another place This is plain in the mean time, that any government, whether fuppofed to be at firft founded in *paternal right, confent of the people*, or the *pofitive appointment of God himfelf*, which can fuperfede either of the other, and fo begin a new government upon a new foundation; I fay, any government began upon either of thefe, can by right of fucceffion come to thofe only, who have the title of him they fucceed to power founded on *contract* can defcend only to him, who has right by that contract power founded on *begetting*, he only can have that *begets*, and power founded on the pofitive *grant* or donation of God, he only can have by right of fucceffion, to whom that grant directs it

§ 97 From what I have faid, I think this is clear, that a right to the ufe of the creatures, being founded originally in the right a man has
to

to subsist and enjoy the conveniencies of life; and the natural right children have to inherit the goods of their parents, being founded in the right they have to the same subsistence and commodities of life, out of the stock of their parents, who are therefore taught by natural love and tenderness to provide for them, as a part of themselves, and all this being only for the good of the proprietor, or heir, it can be no reason for children's inheriting of *rule* and *dominion*, which has another original and a different end. Nor can primogeniture have any pretence to a right of solely inheriting either *property* or *power*, as we shall, in its due place, see more fully. It is enough to have shewed here, that *Adam's property*, or *private dominion*, could not convey any sovereignty or rule to his heir, who not having a right to inherit all his father's possessions, could not thereby come to have any sovereignty over his brethren: and therefore, if any sovereignty on account of his *property* had been vested in *Adam*, which in truth there was not, yet it would have died with him.

§ 98. As *Adam's* sovereignty, if, by virtue of being proprietor of the world, he had any authority over men, could not have been inherited by any of his children over the rest, because they had the same title to divide the inheritance, and every one had a right to a portion of his father's possessions, so neither could *Adam's* sovereignty by right of *fatherhood*, if any such he had, descend to any one of his children · for it being, in our author's account, a right acquired by *begetting* to rule over those he had begotten, it was not a power possible to be inherited, because the right being consequent to, and built on, an act perfectly personal, made that power so too, and impossible

Possible to be inherited for paternal power, being a natural right rising only from the relation of
father and son, is as impossible to be inherited as
the relation itself; and a man may pretend as well
to inherit the conjugal power the husband, whose
heir he is, had over his wife, as he can to inherit the paternal power of a father over his children for the power of the husband being founded on contract, and the power of the father on
begetting, he may as well inherit the power obtained by the conjugal contract, which was only
personal, as he may the power obtained by begetting, which could reach no farther than the
person of the begetter, unless begetting can be a
title to power in him that does not beget

§ 99 Which makes it a reasonable question to
ask, whether *Adam*, dying before *Eve*, his heir,
(suppose *Cain* or *Seth*) should have by right of inheriting *Adam's fatherhood*, sovereign power over
Eve his mother · for *Adam's fatherhood* being nothing but a right he had to govern his children,
because he begot them, he that inherits *Adam's
fatherhood*, inherits nothing, even in our author's
sense, but the right *Adam* had to govern his children, because he begot them · so that the monarchy of the heir would not have taken in *Eve*, or
if it did, it being nothing but the *fatherhood of
Adam* descended by inheritance, the heir must have
right to govern *Eve*, because *Adam* begot her, for
fatherhood is nothing else

§ 100 Perhaps it will be said with our author,
that a man can alien his power over his child;
and what may be transferred by compact, may
be possessed by inheritance I answer, a father
cannot alien the power he has over his child he
may perhaps to some degrees forfeit it, but cannot transfer it, and if any other man acquire it,
it

it is not by the father's grant, but by some act of his own. For example, a father, unnaturally careless of his child, sells or gives him to another man, and he again exposes him, a third man finding him, breeds up, cherishes, and provides for him as his own. I think in this case, no body will doubt, but that the greatest part of filial duty and subjection was here owing, and to be paid to his foster-father, and if any thing could be demanded from the child, by either of the other, it could be only due to his natural father, who perhaps might have forfeited his right to much of that duty comprehended in the command, *Honour your parents*, but could transfer none of it to another. He that purchased, and neglected the child, got by his purchase and grant of the father, no title to duty or honour from the child, but only he acquired it, who by his own authority, performing the office and care of a father, to the forlorn and perishing infant, made himself, by paternal care, a title to proportionable degrees of paternal power. This will be more easily admitted upon consideration of the nature of paternal power, for which I refer my reader to the second book.

§ 101. To return to the argument in hand; this is evident, That paternal power arising only from *begetting*, for in that our author places it alone, can neither be *transferred* nor *inherited*: and he that does not beget, can no more have paternal power, which arises from thence, than he can have a right to any thing, who performs not the condition, to which only it is annexed. If one should ask, by what law has a father power over his children? it will be answered, no doubt, by the law of nature, which gives such a power over them, to him that begets them. It

one

one fhould afk likewife, by what law does our
author's heir come by a right to inherit? I think
it would be anfwered, by the law of nature too:
for I find not that our author brings one word of
fcripture to prove the right of fuch an heir he
fpeaks of Why then the law of nature gives
fathers paternal power over their children, becaufe they did *beget* them, and the fame law of
nature gives the fame paternal power to the heir
over his brethren, who did not beget them:
whence it follows, that either the father has not
his paternal power by begetting, or elfe that the
heir has it not at all, for it is hard to underftand
how the law of nature, which is the law of reafon, can give the paternal power to the father
over his children, for the only reafon of *begetting*;
and to the firft born over his brethren without
this only reafon, *i e* for no reafon at all and if
the eldeft, by the law of nature, can inherit this
paternal power, without the only reafon that gives
a title to it, fo may the youngeftas well is he, and
a ftranger as well as either, for where there is no
reafon for any one, as there is not, but for him that
begets, all have an equal title I am fure our author offers no reafon; and when any body does,
we fhall fee whether it will hold or no.

§ 102 In the mean time it is as good fenfe to
fay, that by the law of nature a man has right
to inherit the property of another, becaufe he
is of kin to him, and is known to be of his
blood, and therefore, by the fame law of nature,
an utter ftranger to his blood has right to inherit
his eftate, as to fay that, by the law of nature,
he that begets them has paternal power over his
children, and therefore, by the law of nature,
the heir that begets them not, has this paternal
power over them, or fuppofing the law of the
land

land gave abfolute power over their children to fuch only who nurfed them, and fed their children themfelves, could any body pretend, that this law gave any one, who did no fuch thing, abfolute power over thofe, who were not his children?

§ 103. When therefore it can be fhewed, that conjugal power can belong to him that is not an hufband, it will alfo I believe be proved, that our author's paternal power, acquired by begetting, may be inherited by a fon, and that a brother, as heir to his father's power, may have paternal power over his brethren, and by the fame rule conjugal power too: but till then, I think we may reft fatisfied, that the paternal power of *Adam*, this fovereign authority of *fatherhood*, were there any fuch, could not defcend to, nor be inherited by, his next heir. *Fatherly power*, I eafily grant our author, if it will do him any good, can never be loft, becaufe it will be as long in the world as there are fathers: but none of them will have *Adam*'s paternal power, or derive their's from him, but every one will have his own, by the fame title *Adam* had his, *viz* by *begetting*, but not by inheritance, or fucceffion, no more than hufbands have their conjugal power by inheritance, from *Adam* And thus we fee, as *Adam* had no fuch *property*, no fuch *paternal power*, as gave him *fovereign* jurifdiction over mankind; fo likewife his fovereignty built upon either of thefe titles, if he had any fuch, could not have defcended to his heir, but muft have ended with him. *Adam* therefore, as has been proved, being neither monarch, nor his imaginary monarchy hereditable, the power which is now in the world, is not that which was *Adam*'s, fince all that *Adam* could have upon our author's grounds, either of *property* or *fatherhood*, neceffarily died

with

with him, and could not be conveyed to pofterity by inheritance In the next place we will confider, whether *Adam* had any fuch heir, to inherit his power, as our author talks of

---

CHAP X.

Of the Heir to Adam's *Monarchical Power.*

§ 104 OUR author tells us, Obfervations, 253 *That it is a truth undeniable, that there cannot be any multitude of men whatfoever, either great or fmall, tho' gathered together from the feveral corners and remoteft regions of the world, but that in the fame multitude, confidered by its felf, there is one man amongft them, that in nature hath a right to be king of all the reft, as being the next heir to* Adam, *and all the other fubjects to him every man by nature is a king or a fubject.* And again, p 20 *If* Adam *himfelf were ftill living, and now ready to die, it is certain that there is one man, and but one in the world, who is next heir* Let this *multitude of men* be, if our author pleafes, all the princes upon the earth, there will then be, by our author's rule, *one amongft them, that in nature hath a right to be king of all the reft, as being the right heir to* Adam ; an excellent way to eftablifh the thrones of princes, and fettle the obedience of their fubjects, by fetting up an hundred, or perhaps a thoufand titles (if there be fo many princes in the world) againft any king now reigning, each as good, upon our author's grounds, as his who wears the crown. If this right of *heir* carry any weight with it, if it be the *ordinance of God*, as our author feems to tell us, *Obfervations*, 244. muft not all be fubject to it, from the higheft to the loweft ? Can thofe who wear
the

the name of princes, without having the right of
being *heirs to* Adam, demand obedience from their
subjects by this title, and not be bound to pay it
by the same law? Either governments in the
world are not to be claimed, and held by this title of *Adam's* heir, and then the starting of it is
to no purpose, the being or not being *Adam's* heir
signifies nothing as to the title of dominion   or
if it really be, as our author says, the true title
to government and sovereignty, the first thing to
be done, is to find out this true heir of *Adam*,
seat him in his throne, and then all the kings and
princes of the world ought to come and resign up
their *crowns* and *scepters* to him, as things that
belong no more to them, than to any of their subjects

§. 105   For either this right in nature, of
Adam's heir, to be king over all the race of men,
(for all together they make one *multitude*) is a
right not necessary to the making of a lawful
king, and so there may be lawful kings without it,
and then king's titles and power depend not on it,
or else all the kings in the world but one are
not lawful kings, and so have no right to obedience   either this title of heir to *Adam* is that
whereby kings hold their crowns, and have a
right to subjection from their subjects, and then
one only can have it, and the rest being subjects
can require no obedience from other men, who are
but their fellow subjects, or else it is not the title
whereby kings rule, and have a right to obedience from their subjects, and then kings are kings
without it, and this dream of the natural sovereignty of *Adam's* heir is of no use to obedience
and government   for if kings have a right to dominion, and the obedience of their subjects, who
are not, nor can possibly be, heirs to *Adam*, what
                                                    use

use is there of such a title, when we are obliged
to obey without it? If kings, who are not heirs
to *Adam*, have no right to sovereignty, we are all
free, till our author, or any body for him, will
shew us *Adam*'s right heir If there be but one
heir of *Adam*, there can be but one lawful king
in the world, and no body in conscience can be
obliged to obedience till it be resolved who that
is, for it may be any one, who is not known to
be of a younger house, and all others have equal
titles If there be more than one heir of *Adam*,
every one is his heir, and so every one has regal
power · for if two sons can be heirs together, then
all the sons are equally heirs, and so all are heirs,
being all sons, or sons sons of *Adam* Betwixt
these two the right of heir cannot stand ; for by
it either but one only man, or all men are kings
Take which you please, it dissolves the bonds of
government and obedience, since, if all men are
heirs, they can owe obedience to no body, if only
one, nobody can be obliged to pay obedience to
him, till he be known, and his title made out.

CHAP XI

Who HEIR?

§ 106 THE great question which in all ages
has disturbed mankind, and brought
on them the greatest part of those mischiefs which
have ruined cities, depopulated countries, and dis-
ordered the peace of the world, has been, not
whether there be power in the world, nor whence
it came, but who should have it. The settling of
this point being of no smaller moment than the
security of princes, and the peace and welfare of
their estates and kingdoms, a reformer of politics,

F   one

one would think, fhould lay this fure, and be very clear in it for if this remain difputable, all
the reft will be to very little purpofe, and the
fkill ufed in dreffing up power with all the
fplendor and temptation abfolutenefs can add to
it, without fhewing who has a right to have it,
will ferve only to give a greater edge to a man's
natural ambition, which of its felf is but too keen.
What can this do but fet men on the more eager-
ly to fcramble, and fo lay a fure and lafting foundation of endlefs contention, and diforder, inftead
of that peace and tranquillity, which is the bufinefs of government, and the end of human fociety ?

§ 107 This defignation of the perfon our author is more than ordinary obliged to take care
of, becaufe he, affirming that *the affignment of
civil power is by divine inflitution,* hath made the
conveyance as well as the power itfelf facred fo
that no confideration, no act or art of man, can
divert it from that perfon, to whom, by this divine right, it is affigned, no neceffity or contrivance can fubftitute another perfon in his room
for if the *affignment of civil power be by divine inflitution,* and *Adam's heir* be he to whom it is thus
affigned, as in the foregoing chapter our autho-
tells us, it wonld be as much facrilege for any
one to be king, who was not *Adam's* heir, as it
would have been amongft the *Jews,* for any one
to have been *prieft,* who had not been of *Aaron's*
pofterity for *not only* the priefthood *in general being by divine inflitution, but the affignment of it* to
the fole line and pofterity of *Aaron,* made it impoffible to be enjoyed or exercifed by any one, but
thofe perfons who were the off-fpring of *Aaron:*
whofe fucceffion therefore was carefully obferved,
and

and by that the perfons who had a right to the priefthood certainly known

§ 108 Let us fee then what care our author has taken, to make us know who is this *heir, who by divine inftitution has a right to be king over all men.* The firft account of him we meet with is, p 12 in thefe words *This fubjection of children, being the fountain of all regal authority, by the ordination of God himfelf, it follows, that civil power, not only in general, is by divine inftitution, but even the affignment of it, fpecifically to the eldeft parents.* Matters of fuch confequence as this is, fhould be in plain words, as little liable, as might be, to doubt or equivocation, and I think, if language be capable of expreffing any thing diftinctly and clearly, that of kindred, and the feveral degrees of nearnefs of blood, is one It were therefore to be wifhed, that our author had ufed a little more intelligible expreffions here, that we might have better known, who it is, to whom the *affignment of civil power* is made by *divine inftitution*; or at leaft would have told us what he meant by *eldeft parents:* for I believe, if land had been affigned or granted to him, and the *eldeft parents* of his family, he would have thought it had needed an interpreter; and it would fcarce have been known to whom next it belonged

§ 109 In propriety of fpeech, (and certainly propriety of fpeech is neceffary in a difcourfe of this nature) *eldeft parents* fignifies either the eldeft men and women that have had children, or thofe who have longeft had iffue; and then our author's affertion will be, that thofe fathers and mothers, who have been longeft in the world, or longeft fruitful, have by *divine inftitution* a right to *civil power* If there be any abfurdity in this, our author muft anfwer for it and if his meaning be different from my explication, he is to be blamed, that he would not fpeak it plainly This I am fure, *parents* cannot fignify heirs male, nor *elaeft parents* an infant child who yet may fometimes be the true heir, if there can be but one And we are hereby ftill as much at a lofs, who *civil power* belongs to, notwithflanding this *affignment by divine inflitution*, as if there had been no fuch *affignment* at all, or our author had faid nothing of it. This of *eldeft parents* leaving us more in the dark, who by *divine inflitution* has a right to *civil power*, than thofe who never heard any thing at all of *heir*, or defcent, of which our author is fo full And though the chief matter of his writing be to teach obedience to thofe who have a right to it, which he tells us is conveyed by defcent, yet who thofe are, to whom this right by defcent belongs, he leaves, like the philofophers ftone in politics, out of the reach of any one to difcover from his writings

§ 110 This obfcurity cannot be imputed to want of language in fo great a mafter of ftyle as Sir *Robert* is, when he is refolved with himfelf what he would fay · and therefore, I fear, finding how laid it would be to fettle rules of defcent by divine inflitution, and how little it would be to his purpofe, or conduce to the clearing and eftablifhing the titles of princes, if fuch rules of defcent were fettled, he chofe rather to content himfelf with doubtful and general terms, which might make no ill found in mens ears, who were willing to be pleafed with them, rather than offer any clear rules of defcent of this *fatherhood* of *Adam*, by which men's confciences might be fa-tisfied to whom it defcended, and know the per-

fons

fons who had a right to regal power, and with it to their obedience

§ 111 How elfe is it poffible, that laying fo much ftrefs, as he does, upon *difcent*, and *Adam's heir, next heir, true heir*, he fhould never tell us what *heir* means, nor the way to know who the *next* or *true heir* is? This, I do not remember, he does any where exprefly handle, but, where it comes in his way, very warily and doubtfully touches, though it be fo neceffary, that without it all difcourfes of government and obedience upon his principles would be to no purpofe, and *fatherly power*, never fo well made out will be of no ufe to any body Hence he tells us, *Obfervations*, 244 *That not only the conftitution of power in general, but the limitation of it to one kind*, (i e) *monarchy, and the determination of it to the individual perfon and line of* Adam, *are all three ordinances of God*, neither Eve nor her children could either limit Adam's power, or join others with him, and what was given unto Adam *was given in his perfon to his pofterity* Here again our author informs us, that the *divine ordinance* hath limited the defcent of *Adam's* monarchical power To whom? To Adam's *line and pofterity*, fays our author A notable *limitation*, a *limitation* to all mankind for if our author can find any one amongft mankind, that is not of the *line* and *pofterity* of *Adam*, he may perhaps tell him, who this next heir of *Adam* is but for us, I defpair how this *limitation* of *Adam's* empire to his *line* and *pofterity* will help us to find out *one heir*. This *limitation* indeed of our author will fave thofe the labour, who would look for him amongft the race of brutes, if any fuch there were, but will very little contribute to the difcovery of *one next heir* amongft men, though it make a fhort and

eafy

eafy determination of the queftion about the defcent of *Adam*'s regal power, by telling us, that
the *line* and *pofterity* of *Adam* is to have it, that is,
in plain *Englifh*, any one may have it, fince there
is no perfon living that hath not the title of being of the *line* and *pofterity* of *Adam* , and while
it keeps there, it keeps within our author's limitation by God's ordinance Indeed, p 19. he
tells us, that *fuch heirs are not only lords of their
own children, but of their brethren* , whereby,
and by the words following, which we fhall confider anon, he feems to infinuate, that the eldeft
fon is *heir* ; but he no where, that I know, fays
it in direct words, but by the inftances of *Cain*
and *Jacob*, that there follow, we may allow this
to be fo far his opinion concerning heirs, that
where there are divers children, the eldeft fon has
the right to be *heir* That primogeniture cannot
give any title to paternal power, we have already
fhewed That a father may have a natural right
to fome kind of power over his children, is eafily granted , but that an elder brother has fo over
his brethren, remains to be proved God or nature has not any where, that I know, placed fuch
jurifdiction in the firft-born , nor can reafon find
any fuch natural fuperiority amongft brethren.
The law of *Mofes* gave a double portion of the
goods and poffeffions to the eldeft ; but we find
not any where that naturally, or by *God's inftitution*, fuperiority or dominion belonged to him,
and the inftances there brought by our author are
but flender proofs of a right to civil power and
dominion in the firft-born, and do rather fhew the
contrary

§ 112 His words are in the forecited place:
And therefore we find God told Cain *of his brother*
Abel ;

Abel ; *his defire fhall be fubject unto thee, and thou fhalt rule over him*   To which I anfwer,

1. Thefe words of God to *Cain*, are by many interpreters, with great reafon, underftood in a quite different fenfe than what our author ufes them in

2. Whatever was meant by them, it could not be, that *Cain*, as elder, had a natural dominion over *Abel*, for the words are conditional, *If thou doft well*, and fo perfonal to *Cain*   and whatever was fignified by them, did depend on his carriage, and not follow his birth-right ; and therefore could by no means be an eftablifhment of dominion in the firft-born in general. for before this *Abel* had his *diftinct territories by right of private dominion*, as our author himfelf confeffes, *Obfervations*, 210 which he could not have had to the prejudice of the heirs title, *if by divine inftitution, Cain* as heir were to inherit all his father's dominion.

3 If this were intended by God as the charter of primogeniture, and the grant of dominion to elder brothers in general as fuch, by right of inheritance, we might expect it fhould have included all his brethren · for we way well fuppofe, *Adam*, from whom the world was to be peopled, had by this time, that thefe were grown up to be men, more fons than thefe two   whereas *Abel* himfelf is not fo much as named , and the words in the original can fcarce, with any good conftruction, be applied to him.

4 It is too much to build a doctrine of fo mighty confequence upon fo doubtful and obfcure a place of fcripture, which may be well, nay better, underftood in a quite different fenfe, and fo can be but an ill proof, being as doubtful as the thing to be proved by it ; efpecially when there

F 4   is

is nothing elfe in fcripture or reafon to be found, that favours or fuppoits it

§ 113 It follows, p 19 *Accordingly when Ja-cob bought his brother's birth-right,* Ifaac *bleffed him thus , Be lord over thy brethren, and let the fons of thy mother bow before thee* Another inftance, I take it, brought by onr author to evince dominion due to birth-right, and an admirable one it is for it muft be no ordinary way of reafoning in a man, that is pleading for the natural power of kings, and againft all compact, to bring for proof of it, an example, where his own account of it founds all the right upon compact, and fettles empire in the younger brother, unlefs buying and felling be no compact, for he tells us, *when Ja-cob bought his brothers birth-right* But paffing by that, let us confider the hiftory itfelf, with what ufe our author makes of it, and we fhall find thefe following miftakes about it

1 That our author reports this, as if *Ifaac* had given *Jacob* this bleffing, immediately upon his purchafing the *birth-right* for he fays, *when Ja-cob bought,* Ifaac *bleffed him* ; which is plainly otherwife in the fcripture , for it appears, there was a diftance of time between, and if we will take the ftory in the order it lies, it muft be no fmall diftance , all *Ifaac*'s fojourning in *Grrar,* and tranfactions with *Abimelech, Gen* xxvi coming between, *Rebecca* being then beautiful, and confequently young , but *Ifaac,* when he bleffed *Jacob,* was old and decrepit and *Efau* alfo complains of *Jacob, Gen* xxvii 36 that *two times* he had fupplanted him , *He took away my birth-right,* fays he, *and behold now he hath taken away my bleffing* , words, that I think fignify diftance of time and difference of action.

2 Another

2 Another miftake of our author's is, th,,t he fuppofes *Ifaac* gave *Jacob the bleffing*, and bid him be *lord over his brethren*, becaufe he had the *birth-right*; for our author brings this example to prove, that he that has the *birth-right*, has thereby a right to *be lord over his brethren*. But it is alfo manifeft by the text, that *Ifaac* had no confideration of *Jacob's* having bought the birth-right; for when he bleffed him, he confidered him not as *Jacob*, but took him for *Efau.* Nor did *Efau* underftand any fuch connection between *birth-right* and the *bleffing*, for he fays, *He hath fupplanted me thefe two times, he took a-way my birth-right, and behold now he hath taken away my bleffing.* whereas had the *bleffing*, which was to be *lord over his brethren*, belonged to the *birth-right*, *Efau* could not have complained of this fecond, as a cheat, *Jacob* having got nothing but what *Efau* had fold him, when he fold him his *birth-right*, fo that it is plain, dominion, if thefe words fignify it, was not underftood to be-long to the *birth-right*

§ 114. And that in thofe days of the patriarchs, dominion was not underftood to be the right of the heir, but only a greater portion of goods, is plain from *Gen* xxi 10. for *Sarah*, taking *Ifaac* to be heir, fays, *Caft out this bondwoman and her fon, for the fon of this bondwoman fhall not be heir with my fon* whereby could be meant nothing, but that he fhould not have a pretence to an equal fhare of his father's eftate after his death, but fhould have his portion prefently, and be gone Accord-ingly we read, *Gen* xxv 5, 6 That *Abraham gave a'l th t he had unto Ifaac, but unto the fons of the concubines which Abraham had, Abraham gave gifts, and fent them away from Ifaac his fon, while he yet lived* That is, *Abraham* having given portions to all his other fons, and fent them away, that

which

which he had referved, being the greateft part of
his fubftance, *Ifaac* as heir poffeffed after his
death · but by being heir, he had no right to be
lord over his brethren , for if he had, why fhould
Sarah endeavour to rob him of one of his *fubjects*,
or leffen the number of his *flaves*, by defiring to
have *Ifhmael* fent away?

§ 115 Thus, as under the law, the privilege
of *birth-right* was nothing but a double portion:
fo we fee that before *Mofes*, in the patriarchs
time, from whence our author pretends to take
his model, there was no knowledge, no thought,
that birth right gave rule or empire, paternal or
kingly authority, to any one over his brethren.
If this be not plain enough in the ftory of *Ifaac*
and *Ifhmael*, he that will look into 1 *Chron* v 12,
may there read thefe words *Reuben was the firf-
born , but forafmuch as he defiled his father's bed,
his birth-right was given unto the fons of Jofeph,
the fon of Ifrael and the genealogy is not to be
reckoned after the birth right , for Judah prevailed
above his brethren, and of him came the chief ruler;
but the birth-right was Jofeph's* What this birth-
right was, *Jacob* bleffing *Jofeph*, *Gen.* xlviii 22.
telleth us in thefe words, *Moreover I have given
thee one portion above thy brethren, which I took
out of the hand of the Amorite, with my fword
and with my bow* Whereby it is not only plain
that the birth-right was nothing but a double portion; but the text in *Chronicles* is exprefs
againft our author's doctrine, and fhews that
dominion was no part of the birth-right, for it
tells us, that *Jofeph* had the birth-right, but *Judah* the dominion. One would think our author
were very fond of the very name of *birth-right*,
when he brings this inftance of *Jacob* and *Efau*,
to prove that dominion belongs to the heir over
his brethren.

§. 116.

§. 116. 1 Becaufe it will be but an ill example to prove, that dominion by God's ordination belonged to the eldeft fon, becaufe *Jacob* the youngeft here had it, let him come by it how he would: for if it prove any thing, it can only prove, againft our author, that the *affignment of dominion to the eldeft is not by divine inftitution,* which would then be unalterable: for if by the law of God, or nature, abfolute power and empire belongs to the eldeft fon and his heirs, fo that they are fupreme monarchs, and all the reft of their brethren flaves, our author gives us reafon to doubt whether the eldeft fon has a power to part with it, to the prejudice of his pofterity, fince he tell us, *Obfervations,* 158 That *in grants and gifts that have their original from God or nature, no inferior power of man can limit, or make any law of prefcription againft them*

§ 117 2 Becaufe this place, *Gen* xxvii 29. brought by our author, concerns not at all the dominion of one brother over the other, nor the fubjection of *Efau* to *Jacob.* for it is plain in the hiftory, that *Efau* was never fubject to *Jacob*, but lived apart in mount *Seir*, where he founded a diftinct people and government, and was himfelf prince over them, as much as *Jacob* was in his own family. This text, if confidered, can never be underftood of *Efau* himfelf, or the perfonal dominion of *Jacob* over him. for the words *brethren* and *fons of thy mother*, could not be ufed literally by *Ifaac*, who knew *Jacob* had only one brother, and thefe words are fo far from being true in a literal enfe, or eftablifhing any dominion in *Jacob* over *Efau*, that in the ftory we find the quite contrary, for *Gen* xxxii *Jacob* feveral times calls *Efau* lord, and himfelf his fervant, and *Gen.* xxxiii. *he bowed himfelf feven times to the ground to* Efau Whether *Efau* then were a fubject and vaffal (nay, as our author tells us, all fubjects arc flaves) to *Jacob*, and *Jacob* his fovereign prince by birth-right, I leave the reader to judge ; and to believe if he can, that thefe words of *Ifaac, Be lord over thy brethren, and let thy mother's fons bow down to thee*, confirmed *Jacob* in a fovereignty over *Efau*, upon the account of the *birth-right* he had got from him.

§ 118 He that reads the ftory of *Jacob* and *Efau,* will find there was never any jurifdiction or authority, that either of them had over the other after their father's death they lived with the friendfhip and equality of brethren, neither *lord,* neither *flave,* to his brother ; but independent each of other, were both heads of their diftinct families, where they received no laws from one another, but lived feparately, and were the roots out of which fprang two diftinct people under two diftinct governments. This bleffing then of *Ifaac,* whereon our author would build the dominion of the elder brother, fignifies no more, but what *Rebecca* had been told from God, *Gen* xxv 23 *Two nations are in thy womb, and two manner of people fhall be feparated from thy bowels, and the one people fhall be ftronger than the other people, and the elder fhall ferve the younger ,* and fo *Jacob* bleffed *Judah, Gen* xlix and gave him the *fcepter* and *dominion,* from whence our author might have argued as well, that jurifdiction and dominion belongs to the third fon over his brethren, as well as from this bleffing of *Ifaac,* that it belonged to *Jacob* both thefe places contain only predictions of what fhould long after happen to their pofterities, and not any declaration of the right of inheritance to dominion in either And thus we have our author's two great and only arguments

guments to prove, that *heirs are lords over their brethren*

1 Becaufe God tells *Cain, Gen* iv. that however fin might fet upon him, he ought or might be mafter of it · for the moft learned interpreters underftood the words of fin, and not of *Abel,* and give fo ftrong reafons for it, that nothing can convincingly be inferred, from fo doubtful a text, to our author's purpofe

2 Becaufe in this of *Gen* xxvii *Ifaac* foretels that the *Ifraelites,* the pofterity of *Jacob,* fhould have dominion over the *Edomites,* the pofterity of *Ifau*, therefore fays our author, *heirs are lords of their brethren* I leave any one to judge of the conclufion.

§ 119 And now we fee how our author has provided for the defcending, and conveyance down of *Adam*'s monarchical power, or paternal dominion to pofterity, by the inheritance of his *heir,* fucceeding to all his father's authority, and becoming upon his death as much lord as his father was, *not only over his own children, but over his brethren,* and all defcended from his father, and fo *in infinitum* But yet who this heir is, he does not once tell us, and all the light we have from him in this fo fundamental a point, is only, that in his inftance of *Jacob,* by ufing the word *birthright,* as that which paffed from *Efau* to *Jacob,* he leaves us to guefs, that by heir, he means the eldeft fon, though I do not remember in any where mentions exprefly the title of the firft born, but all along keeps himfelf under the fhelter of the indefinite term *heir* But taking it to be his meaning, that the eldeft fon is heir, (for if the eldeft be not, there will be no pretence why the fons fhou'd not be all *heirs* alike) and fo by right of primogeniture has dominion over his brethren;

this

this is but one step towards the settlement of succession, and the difficulties remain still as much as
ever till he can shew us who is meant by right
heir, in all those cases which may happen where
the present possessor hath no son This he silent-
ly passes over, and perhaps wisely too · for what
can be wiser, after one has affirmed, that *the person having that power, as well as the power and form
of government, is the ordinance of God, and by divine
institution,* vid *Observations,* 254 p 12 than to be
careful, not to start any question concerning the person, the resolution whereof will certainly lead him
into a confession, that God and nature hath determined nothing about him? And if our author
cannot shew who by right of nature, or a clear
positive law of God, has the next right to inherit
the dominion of this natural monarch he has been
at such pains about, when he died without a
son, he might have spared his pains in all the
rest, it being more necessary for the settling men's
consciences, and determining their subjection and
allegiance, to shew them who by original right,
superior and antecedent to the will, or any act of
men, hath a title to this *paternal jurisdiction,*
than it is to shew that by nature there was such
a *jurisdiction,* it being to no purpose for me to
know there is such a *paternal power,* which I
ought, and am disposed to obey, unless, where
there are many pretenders, I also know the person that is rightfully invested and endowed with
it

§ 120 For the main matter in question being
concerning the duty of my obedience, and the
obligation of conscience I am under to pay it to
him that is of right my lord and ruler, I must
know the person that this right of paternal power
resides in, and so impowers him to claim obedience
from

from me for let it be true what he fays, p. 12.
That *civil power not only in general is by divine
inftitution, but even the affignment of it fpecially to
the eldeft parents*, and *Obfervations*, 254 *That
not only the power or right of government, but the
form of the power of governing, and the perfon
having that power, are all the ordinance of God*;
yet unlefs he fhew us in all cafes who is this perfon, *ordained* by God, who is this *eldeft parent*;
all his abftract notions of monarchical power will
fignify juft nothing, when they are to be reduced
to practice, and men are confcientioufly to pay
their obedience for *paternal jurifdiction* being
not the thing to be obeyed, becaufe it cannot
command, but is only that which gives one man
a right which another hath not, and if it come
by inheritance, another man cannot have, to
command and be obeyed ; it is ridiculous to fay,
I pay obedience to the *paternal power,* when I
obey him, to whom paternal power gives no
right to my obedience for he can have no divine right to my obedience, who cannot fhew
h s divine right to the power of ruling over me,
as well as that by divine right there is fuch a
power in the world

§ 121 And hence not being able to make out
any prince's title to government, as heir to *Adam,*
which therefore is of no ufe, and had been better
let alone, he is fain to refolve all into prefent poffeffion, and makes civil obedience as due to an
ufurper, as to a lawful king , and thereby the
ufurper's title as good His words are, *Obfervations,* 253 and they deferve to be remembered:
*If an ufurper difpoffefs the true heir, the fubjects
obedience to the fatherly power muft go along, and
wait upon God's providence* But I fhall leave his
title of ufurpers to be examined in its due place,
and

and defire my fober reader to confider what thanks princes owe fuch politics as this, which can fuppofe *paternal power* (*i e*) a right of government in the hands of a *Cade*, or a *Cromwell*, and fo all obedience being due to paternal power, the obedience of fubjects will be due to them, by the fame right, and upon as good grounds, as it is to lawful princes, and yet this, as dangerous a doctrine as it is, muft neceffarily follow from making all political power to be nothing elfe, but *Adam's* paternal power by right and divine *inftitution*, defcending from him without being able to fhew to whom it defcended, or who is heir to it

§ 122 To fettle government in the world, and to lay obligations to obedience on any man's confcience, it is as neceffary (fuppofing with our author that all power be nothing but the being poffeffed of *Adam's fatherhood*) to fatify him, who has a right to this *power*, this *fatherhood*, when the poffeffer dies without fons to fucceed immediately to it, as it was to tell him, that upon the death of the father, the eldeft fon had a right to it for it is ftill to be remembered, that the great queftion is, (and that which our author would be thought to contend for if he did not fometimes forget it) what perfons have a right to be obeyed, and not whether there be a power in the world, which is to be called *paternal*, without knowing in whom it refides for fo it be a power, *i e* right to govern, it matters not, whether it be termed *paternal* or *regal*, *natural* or *acquir'd*, whether you call it *fupreme fatherhood*, or *fupreme brotherhood*, will be all one, provided we know who has it

§ 123 I go on then to afk, whether the inheriting of this *paternal power*, this *fupreme fatherhood*

therhood, the grandson by a daughter hath a right before a nephew by a brother? Whether the grandson by the eldest son, being an infant, before the younger son, a man and able? Whether the daughter before the uncle? or any other man, descended by a male line? Whether a grandson by a younger daughter, before a grand-daughter by an elder daughter? Whether the elder son by a corcubine, before a younger son by a wife? From whence also will arise many questions of legitimation, and what in nature is the difference betwixt a wife and a concubine? for as to the municipal or positive laws of men, they can signify nothing here   It may farther be asked, Whether the eldest son, being a fool, shall inherit this *paternal power*, before the younger, a wise man? and what degree of folly it must be that shall exclude him? and who shall be judge of it? Whether the son of a fool, excluded for his folly, before the son of his wife brother who reigned? Who has the *paternal power* whilst the widow-queen is with child by the deceased king, and no body knows whether it will be a son or a daughter? Which shall be heir of the two male-twins, who by the dissection of the mother were laid open to the world? Whether a sister by the half blood, before a brother's daughter by the whole blood?

§ 124 These, and many more such doubts, might be proposed about the titles of succession, and the right of inheritance, and that not as idle speculations, but such as in history we shall find have concerned the inheritance of crowns and kingdoms, and if our's want them, we need not go farther for famous examples of it, than the other kingdom in this very island, which having been fully related by the ingenuous and
learned

learned author of *Patriarcha non Monarcha*, I need say no more of Till our author hath refolved all the doubts that may arife about the next heir, and fhewed that they are plainly determined by the law of nature, or the revealed law of God, all his fuppofitions of a *monarchical, abfolute, fupreme, paternal power* in *Adam*, and the defcent of that power to his heirs, would not be of the leaft u'e to eftablifh the authority, or make out the title, of any one prince now on earth ; but would rather unfettle and bring all into queftion for let our author tell us as long as he pleafes, and let all men believe it too, that *Adam* had a *paternal*, and thereby a *monarchical power*; that this (the only *power* in the world) *defcended to his heirs*, and that there is no other power in the world but this : let this be all as clear demonftration, as it is manifeft error, yet if it be not paft doubt, to whom this *paternal power defcends*, and whofe now it is, no body can be under any obligation of *obedience*, unlefs any one will fay, that I am bound to pay obedience to *paternal power* in a man who has no more *paternal power* than I myfelf , which is all one as to fay, I obey a man, becaufe he has a right to govern; and if I be afked, how I know he has a right to govern, I fhould anfwer, it cannot be known, that he has any at all for that cannot be the reafon of my obedience, which I know not to be fo; much lefs can that be a reafon of my obedience, which no body at all can know to be fo.

§ 125 And therefore all this ado about *Adam's fatherhood*, the greatnefs of its power, and the neceffity of its fuppofal, helps nothing to eftablifh the power of thofe that govern, or to determine the obedience of fubjects who are to obey, if they cannot tell whom they are to obey, or it cannot

be

be known who are to govern, and who to obey.
In the ftate the world is now, it is irrecoverably
ignorant, who is *Adam*'s heir   This *fatherhood*,
this *monarchical power of Adam*, defcending to
his heirs, would be of no more ufe to the government of mankind, than it would be to the
quieting of men's oonfciences, or fecuring their
healths, if our author had affured them, that
Adam had a *power* to forgive fins, or cure difeafes,
which by divine inftitution defcended to his *heir*,
whilft this heir is impoffible to be known   And
fhould not he do as rationally, who upon this affurance of our author went and corfeffed his fins,
and expected a good abfolution, or took phyfic
with expectation of health, from any one who
had taken on himfelf the name of prieft or phyfician, or thruft himfelf into thofe employments,
faying, I acquiefce in the abfolving power defcending from *Adam*, or I fhall be cured by the
medicinal power defcending from *Adam*; as he
who fays, I fubmit to and obey the *paternal power*
defcending from *Adam*, when it is confeffed all
thefe powers defcend only to his fingle heir, and
that heir is unknown?

§ 126 It is true, the civil lawyers have pretended to determine fome of thefe cafes concein-
ing the fucceffion of princes; but by our author's
principles, they have meddled in a matter that
belongs not to them   for if all political power be
derived only from *Adam*, and be to defcend only
to his fucceffive heirs, by the *ordinance of God*,
and *divine inftitution*, this is a right antecedent
and paramount to all government, and therefore
the pofitive laws of men cannot determine that,
which is itfelf the foundation of all law and government, and is to receive its rule only from
the law of God and nature.   And that being filent

lent in the cafe, I am apt to think there is no fuch right to be conveyed this way? I am fure it would be to no purpofe if there were, and men would be more at a lofs concerning government, and obedience to governors, than if there were no fuch right, fince by pofitive laws and compact, which *divine inftitution* (if there be any) fhuts out, all thefe endlefs inextricable doubts can be fafely provided againft but it can never be underftood, how a divine natural right, and that of fuch moment as is all order and peace in the world, fhould be conveyed down to pofterity, without any plain natural or divine rule concerning it And there would be an end of all civil government, if the *affignment* of civil power were by *divine inftitution* to the heir, and yet *by that divine inftitution* the perfon of the heir could not be known. This *paternal regal power* being by divine right only his, it leaves no room for human prudence, or confent, to place it any where elfe; for if only one man hath a divine right to the obedience of mankind, no body can claim that obedience, but he that can fhew that right; nor can men's confciences by any other pretence be obliged to it And thus this doctrine cuts up all government by the roots

§ 127 Thus we fee how our author, laying it for a fure foundation, that the very *perfon* that is to rule, is the *ordinance* of God, and by *divine inftitution*, tells us at large, only that this perfon is the *heir*, but who this heir is, he leaves us to guefs, and fo this *divine inftitution*, which affigns it to a perfon whom we have no rule to know, is juft as good as an affignment to no body at all. But whatever our author does, *divine inftitution* makes no fuch ridiculous affignments nor can God be fuppofed to make it a facred law, that
one

one certain perfon fhould have a right to fomething, and yet not give rules to mark out, and
know that perfon by, or give an *heir* a divine
right to power, and yet not point out who that
heir is It is rather to be thought, that an *heir*
had no fuch right by *divine inftitution*, than that
God fhould give fuch a right to the *heir*, but yet
leave it doubtful and undeterminable who fuch
heir is.

§ 128 If God had given the land of *Canaan*
to *Abrahom*, and in general terms to fome body
after him, without naming his feed, whereby it
might be known who that fomebody was, it
would have been as good and ufeful an affignment,
to determine the right to the land of *Canaan*, as
it would be the determining the right of crowns,
to give empire to *Adam* and his fucceffive heirs
after him, without telling who his heir is · for
the word *heir*, without a rule to know who it is,
fignifies no more than fome body, I know not
whom   God making it a *divine inftitution*, that
men fhould not marry thofe who were *near of kin*,
thinks it not enough to fay, *None of you fhall ap-
proach to any that is near of kin to him, to uncover
her nakednefs*; but moreover, gives rules to
know who are thofe *near of kin*, forbidden by
divine inftitution; or elfe that law would have
been of no ufe, it being to no purpofe to lay reftraint, or give privileges to men, in fuch general
terms, as the particular perfon concerned cannot
be known by   But God not having any where
faid, the next heir fhall inherit all his father's
eftate or dominion, we are not to wonder, that
he hath no where appointed who that heir fhould
be, for never having intended any fuch thing,
never defigned any heir in that fenfe, we cannot
expect he fhould any where nominate, or appoint
any

any perſon to it, as we might, had it been otherwiſe And therefore in ſcripture, though the
word *heir* occur, yet there is no ſuch thing as
heir in our author's ſenſe, one that was by right
of nature to inherit all that his father had, excluſive of his brethren Hence *Sarah* ſuppoſes,
that if *Iſhmael* ſtaid in the houſe, to ſhare in
Abraham's eſtate after his death, this ſon of a
bond-woman might be heir with *Iſaac*, and
therefore, ſays ſhe, *caſt out this bond-woman and
her ſon, for the ſon of this bond-woman ſhall not
be heir with my ſon* · but this cannot excuſe our
author, who telling us there is, in every number
of men, one who is right and next *heir* to *Adam*,
ought to have told us what the laws of deſcent
are but he having been ſo ſparing to inſtruct us
by rules, how to know who is *heir*, let us ſee in
the next place, what his hiſtory out of ſcripture,
on which he pretends wholly to build his government, gives us in this neceſſary and fundamental point

§ 129. Our author, to make good the title of
his book, p 13 begins his hiſtory of the deſcent
of *Adam*'s regal power, p 13. in theſe words
This lordſhip which Adam *by command had over
the whole world, and by right deſcending from him,
the patriarchs did enjoy, was a large*, &c How
does he prove that the patriarchs by deſcent did
enjoy it ? for *dominion of life and death*, ſays he,
we find Judah *the father pronounced ſentence of
death againſt* Thamar *his daughter in law for playing the harlot*, p 13. How does this prove that
Judah had abſolute and ſovereign authority ? *he
pronounced ſentence of death*. The pronouncing
of ſentence of death is not a certain mark of
ſovereignty, but uſually the office of inferior ma-
giſtrates. The power of making laws of life and
death

death is indeed a mark of sovereignty, but pronouncing the sentence according to those laws may
be done by others, and therefore this will but ill
prove that he had sovereign authority · as if one
should say, *Judge Jefferies* pronounced sentence of
death in the late times, therefore *Judge Jefferies*
had sovereign authority. But it will be said,
Judah did it not by commission from another, and
therefore did it in his own right. Who knows
whether he had any right at all ? Heat of passion
might carry him to do that which he had no authority to do *Judah had dominion of life and
death* how does that appear ? He exercised it,
he *pronounced sentence of death against* Thamar .
our author thinks it is very good proof, that because he did it, therefore he had a right to do it:
he lay with her also by the same way of proof,
he had a right to do that too If the consequence
be good from doing to a right of doing, *Abfalom*
too may be reckoned amongst our author's sovereigns, for he pronounced such a sentence of
death against his brother *Amnon,* and much upon
a like occasion, and had it executed too, if that
be sufficient to prove a dominion of life and
death

But allowing this all to be clear demonstration
of sovereign power, who was it that had this
lordship by right descending to him from Adam, *as
large and ample as the absolutest dominion of any
monarch ? Judah,* says our author, *Judah* a
younger son of *Jacob,* his father and elder brethren living , so that if our author's own proof
be to be taken, a younger brother may, in the
life of his father and elder brothers, *by right of
descent, enjoy* Adam's *monarchical power ;* and if
one so qualified may be monarch by descent, why
may not every man ? if *Judah,* his father and
elder

elder brother living, were one of *Adam*'s heirs, I know not who can be excluded from this inheritance, all men by inheritance may be monarchs as well as *Judah*.

§ 130 *Touching war, we see that* Abraham *commanded an army of* 318 *soldiers of his own family, and* Esau *met his brother* Jacob *with* 400 *men at arms · for matter of peace,* Abraham *made a league with* Abimelech, *&c.* p 13 Is it not possible for a man to have 318 men in his family, without being heir to *Adam?* A planter in the *West-Indies* has more, and might, if he pleased, (who doubts?) muster them up and lead them out against the *Indians,* to seek reparation upon any injury received from them, and all this without the *absolute dominion of a monarch, descending to him from* Adam Would it not be an admirable argument to prove, that all power by God's institution descended from *Adam* by inheritance, and that the very person and power of this planter were the *ordinance of God,* because he had power in his family over servants, born in his house, and bought with his money ` For this was just *Abraham*'s case, those who were rich in the *patriarch*'s days, as in the *West Indies* now, bought *men* and *maid servants,* and by their increase, as well as purchasing of new, came to have large and numerous families, which though they made use of in war or peace, can it be thought the power they had over them was an inheritance descended from *Adam,* when it was the purchase of their money? A man's riding in an expedition against an enemy, his horse bought in a fair would be as good a proof that the owner *enjoyed the lordship which* Adam *by command had over the whole world, by right descending to him,* as *Abraham*'s leading out the servants of his family is,

that

that the *patriarchs* enjoyed this lordſhip by deſcent from *Adam* ſince the title to the power, the maſter had in both caſes, whether over ſlaves or horſes, was only from his purchaſe, and the getting a dominion over any thing by bargain and money, is a new way of proving one had it by deſcent and inheritance

§. 131 *But making war and peace are marks of ſovereignty* Let it be ſo in politic ſocieties. may not therefore a man in the *Weſt Indies,* who hath with him ſons of his own, friends, or companions, ſoldiers under pay, or ſlaves bought with money, or perhaps a band made up of all theſe, make war and peace, if there ſhould be occaſion, and *ratify the articles too with an oath,* without being a ſovereign, an abſolute king over thoſe who went with him? He that ſays he cannot, muſt then allow many maſters of ſhips, many private planters, to be abſolute monarchs, for as much as this they have done War and peace cannot be made for politic ſocieties, but by the ſupreme power of ſuch ſocieties; becauſe war and peace, giving a different motion to the force of ſuch a politic body, none can make war or peace, but that which has the direction of the force of the whole body, and that in politic ſocieties is only the ſupreme power In voluntary ſocieties for the time, he that has ſuch a power by conſent, may make war and peace, and ſo may a ſingle man for himſelf, the ſtate of war not conſiſting in the number of *partiſans,* but the enmity of the parties, where they have no ſuperior to appeal to.

§ 132 The actual making of war or peace is no proof of any other power, but only of diſpoſing thoſe to exerciſe or ceaſe acts of enmity for whom he makes it; and this power in many

G caſes

cases any one may have without any politic supremacy and therefore the making of war or peace will not prove that every one that does so is a politic ruler, much less a king, for then common-wealths must be kings too, for they do as certainly make war and peace as monarchical government

§ 133 But granting this a *mark of sovereignty* in *Abraham*, is it a proof of the descent to him of *Adam's sovereignty* over the whole world? If it be, it will surely be as good a proof of the *descent of Adam's lordship* to others too And then common-wealths, as well as *Abraham*, will be *heirs of Adam*, for they make *war and peace*, as well as he If you say, that the *lordship of Adam* doth not by right descend to common-wealths, though they make war and peace, the same say I of *Abraham*, and then there is an end of your argument if you stand to your argument, and say those that do make war and peace, as common-wealths do without doubt, do *inherit* Adam's *lordship*, there is an end of your monarchy, unless you will say, that common wealths *by descent* enjoying Adam's *lordship* are monarchies; and that indeed would be a new way of making all the government in the world monarchical

§ 134 To give our author the honour of this new invention, for I confess it is not I have first found it out by tracing his principles, and so charged it on him, it is fit my readers know that (as absurd as it may seem) he teaches it himself, p. 23 where he so generously says, *In all kingdoms and common wealths in the world, whether the prince be the supreme father of the people, or but the true heir to such a father, or come to the crown by usurpation or election, or whether some few or a multitude govern the common wealth, yet still the* authority

authority that is in any one, or in many, or in all those, is the only right, and natural authority of a supreme father, which right of *fatherhood*, he often tells us, is *regal and royal authority*; is particularly, p 12. the page immediately preceding this instance of *Abraham* This regal authority, he says, those that govern common-wealths have; and if it be true, that regal and royal authority be in those that govern common wealths, it is as true that common-wealths are governed by kings, for if regal authority be in him that governs, he that governs must needs be a king, and so all common-wealths are nothing but down-right monarchies, and then what need any more ado about the matter? The government of the world are as they should be, there is nothing but monarchy in it This, without doubt, was the surest way our author could have found, to turn all other governments, but monarchical, out of the world

§ 135 But all this scarce proves *Abraham* to have been a king as heir to *Adam* If by inheritance he had been king, *Lot*, who was of the same family, must needs have been his subject, by that title before the servants in his family; but we see they lived as friends and equals, and when their herdsmen could not agree, there was no pretence of jurisdiction or superiority between them, but they parted by consent, *Gen* xiii hence he is called both by *Abraham*, and by the text, *Abraham's brother*, the name of friendship and equality, and not of jurisdiction and authority, though he were really but his nephew And if our author knows that *Abraham* was *Adam's* heir, and a king, it was more, it seems, than *Abraham* himself knew, or his servant whom he sent a wooing for his son, for when he sets out the ad-

G 2 vantage,

vantages of the match, xxiv *Gen.* 35 thereby to prevail with the young woman and her friends, he says, *I am Abraham's servant, and the Lord hath blessed my master greatly, and he is become great ; and he hath given him flocks and herds, and silver and gold, and men servants and maid-servants, and camels and asses, and Sarah, my master's wife, bare a son to my master when she was old, and unto him hath he given all he hath* Can one think that a discreet servant, that was thus particular to set out his master's greatness, would have omitted the crown *Isaac* was to have, if he had known of any such ? Can it be imagined he should have neglected to have told them on such an occasion as this, that *Abraham* was a king, a name well known at that time, for he had nine of them his neighbours, if he or his master had thought any such thing, the likeliest matter of all the rest, to make his errand successful ?

§ 136 But this discovery it seems was reserved for our author to make 2 or 3000 years after, and let him enjoy the credit of it, only he should have taken care that some of *Adam's* land should have descended to this his *heir*, as well as all *Adam's* lordship for though this lordship which *Abraham*, (if we may believe our author) as well as the other patriarchs, *by right descending to him, did enjoy, was as large and ample as the absolutest dominion of any monarch which hath been since the creation*, yet his estate, his territories, his dominions were very narrow and scanty, for he had not the possession of a foot of land, till he bought a field and a cave of the sons of *Heth* to bury *Sarah* in

§ 137 The instance of *Esau* joined with this of *Abraham*, to prove that the *lordship which* Adam had over *the whole world, by right descending from him, the patriarchs did enjoy,* is yet more
pleasant

pleafant than the former. *Efau met his brother* Jacob *with* 400 *men at arms*, he therefore was a king by right of heir to *Adam* Four hundred armed men then, however got together, are e- nough to prove him that leads them, to be a king and *Adam*'s heir There have been tories in *Ireland*, (whatever there are in other countries) who would have thanked our author for fo honou- rable an opinion, of them, efpecia ly if there had been no body near with a better title of 500 armed men, to queftion their royal authority of 400 It is a fhame for men to trifle fo, to fay no worfe of it, in fo ferious an argument Here *Efau* is brought as a proof that *Adam*'s lordfhip, *Adam's absolute dominion, as large as that of any monarch, defcended by right to the patriarchs,* and in this very *chap* p 19 *Jacob* is brought as an inftance of one, that by *birth-right was lord over his brethren* So we have here two brothers ab- folute monarchs by the fame title, and at the fame time heirs to *Adam*; the eldeft, heir to *Adam*, becaufe he met his brother with 400 men; and the youngeft, heir to *Adam* by *birth-right :* Efau *enjoyed the lordfhip which* Adam *had over the whole world by right defcending to him, in as large and ample manner, as the abfoluteft dominion of any monarch*, and at the fame time, *Jacob lord over him, by the right heirs have to be lords over their brethren.* Rifum teneatis ? I never, I confefs, met with any man of parts fo dextrous as Sir *Robert* at this way of arguing but it was his misfortune to light upon an *hypothefis,* that could not be ac- commodated to the nature of things, and human affairs; his principles could not be made to agree with that conftitution and order, which God had fettled in the world, and therefore muft needs of- ten clafh with common fenfe and experience

G 3 § 138.

§ 138 In the next section, he tells us, *This patriarchal power continued not only till the flood, but after it, as the name patriarch doth in part prove* The word patriarch doth more than *in part prove*, that *patriarchal power* continued in the world as long as there were patriarchs, for it is neceffary that patriarchal power fhould be whilft there are patriarchs as it is neceffary there fhould be paternal or conjugal power whilft there are fathers or hufbands, but this is but playing with names That which he would fallaciously infinuate is the thing in queftion to be proved, *viz that the lordfhip which Adam had over the world*, the fuppofed abfolute univerfal dominion of *Adam* by *right defcending from him, the patriarchs did enjoy* It he affirms fuch an abfolute monarchy continued to the flood, in the world, I would be glad to know what records he has it from, for I confefs I cannot find a word of it in my Bible if by *patriarchal power* he means any thing elfe, it is nothing to the matter in hand And how the name *patriarch* in fome part proves, that thofe, who are called by that name, had abfolute monarchical power, I confefs, I do not fee, and therefore I think needs no anfwer till the argument from it be made out a little clearer

§ 139 *The three fons of* Noah *had the world,* fays our author, *divided amongft them by their father, for of them was the whole world overfpread,* p 14 The world might be overfpread by the offspring of *Noah's* fons, though he never divided the world amongft them, for the earth might be replenifhed without being divided. fo that all our author's argument here proves no fuch divifion However, I allow it to him, and then afk, the world being divided amongft them, which of the three was *Adam's* heir ? If *Adam's lordfhip, Adam's monarchy*,

monarchy, by right defcended only to the eldeſt, then the other two could be but his *ſubjects*, his *ſlaves* if by right it defcended to all three brothers, by the ſame right, it will defcend to all mankind, and then it will be impoſſible what he ſays, p 19 that *heirs are lords of their brethren*, ſhould be true, but all brother, and confequently all men, will be equal and independent, all heirs to *Adam's* monarchy, and confequently all monarchs too, one as much as another But it will be ſaid, *Noah* their father divided the world amongſt them, ſo that our author will allow more to *Noah*, than he will to God almighty, for *Obſervations*, 211 he thought it hard, that God himſelf ſhould give the world to *Noah* and his ſons, to the prejudice of *Noah's* birth right his words are, *Noah was left ſole heir to the world why ſhould it be thought that God would diſinherit him of his birth-right, and make him, of all men n the world, the only tenant in common with his children ?* and yet here he thinks it fit that *Noah* ſhould diſinherit *Shem* of his birth-right, and divide the world betwixt him and his brethren ; ſo that this *birth-right*, when our author pleaſes, muſt, and when he pleaſes muſt not, be ſacred and inviolable

§ 140 If *Noah* did divide the world between his ſons, and his aſſignment of dominions to them were good, there is an end of divine inſtitution, all our author's diſcourfe of *Adam's* heir, with whatſoever he builds on it, is quite out of doors, the natural power of kings falls to the ground, and then *the form of the power governing, and the perſon having that power, will not be* as he ſays they are, *Obſervations*, 254) *the ordinance of God, but they will be ordinances of man ·* for if the right of the heir be the ordinance of

G 4 God,

a divine right, no man, father or not father, can alter it if it be not a divine right, it is only human, depending on the will of man and so where human inflitution gives it not, the fiftborn has no right at all above his brethren, and men may put government into what hands, and under what form, they pleafe

§ 141 He goes on, *Moft of the civileft nations of the earth labou to fetch their original from fome of the fons, or nephews of* Noah, p 14   How many do moft of the civileft nations amount to? and who are they? I fear the *Chinefes*, a very great and civil people, as well as feveral other people of the *Eaft, Weft, North,* and *South,* trouble not themfelves much about this matter. All that beleve the Bible, which I belive are our author's *moft of the civileft nations,* muft neceffarily derive themfelves from *Noah,* but for the reft of the world, they think little of his fons or nephews But if the heralds and antiquaries of all nations, for it is thefe men generally that labour to find out the originals of nations, or all the nations themfelves, *fhould labour to fetch their original from fome of the fons or nephews of* Noah, what would this be to prove, that the *lordfhip which* Adam *had over the whole world, by right defcended to the patriarchs?* Whoever, nations, or races of men, *labour to fetch their original from,* may be concluded to be thought by them, men of renown, famous to pofterity, for the greatnefs of their virtues and actions, but beyond thefe they look not, nor confider who they were heirs to, but look on them as fuch as raifed themfelves, by their own virtue, to a degree that would give a luftre to thofe who in future ages could pretend to derive themfelves from them.   But if it were *Ogyges, Hercules, Brama, Tamberlain,*

Tamberlain, *Pharamond* ; nay, if *Jupiter* and *Saturn* were the names, from whence divers races of men, both ancient and modern, have laboured to derive their original ; will that prove, that those men *enjoyed the lordship of* Adam, *by right descending to them?* If not, this is but a flourish of our author's to mislead his reader, that in itself signifies nothing

§ 142 To as much purpose is what he tells us, p 15 concerning this division of the world, *That some say it was by* Lot, *and others that* Noah *failed round the* Mediterranean *in ten years, and divided the world into* Asia, Africk *and* Europe, portions for his three sons *America* then, it seems, was left to be his that could catch it Why our author takes such pains to prove the division of the world by *Noah* to his sons, and will not leave out an imagination, though no better than a dream, that he can find any where to favour it, is hard to guess, since such a *division*, if it prove any thing, must necessarily take away the title of *Adam*'s heir ; unless three brothers can all together be heirs of *Adam* ; and therefore the following words, *Howsoever the manner of this division be uncertain, yet it is most certain the division itself was by families from* Noah *and his children, over which the parents were heads and princes*, p 15 if allowed him to be true, and of any force to prove, that all the power in the world is nothing but the lordship of Adam's descending by right, they will only prove, that the fathers of the children are all heirs to this lordship of *Adam* for if in those days *Chem* and *Japhe*, and other parents, besides the eldest son, were heads and princes over their families, and had a right to divide the earth by families, what hinders younger brothers, being fathers of families, from

having

having the fame right? If *Cham* and *Japhet* were princes by right defcending to them, notwith-ftanding any title of heir in their eldeft brother, younger brothers by the fame right defcending to them are princes now, and fo all our author's natural power of kings will reach no farther than their own children, and no kingdom, by this natural right, can be bigger than a family   for either this *lordfhip of* Adam *over the whole world,* by right defcends only to the eldeft fon, and then there can be but one heir, as our author fays, p 19 or elfe, it by right defcends to all the fons equally, and then every father of a family will have it, as well as the three fons of *Noah*. take which you will, it deftroys the prefent go-vernments and kingdoms, that are now in the world, fince whoever has this *natural power of a king,* by right defcending to him, muft have it, either as our author tells us *Cain* had it, and be lord over his brethren, and fo be alone king of the whole world, or elfe, as he tells us here, *Shem, Cham* and *Japhet* had it, three brothers, and fo be only prince of his own family, and all families independent one of another · all the world muft be only one empire by the right of the next heir, or elfe every family be a diftinct government of itfelf, by the *lordfhip of* Adam's *defcending to parents of families.* And to this on-ly tend all the proofs he here gives us of the defcent of *Adam's* lordfhip for continuing his ftory of this defcent, he fays,

§ 143 *In the difperfion of* Babel, *we muft cer-tainly find the eftablifhment of royal power, through-out the kingdoms of the world,* p 14 If you muft find it, pray do, and you will help us to a new piece of hiftory. but you muft fhew it us before

we

we fhall be bound to believe, that regal power was eftablifhed in the world upon your principles: for, that regal power was eftablifhed *in the kingdoms of the world,* I think no body will difpute ; but that there fhould be kingdoms in the world, whofe feveral kings enjoyed their crowns, *by right defcending to them from* Adam, that we think not only *apocryphal,* but alfo utterly impoffible. If our author has no better foundation for his monarchy than a fuppofition of what was done at the difperfion of *Babel,* the monarchy he erects thereon, whofe top is to reach to heaven to unite mankind, will ferve only to divide and fcatter them as that tower did, and, inftead of eftablifhing civil government and order in the world, will produce nothing but confufion

§ 144 For he tells us, the *nations* they were divided into, *were diftinct families, which had fathers for rulers over them, whereby it appears, that even in the confufion, God was careful to preferve the fatherly authority, by diftributing the diverfity of languages according to the diverfity of families,* p 14. It would have been a hard matter for any one but our author to have found out fo plainly, in the text he here brings, that all the nations in that difperfion were governed by *fathers,* and that *God was careful to preferve the fatherly authority.* The words of the text are, *Thefe are the fons of Shem after their families, after their tongues in their lands, after their nations ;* and the fame thing is faid of *Cham* and *Japhet,* after an enumeration of their pofterities, in all which there is not one word faid of their governors, or forms of government; of *fathers,* or *fatherly authority* But our author, who is very quick fighted to fpy out *fatherhood,* where no body elfe could fee any the leaft glimpfes of it, tells

tells us positively their *rulers were fathers, and God was careful to preserve the fatherly authority*; and why? Because those of the same family spoke the same language, and so of necessity in the division kept together Just as if one should argue thus *Hannibal* in his army, consisting of divers nations, kept those of the same language together, therefore fathers were captains of each band, and *Hannibal* was careful of the *fatherly authority* or in peopling of *Carolina*, the *English*, *French*, *Scotch* and *Welch* that are there, plant themselves together, and by them the country is divided *in their lands after their tongues, after their families, after their nations*, therefore care was taken of the *fatherly authority* or because, in many parts of *America*, every little tribe was a distinct people, with a different language, one should infer, that therefore *God was careful to preserve the fatherly authority*, or that therefore their rulers *enjoyed* Adam's *lordship by right descending to them*, though we know not who were their governors, nor what their form of government, but only that they were divided into little independent societies, speaking different languages

§ 115 The scripture says not a word of their rulers or forms of government, but only gives an account, how mankind came to be divided into distinct languages and nations, and therefore it is not to argue from the authority of scripture, to tell us positively, *fathers* were their *rulers*, when the scripture says no such thing, but to set up fancies of one's own brain, when we confidently aver matter of fact, where records are utterly silent Upon a like ground, *i e* none at all, he says, *That they were not confused multitudes*

without

*without heads and governors, and at liberty to choose
what governors or governments they pleased*

§. 146 For I demand, when mankind were
all yet of one language, all congregated in the
plain of *Shinar*, were they then all under one
monarch, *who enjoyed the lordship of* Adam *by
right descending to him?* If they were not, there
were then no thoughts, it is plain, of *Adam's
heir*, no right to government known then upon
that title, no care taken, by God or man, of
Adam's fatherly authority If when mankind
were but one people, dwelt all together, and
were of one language, and were upon building
a city together, and when it was plain, they
could not but know the right heir, for *Shem* lived
till *Isaac's* time, a long while after the division
at *Babel*, if then, I say, they were not under the
monarchical government of *Adam's* fatherhood,
by right descending to the heir, it is plain there
was no regard had to the *fatherhood*, no monarchy
acknowledged due to *Adam's heir*, no empire of
Shem's in *Asia*, and consequently no such division
of the world by *Noah*, as our author has talked
of As far as we can conclude any thing from
scripture in this matter, it seems from this place,
that if they had any government, it was rather a
common-wealth than an absolute monarchy for
the scripture tells us, *Gen* xi. *They said* it was
not a prince commanded the building of this city
and tower, it was not by the command of one
monarch, but by the consultation of many, a
free people, *let us build us a city* they built it
for themselves as free-men, not as slaves for their
lord and master *that we be not scattered abroad;*
having a city once built, and fixed habitations to
settle our abodes and families This was the consultation and design of a people, that were at liberty

berty to part afunder, but defired to keep in one body, and could not have been either neceffary or likely in men tied together under the government of one monarch, who if they had been, as our author tells us, all *flaves* under the abfolute demi- nion of a monarch, needed not have taken fuch care to hinder themfelvess from wandering out of the reach of his dominion I demand whether this be not plainer in fcripture than any thing of *Adam's heir or fatherly authority?*

§ 147 But it being, as God fays, *Gen* vi 6 one people, they had one ruler, one king by na- tural right, abfolute and fupreme over them, *what care had God to preferve the paternal authori- ty of the fupreme fatherhood,* if on a fudden he fuffer 72 (for fo many our author talks of) *diftinct nations* to be erected out of it, under diftinct go- vernors, and at once to withdraw themfelves from the obedience of their fovereign? This is to intitle God's care how, and to what we pleafe Can it be fenfe to fay, that God was careful to preferve the *fatherly authority* in thofe who had it not? for if thefe were fubjects under a fupreme prince, what authority had they? Was it an in- ftance of God's care to preferve the *fatherly au- thority,* when he took away the true *fupreme fa- therhood* of the natural monarch? Can it be reafon to fay, that God, for the prefervation of *fatherly authority,* lets feveral new governments with their governors ftart up, who could not all have *fatherly authority?* And is it not as much reafon to fay, that God is careful to deftroy *fa- therly authority,* when he fuffers one, who is in poffeffion of it, to have his government torn in pieces, and fhared by feveral of his fubjects? Would it not be an argument juft like this, for monarchical government, to fay, when any mo-

narchy

narchy was fhattered to pieces, and divided a-
mongft revolted fubjects, that God was careful
to preferve monarchical power, by rending a
fettled empire into a multitude of little governments? If any one will fay, that what happens in
providence to be preferved, God is careful to
preferve as a thing therefore to be efteemed by
men as neceffary or ufeful, it is a peculiar propriety of fpeech, which every one will not think
fit to imitate: but this I am fure is impoffible to
be either proper, or true fpeaking, that *Shem*, for
example, (for he was then alive) fhould have *fatherly authority*, or fovereignty by right of *fatherhood*, over that one people at *Babel*, and that
the next moment, *Shem* yet living, 72 others
fhould have *fatherly authority*, or fovereignty by
right of fatherhood, over the fame people, divided into fo many diftinct governments either thefe
72 fathers actually were rulers, juft before the
confufion, and then they were not one people,
but that God himfelf fays they were, or elfe they
were a common wealth, and then where was
monarchy? or elfe thefe 72 fathers had *fatherly
authority*, but knew it not Strange! that *fatherly authority* fhould be the only original of
government amongft men, and yet all mankind
not know it, and ftranger yet, that the confufion
of tongues fhould reveal it to them all of a fudden, that in an inftant thefe 72 fhould know that
they had *fatherly power*, and all others know that
they were to obey it in them, and every one
know that particular *fatherly authority* to which
he was a fubject He that can think this arguing
from fcripture, may from thence make out what
model of an *Eutopia* will beft fuit with his fancy
or intereft, and this *fatherhood*, thus difpofed of,
will juftify both a prince who claims an univerfal
monarchy,

monarchy, and his fubjects, who, being fathers
of families, fhall quit all fubjection to him, and
canton his empire into lefs governments for themfelves, for it will always remain a doubt in
which of thefe the fatherly authority refided, till
our author refolves us, whether *Sh m*, who was
then alive, or thefe 72 new princes, beginning fo
many new empires in his dominions, and over his
fubjects, had right to govern, fince our author
tells us, that both one and the other had *fatherly*
which is fupreme authority, and are brought in
by him as inftances of thofe who did *enjoy the
lordfhips of* Adam *by right defcending to them,
which was as large and ample as the abfolutefl dominion of any monarch* This at leaft is unavoidable, that if *God was careful to preferve the
fatherly authority, in the 72 new-erected nations*,
it neceffarily follows, that he was as careful to
deftroy all pretences of *Adam's* heir ; fince he
took care, and therefore did preferve the fatherly
authority in fo many, at leaft 71, that could not
poffibly be *Adam's* heirs, when the right heir (if
God had ever ordained any fuch inheritance)
could not but be known, *Shem* then living, and
they being all one people.

§ 148 *Nimrod* is his next inftance of enjoying this patriarchal power, p 16 but I know not
for what reafon our author feems a little unkind
to him, and fays, that he *againfl right enlarged
his empire, by feizing violently on the rights of other
lords of families* Thefe *lords of families* here
were called *fathers of families*, in his account
of the difperfion at *Babel* but it matters not how
they were called, fo we know who they are, for
this fatherly authority muft be in them, either as
heirs to *Adam*, and fo there could not be 72, nor
above one at once, or elfe as natural parents over
their

their children, and so every father will have *paternal authority* over his children by the same right, and in as large extent as those 72 had, and so be independent princes over their own offspring. Taking his *lords of families* in this latter sense, (as it is hard to give those words any other sense in this place) he gives us a very pretty account of the original of monarchy, in these following words, p 16 *And in this sense he may be said to be the author and founder of monarchy*, viz As against right seizing violently on the rights of fathers over their children , which paternal authority, if it be in them, by right of nature, (for else how could those 72 come by it?) no body can take from them without their own consents, and then I desire our author and his friends to consider, how far this will concern other princes, and whether it will not, according to his conclusion of that paragraph, resolve all regal power of those, whose dominions extend beyond their families, either into tyranny and usurpation, or election and consent of fathers of families, which will differ very little from consent of the people.

§ 149 All his instances, in the next *section*, p. 17 of the 12 dukes of *Edom*, the nine kings in a little corner of *Asia* in *Abraham*'s days, the 31 kings in *Canaan* destroyed by *Joshua*, and the care he takes to prove that these were all sovereign princes, and that every town in those days had a king, are so many direct proofs against him, that it was not the *lordship* of Adam *by right descending* to them, that made kings for if they had held their royalties by that title, either there must have been but one sovereign over them all, or else every father of a family had been as good a prince, and had as good a claim to royalty, as these:

thefe for if all the fons of *Efau* had each of
them, the younger as well as the eldeft, the
right of *fatherhood*, and fo were fovereign princes
after their fathers death, the fame right had their
fons after them, and fo on to all pofterity ; which
will limit all the natural power of fatherhood,
only to be over the iffue of their own bodies and
their defcendents, which power of fatherhood
dies with the head of each family, and makes
way for the like power of fatherhood to take
place in each of his fons over their refpective
pofterities whereby the power of fatherhood will
be preferved indeed, and is intelligible, but will
not be at all to our author's purpofe   None of
the inflances he brings are proofs of any power
they had, as heirs of *Adam*'s paternal authority
by the title of his fatherhood defcerding to
them ; no, nor of any power they had by virtue
of their own   for *Adam's fatherhood* being over
all mankind, it could defcend but to one at
once, and from him to his right heir only, and fo
there could by that title be but one king in the
world at a time   and by right of fatherhood, not
defcending from *Adam*, it muft be only as they
themfelves were fathers, and fo could be over
none but their own pofterity   So that if thofe
12 dukes of *Edom* ; if *Abraham* and the nine kings
his neighbours ; if *Jacob* and *Efau*, and the 31
kings in *Canaan*, the 72 kings mutilated by *Ado-
nibefeck*, the 32 kings that came to *Benhadad*,
the 70 kings of *Greece* making war at *Troy*, were,
as our author contends, all of them fovereign
princes ; it is evident that kings derived their
power from fome other original *than fatherhood*,
fince fome of thefe had power over more than
their own pofterity, and it is demonftration, they
could not be all heirs to *Adam*   for I challenge
                                                    any

any man to make any pretence to power by right of *fatherhood*, either intelligible or possible in any one, otherwise, than either as *Adam*'s heir, or as progenitor over his own descendents, naturally sprung from him. And if our author could shew that any one of these princes, of which he gives us here so large a catalogue, had his authority by either of these titles, I think I might yield him the cause, though it is manifest they are all impertinent, and directly contrary to what he brings them to prove, *viz* *That the lordship which A-dam had over the world by right descended to the patriarchs*

§ 150 Having told us, p 16, '*That the patriarchal government continued in* Abraham, Isaac, *and* Jacob, *until the* Egyptian *bordage*, p 17 he tells us, *By manifest footsteps we may trace this paternal government unto the* Israelites *coming into* Egypt, *where the exercise of supreme patriarchal government was intermitted, because they were in subjection to a stronger prince* What these footsteps are of paternal government, in our author's sense, i e of absolute monarchical power descending from *Adam*, and exercised by right of *fatherhood*, we have seen, that is for 2290 years no footsteps at all ; since in all that time he cannot produce any one example of any person who claimed or exercised regal authority by right of *fatherhood*, or shew any one who being a king was *Adam*'s heir all that his proofs amount to, is only this, that there were fathers, patriarchs and kings, in that age of the world, but that the fathers and patriarchs had any absolute power, or by what titles those kings had their's, and of what extent it was, the scripture is wholly silent , it is manifest by right of *fatherhood* they

neither

neither did, nor could claim any title to dominion and empire

§ 151. To say, *that the exercife of fupreme patriarchal government was intermitted, becaufe they were in fubjeffion to a ftronger prince,* proves nothing but what I before fufpected, *viz* That *patriarchal jurifdiffion or government is a* fallacious expreffion, and does not in our author fignify (what he would yet infinuate by it) *paternal* and *regal power,* fuch an abfolute foveregnty as he fuppofes was in *Adam*

§ 152 For how can he fay that *patriarchal jurifdiffion was intermitted in Egypt,* where there was a king, under whofe regal government the *Ifraelites* were, if *patriarchal* were *abfolute monarchical jurifdiffion?* And if it were not, but fomething elfe, why does he make fuch ado about a power not in queftion, and nothing to the purpofe? The exercife of *patriarchal* jurifdiffion, if *patriarchal* be *regal,* was not intermitted whilft the *Ifraelites* were in *Egypt* It is true, the exercife of *regal* power was not then in the hands of any of the promifed feed of *Abraham,* nor before neither that I know, but what is that to the intermiffion of *regal authority, as defcending from* Adam, unlefs our author will have it, that this chofen line of *Abraham* had the right of inheritance to *Adam's* lordfhip? and then to what purpofe are his inftances of the 72 rulers, in whom the fatherly authority was preferved in the confufion at *Babel?* Why does he bring the 12 princes fons of *Ifmael;* and the dukes of *Edom,* and join them with *Abraham, Ifaac,* and *Jacob,* as examples of the exercife of true *patriarchal government,* if the exercife of *patriarchal jurifdiction* were intermitted in the world, whenever the heirs of *Jacob* had not fupreme power? I fear,

fear, *supreme patriarchal jurisdiction* was not only *intermitted,* but from the time of the *Egyptian* bondage quite lost in the world, since it will be hard to find, from that time downwards, any one who exercised it as an inheritance descending to him from the patriarchs *Abraham, Isaac,* and *Jacob* I imagined monarchical government would have served his turn in the hands of *Pharaoh,* or any body But one cannot easily discover in all places what his discourse tends to, as particularly in this place it is not obvious to guess what he drives at, when he says, *the exercise of supreme patriarchal jurisdiction* in *Egypt,* or how this serves to make out the descent of *Adam's* lordship to the patriarchs, or any body else

§ 153 For I thought he had been giving us out of scripture, proofs and examples of monarchical government, founded on paternal authority, descending from *Adam*, and not an history of the *Jews* amongst whom yet we find no kings, till many years after they were a people · and when kings were their rulers, there is not the least mention or room for a pretence that they were heirs to *Adam,* or kings by paternal authority. I expected, talking so much as he does of scripture, that he would have produced thence a series of monarchs, whose titles were clear to *Adam's fatherhood,* and who, as heirs to him, owned and exercised paternal jurisdiction over their subjects, and that this was the true patriarchical government, whereas he neither proves, that the patriarchs were kings ; nor that either kings or patriarchs were heirs to *Adam,* or so much as pretended to it and one may as well prove, that the patriarchs were all absolute monarchs, that the power both of patriarchs and kings was only paternal, and that this power descended

ſcended to them from *Adam* I ſay all theſe propoſitions may be as well proved by a con-fuſed account of a multitude of little kings in the *Weſt-Indies*, out of *Ferdinando Soto*, or any of our late hiſtories of the *Northern America*, or by our author's 70 kings of *Greece*, out of *Homer*, as by any thing he brings out of ſcripture, in that multitude of kings he has reckoned up

§ 154 And methinks he ſhould have let *Homer* and his wars of *Troy* alone, ſince his great zeal to truth or monarchy carried him to ſuch a pitch of tranſport againſt *philoſophers* and *poets*, that he tells us in his preface, that there *are too many in theſe days, who pleaſe themſelves in running after the opinions of philoſophers and poets, to find out ſuch an original of government, as might promiſe them ſome title to liberty, to the great ſcandal of Chriſ-tianity, and bringing in of atheiſm* And yet theſe heathens, philoſopher *Ariſtoth*, and poet *Homer*, are not rejected by our zealous Chriſtian politici-an, whenever they offer any thing that ſeems to ſerve his turn ; whether *to the great ſcandal of* Chriſtianity *and bringing in of* atheiſm, let him look. This I cannot but obſerve, in authors who it is viſible write not for truth, how ready zeal for intereſt and party is to entitle *Chriſtianity* to their deſigns, and to charge *atheiſm* on thoſe who will not without examining ſubmit to their doc-trines, and blindly ſwallow their nonſenſe

But to return to his ſcripture hiſtory, our au-thor farther tells us, p 18 that *after the return of the* Iſraelites *out of* bondage, *God, out of a ſpe-cial care of them, choſe* Moſes *and* Joſhua *ſuccef-ſively to govern as princes in the place and ſtead of the ſupreme fathers* If it be true, that they re-turned out of bondage, it muſt be into a ſtate of freedom,

freedom, and muft imply, that both before and
at'er this *bondage* they were free, unlefs our author will fay, that changing of mafters is returning *out of bondage*, or that a flave *returns out of
bondage*, when he is removed from one galley to
another If then they *returned out of bondage*,
it is plain that in thofe days, whatever our author
in his preface fays to the contrary, there were
difference between a *fon*, a *fubject*, and a *flave*;
and that neither the *patriarchs* before, nor their
rulers after this *Egyptian bondage*, numbered their
fons or *fubjects* amongft their *poffeffions*, and difpofed of them with as abfolute a dominion, as they
did *their other goods*

§ 155 'This is evident in *Jacob*, to whom
Reuben offered his two fons as pledges, and *Judah* was at laft furety for *Benjamins* fafe return
out of *Egypt* which all had been vain, fuperflu-
ous, and but a fort of mockery, if *Jacob* had had
the fame power over every one of his family, as
he had over his ox or his afs, as an *owner* over
his *fubftance*; and the offers that *Reuben* or *Judah* made had been fuch a fecurity for returning
of *Benjamin*, as if a man fhould take two lambs
out of his lord's flock, and offer one as fecurity,
that he will fafely reftore the other

§ 156 When they were out of this *bondage*,
what then? *God out of a fpecial care of them, the
Ifraelites* It is well that once in his book he will
allow God to have any care of the people; for in
other places he fpeaks of mankind, as if God had
no care of any part of them, but only of their
monarchs, and that the reft of the people, the focieties of men, were made as fo many herds of
cattle, only for the fervice, ufe, and pleafure of
their princes

§ 157

§ 157. *Chose* Moses *and* Joshua *successively to govern as princes*; a shrewd argument our author has found out to prove God's care of the fatherly authority, and *Adam*'s heirs, that here, as an expression of his care of his own people, he chooses those for princes over them, that had not the least pretence to either The persons chosen were, *Moses* of the tribe of *Levi*, and *Joshua* of the tribe of *Ephraim*, neither of which had any title of *fatherhood* But says our author, they were in the place and stead of the supreme fathers If God had any where as plainly declared his choice of such *fathers* to be rulers, as he did of *Moses* and *Joshua*, we might believe *Moses* and *Joshua* were in *their place and stead* but that being the question in debate, till that be better proved, *Moses* being chosen by God to be ruler of his people, will no more prove that government belonged to *Adam's heir*, or to the *fatherhood*, than God's choosing *Aaron* of the tribe of *Levi* to be priest, will prove that the priesthood belonged to *Adam*'s heir, or the *prime fathers*. since God would choose *Aaron* to be priest, and *Moses* ruler in *Israel*, though neither of those offices were settled on *Adam*'s heir, or the *fatherhood*

§ 158 Our author goes on, *and after them likewise for a time he raised up judges, to defend his people in time of peril*, p 18 This proves fatherly authority to be the original of government, and that it descended from *Adam* to his heirs, just as well as what went before only here our author seems to confess, that these judges, who were all the governors they then had, were only men of valour, whom they made their generals to defend them in time of peril; and cannot God

rai t

raife up fuch men, unlefs fatherhood have a title to government?

But fays our author, *when God gave the Ifraelites kings, he re-eftablifhed the antient and prime right of lineal fucceffion to paternal government,* p 18

§ 160 How d d God *re-eftablifh* it? by a law, a pofitive command? We find no fuch thing Our author means then, that when God gave them a king, in giving them, a king, he *re-eftablifhed the right, &c.* To re-eftablifh *de facto* the right of lineal fucceffion to paternal government, to put a man in poffeffion of that government which his fathers did enjoy, and he b, lineal fucceffion had a right to for, firft, if it were another government than what his anceftors had, it was not fucceeding to an *antient right,* but beginning a new one for if a prince fhould give a man, befides his antient patrimony, which for fome ages his family had been diffeized of, an additional eftate, never before in the poffeffion of his anceftors, he could not be faid to *re-eftablifh the right of lineal fucceffion* to any more than what had been formerly enjoyed by his anceftors If therefore the power the kings of *Ifrael* had, were any thing more than *Ifaac* or *Jacob* had, it was not the *re-eftablifhing* in them the right of fucceffion to a power, but giving them a new power, however you pleafe to call it, *paternal* or not. and whether *Ifaac* and *Jacob* had the fame power that the kings of *Ifrael* had, I defire any one, by what has been above faid, to confider, and I do not think they will find, that either *Abraham, Ifaac,* or *Jacob,* had any regal power at all

§ 161 Next, there can be no *re-eftablifhment* of *the prime and antient right of lineal fucceffion* to any thing, unlefs he, that is put in poffeffion of

H

it, has the right to fucceed, and be the true and next heir to him he fucceeds to Can that be a re-eftablifhment, which begins in a new family? or that the *re-eftablifhment of an antient right of lineal fucceffion,* when a crown is given to one, who has no right of fucceffion to it, and who, if the lineal fucceffion had gone on, had been out of all poffibility of pretence to it? *Saul,* the firft king God gave the *Ifraelites,* was of the tribe of *Benjamin* Was the *antient and prime right of lineal fucceffion re-eftablifhed* in him? The next was *David,* the youngeft fon of *Jeffe,* of the pofterity of *Judah, Jacob's third fon* Was the *antient and prime right of lineal fucceffion to paternal government re-eftablifhed* in him? or in *Solomon,* his younger fon and fucceffor in the throne? or in *Jeroboam* over the ten tribes? or in *Athaliah,* a woman who reigned fix years an utter ftranger to the royal blood? *If the antient and prime right of lineal fucceffion to paternal government were re-eftablifhed* in any of thefe or their pofterity, *the antient and prime right of lineal fucceffion to paternal government* belongs to younger brothers as well as elder, and may be re-eftablifhed in any man living, for whatever younger brothers, by *ancient and prime right of lineal fucceffion,* may have as well as the elder, that every man living may have a right to, by lineal fucceffion, and Sir *Robert* as well as any other. And fo what a brave right of lineal fucceffion, to his *paternal* or *regal* government, our author has *re-eftablifhed,* for the fecuring the rights and inheritance of crowns, where every one may have it, let the world confider

§ 162 But fays our author however, p 19. *Whenfoever God made choice of any fpecial perfon to be king, he intended that the iffue alfo fhould have benefit thereof, as being comprehended fufficiently in the*

the perfon of the father, altho' the father was only named in the grant. This yet will not help out fucceffion, for if, as our author fays, the benefit of the gra' 'e intended to the *iffue* of the grantee, this will not direct the fucceffion, fince, if God give any thing to a man and his *iffue* in general, the claim cannot be to any one of that *iffue* in particular, every one that is of his race will have an equal right. If it be faid, our author meant *heir*, I believe our author was as willing as any body to have ufed that word, if it would have ferved his turn. but *Solomon*, who fucceeded *David* in the throne, being no more his heir than *Jeroboam*, who fucceeded him in the government of the ten tribes, was his iffue, our author had reafon to avoid faying, That God intended it to the *heirs* when that would not hold in a fucceffion, which our author could not except againft, and fo he has left his fucceffion as undetermined, as if he had faid nothing about it: for if the regal power be given by God to a man and his *iffue*, as the land of *Canaan* was to *Abraham* and his feed, muft they not all have a title to it, all fhare in it? And one may as well fay, that by God's grant to *Abraham* and his feed, the land of *Canaan* was to belong only to one of his feed exclufive of all others, as by God's grant of dominion to a man and *his iffue*, this dominion was to belong in peculiar to one of his *iffue* exclufive of all others.

§ 163. But how will our author prove that whenfoever God made choice of any fpecial perfon to be a king, he intended that *the* (I fuppofe he means his) *iffue alfo fhould have benefit thereof?* has he fo foon forgot *Mofes* and *Jofhua*, whom in this very *fection*, he fays, God out of a fpecial care chofe to govern as princes, and the judges that God

H 2

raised up ? Had not these princes, having the authority of the *supreme fatherhood*, the same power that the kings had, and being specially chosen by God himself, should not their *issue* have the benefit of that choice, as well as *David's* or *Solomon's*? If these had the paternal authority put into their hands immediately by God, why had not their *issue* the benefit of this grant in succession to this power ? or if they had it as *Adam's* heirs, why did not their heirs enjoy it after them by right descending to them ? for they could not be heirs to one another. Was the power the same, and from the same original, in *Moses*, *Joshua* and the *Judges*, as it was in *David* and the *Kings*, and was it inheritable in one, and not in the other ? If it was not *paternal authority*, then God's own people were governed by those that had not *paternal authority*, and those governors did well enough without it. If it were *paternal authority*, and God chose the persons that were to exercise it, our author's rule fails, that *whensoever God makes choice of any person to be supreme ruler* (for I suppose the name king has no spell in it, it is not the title, but the power makes the difference) *he intends that the issue also should have the benefit of it*, since from their coming out of *Egypt* to *David's* time, 400 years, the *issue* was never *so sufficiently comprehended in the person of the father*, as that any son, after the death of his father, succeeded to the government amongst all those judges that judged *Israel*. If, to avoid this, it be said, God always chose the person of the successor, and so, transferring the *fatherly authority* to him, excluded his issue from succeeding to it, that is manifestly not so in the story of *Jephtha*, where he articled with

the

the people, and they made him judge over them, as is plain, *Jig* II

§ 164 It is in vain then to say, that *whenso-ever God chooses any special person* to have the exercise of *paternal authority*, (for if that be not to be king, I desire to know the difference be-tween a king and one having the exercise of *pa-ternal authority*) *he intends the issue also should have the benefit of it*, since we find the authority, the judges had, ended with them, and descended not to their *issue*, and if the judges had not *pater-nal authority*, I fear it will trouble our author, or any of the friends to his principles, to tell who had then the *paternal authority*, that is, the govern-ment and supreme power amongst the *Israelites*, and I suspect they must confess that the chosen people of God continued a people several hun-dreds of years, without any knowledge or thought of this *paternal authority*, or any appearance of monarchical government at all

§ 165 To be satisfied of this, he need but read the story of the *Levite*, and the war there-upon with the *Benjamites*, in the three last *chap-ters* of *Judges*, and when he finds, that the *Levite* appeals to the people for justice that it was the tribes and the congregation, that debated, resolved, and directed all that was done on that occasion, he must conclude either that *God* was not *careful to preserve the fatherly authority* amongst his own chosen people; or else that the *fatherly authority* may be preserved, where there is no monarchical government if the latter, then it will follow, that though *fatherly authority* be ne-ver so well proved, yet it will not infer a necessi-ty of monarchical government, if the former, it will be seem very strange and improbable, that

God

God fhou'd ordain *fatherly authority* to be fo facred amongft the fons of men, that there could
be no power, or government without it, and yet
that amongft his own people, even whilft he
is providing a government for them, and therein
prefcribes rules to the feveral ftates and relations
of men, as great and fundamental one, this
moft weighty and neceffary of all the reft, fhould
be concealed, and lie neglected for 400 years
after

§ 166 Before I leave this, I muft afk how our
author knows that *whenfoever God makes choice of
any fpecial perfon to be king, he intends that the iffue
fhould have the benefit thereof?* Does God by the
law of nature or revelation fay fo? By the fame
law alfo he muft fay, which of his *iffue* muft enjoy the crown in fucceffion, and fo point out the
heir, or elfe leave his *iffue* to divide or fcramble
for the government both alike abfurd, and fuch
as will deftroy the benefit of fuch grant to the
iff When any fuch declaration of God's intention is produced, it will be our duty to believe
God intends it fo, but till that be done, our author muft fhew us fome better warrant, before
we fhall be obliged to receive him as the authen-
tic revealer of God's intentions

§ 167 *The iffue,* fays our author, *is comprehended fufficiently in the perfon of the father, although the father only was named in the grant* and
yet God, when he gave the land of *Canaan* to *A-
braham, Gen* xiii 15 thought fit to put *his feed*
into the grant too fo the priefthood was given to
Aaron and his feed, and the crown God gave not
only to *David,* but *his feed* alfo and however our
author affures us that *God intends, that the iffue fhould
have the benefit of it, when he choofes any perfon to
be king,* yet we fee that the kingdom which he
gave

gave to *Saul*, without mentioning his feed after him, never came to any of his *iffue* and why, when God chose a perfon to be king, he should intend that his *iffue* should have the benefit of it, more than when he chose one to be judge in *Ifrael*, I would fain know a reafon, or why does a grant of *fatherly authority* to a king more comprehend the *iffue*, than when a like grant is made to a judge? Is *paternal authority* by right to defcend to the *iffue* of one, and not of the other? There will need fome reafon to be shewn of this difference, more than the name, when the thing given is the fame *fatherly authority*, and the manner of giving it, God's choice of the perfon, the fame too; for I fuppofe our author, when he fays, *God raifed up judges*, will by no means allow, they were chofen by the people

§ 168 But fince our author has fo confidently affured us of the care of God to preferve the *fatherhood*, and pretends to build all he fays upon the authority of the fcripture, we may well expect that the people, whofe law, conftitution and hiftory is chiefly contained in the fcripture, should furnish him with the cleareft inftances of God's care of preferving the fatherly authority, in that people who it is agreed he had a moft peculiar care of Let us fee then what ftate this *paternal authority* or government was in amongft the *Jews*, from their beginning to be a people It was omitted, by our author's confeffion, from their coming into *Egypt*, till their return out of that bondage, above 200 years from thence till God gave the *Ifraelites* a king, about 400 years more, our author gives but a very flender account of it, nor indeed all that time are there the leaft footfteps of paternal or regal government amongft them But

then

then fays our author, *God re-eſtabliſhed the ancient
and prime right of lineal ſucceſſion to paternal government*

§. 169 What a *lineal ſucceſſion to paternal government* was then eſtabliſhed, we have already
feen   I only now confider how long this laſted,
and that was to their captivity, about 500 years
from thence to their deſtruction by the *Romans*,
above 650 years after, the *ancient and prime right
of lineal ſucceſſion to paternal government* was again
left, and they continued a people in the promiſed
land without it   So that of 1750 years that they
were God's peculiar people, they had hereditary
kingly government amongſt them not one third
of the time , and of that time there is not the
leaſt footſtep of one moment of *paternal government, nor the re-eſtabliſhment of the antient and
prime right of lineal ſucceſſion to it,* whether we
ſuppoſe it to be derived, as from its fountain, from
David, Saul, Abraham, or, which upon our author's principles is the only true, from *Adam.*

O F

CIVIL-GOVERNMENT.

BOOK II

CHAP I

§ 1 IT having been shewn in the foregoing discourse,

1 That *Adam* had not, either by natural right of fatherhood, or by positive donation from God, any such authority over his children, or dominion over the world, as is pretended

2 That if he had, his heirs, yet, had no right to it ·

3 That if his heirs had, there being no law of nature nor positive law of God that determines which is the right heir in all cases that may arise, the right of succession, and consequently of bearing rule, could not have been certainly determined

4 That if even that had been determined, yet the knowledge of which is the eldest line of *Adam*'s posterity, being so long since utterly lost, that in the races of mankind and families of the world, there remains not to one above another, the least pretence to be the eldest house, and to have the right of inheritance .

H 5

All

All thefe premifes having, as I think, been cleaily made out, it is impoffible that the rulers now on earth fhould make any benefit, or derive any the leaft fhadow of authority from that, which is held to be the fountain of all power, *Adam's private dominion and paternal jurifdiction*, fo that he that will not give juft occafion to think that all government in the world is the product only of force and violence, and that men live together by no other rules but that of beafts, where the ftrongeft carries it, and fo lay a foundation for perpetual difordei and mifchief, tumult, fedition and rebellion, (things that the followers of that hypothefis fo loudly cry out againft) muft of neceffity find out another rife of government, another original of political power, and another way of defigning and knowing the perfons that have it, than what Sir *Robert Filmer* hath taught us.

§ 2. To this purpofe, I think it may not be amifs, to fet down what I take to be political power; that the power of a *magiftrate* over a fubject may be diflinguifhed from that of a *father* over his children, a *mafter* over his fervant, a *hufband* over his wife, and a *lord* over his flave. All which diflinct poweis happening fometimes together in the fame man, if he be confidered under thefe different relations, it may help us to diflinguifh thefe powers one from another, and fhew the difference betwixt a ruler of a commonwealth, a father of a family, and a captain of a galley.

§ 3. *Political power*, then, I take to be a *right* of making laws with penalties of death, and confequently all lefs penalties, for the regulating and preferving of property, and of employing the force of the community, in the execution of fuch laws,

laws, and in the defence of the common-wealth
from foreign injury, and all this only for the
public good

CHAP II.

Of the State of Nature

§. 4 TO understand political power right,
and derive it from its original, we must
consider, what state all men are naturally in, and
that is, a *state of perfect freedom* to order their
actions, and dispose of their possessions and persons, as they think fit, within the bounds of the
law of nature, without asking leave, or depending upon the will of any other man.

A *state* also *of equality*, wherein all the power
and jurisdiction is reciprocal, no one having more
than another; there being nothing more evident
than that creatures of the same species and rank,
promiscuously born to all the same advantages
of nature, and the use of the same faculties,
should also be equal one amongst another without
subordination or subjection, unless the lord and
master of them all should, by any manifest declaration of his will, set one above another, and
confer on him, by an evident and clear appointment, an undoubted right to dominion and sovereignty

§ 5 This *equality* of men by nature, the judicious *Hooker* looks upon as so evident in itself,
and beyond all question, that he makes it the
foundation of that obligation to mutual love
amongst men, on which he builds the duties they
owe one another, and from whence he derives
the

the great maxims *of justice* and *charity*. His
words are,

*The like natural inducement hath brought men to
know that it is no less their duty, to love others
than themselves, for seeing those things which are
equal, must needs all have one measure; if I cannot but wish to receive good, even as much at every
man's hands, as any man can wish unto his own
soul, how should I look to have any part of my desire herein satisfied, unless myself be careful to satisfy the like desire, which is undoubtedly in other
men, being of one and the same nature? To have
any thing offered them repugnant to this desire, must
needs in all respects grieve them as much as me;
so that if I do harm, I must look to suffer, there
being no reason that others should shew greater measure of love to me, than they have by me shewed
unto them my desire therefore to be loved of my
equals in nature, as much as possible may be, im-
poseth upon me a natural duty of bearing to them-
ward fully the like affection; from which relation
of equality between ourselves and them that are as
ourselves, what several rules and canons natural
reason hath drawn, for direction of life, no man is
ignorant* Eccl Pol Lib 1.

§ 6 But though this be *a state of liberty* yet it
is not a state of licence though man in that state
have an uncontroulable liberty to difpofe of his
perfon or poffeffions, yet he has not liberty to
deftroy himfelf, or fo much as any creature in
his poffeffion, but where fome nobler ufe than its
bare prefervation calls for it. The *state of nature* has a law of nature to govern it, which
obliges every one: and reafon, which is that law,
teaches all mankind, who will but confult it, that
being all *equal and independent*, no one ought to
harm another in his life, health, liberty, or poffeffions;

seſſions for men being all the workmanſhip of one omnipotent, and infinitely wiſe maker, all the ſervants of one ſovereign maſter, ſent in- into the world by his order, and about his buſi- neſs; they are his property, whoſe workmanſhip they are, made to laſt during his, not one ano- ther's pleaſure. and being furniſhed with like fa- culties, ſharing all in one community of nature, there cannot be ſuppoſed any ſuch *ſubordination* among us, that may authorize us to deſtroy one another, as if we were made for one another's uſes, as the inferior ranks of creatures are for our's Every one, as he is *bound to preſerve him- ſelf*, and not to quit his ſtation wilfully, ſo by the like reaſon, when his own preſervation comes not in competition, ought he, as much as he can, *to preſerve the reſt of mankind*, and may not, un- leſs it be to do juſtice on an offender, take away, or impair the life, or what tends to the preſerva- tion of the life, the liberty, health, limb, or goods of another.

§ 7 And that all men may be reſtrained from invading others rights, and from doing hurt to one another, and the law of nature be obſerved, which willeth the peace and *preſervation of all mankind*, the *execution* of the law of nature is, in that ſtate, put into every man's hands, where- by every one has a right to puniſh the tranſgreſ- ſors of that law to ſuch a degree, as may hinder its violation. for the *law of nature* would, as all other laws that concern men in this world, be in vain, if there were no body that in the ſtate of nature had a *power to execute* that law, and there- by preſerve the innocent, and reſtrain offenders. And if any one in the ſtate of nature may puniſh another for any evil he has done, every one may do ſo. for in that *ſtate of perfect equality*, where naturally

naturally there is no fuperiority or jurifdiction
of one over another, what any may do in profe-
cution of that law, every one muſt needs have a
right to do

§. 8 And thus, in the ſtate of nature, *one man
comes by a power over another* ; but yet no abſolute
or arbitrary power, to uſe a criminal, when he
has got him in his hands, according to the paf-
ſionate heats, or boundleſs extravagancy of his
own will , but only to retribute to him, ſo far as
calm reaſon and conſcience dictate, what is pro-
portionate to his tranſgreſſion, which is ſo much
as may ſerve for *reparation* and *reſtraint* for
theſe two are the only reaſons, why one man may
lawfully do harm to another, which is that we
call *puniſhment* In tranſgreſſing the law of nature, the offender declares himſelf to live by another rule than that of reaſon and common equity,
which is that meaſure God has ſet to the actions of men, for their mutual ſecurity, and ſo
he becomes dangerous to mankind, the tye,
which is to ſecure them from injury and violence,
being ſlighted and broken by him Which being
a treſpaſs againſt the whole ſpecies, and the peace
and ſafety of it, provided for by the law of nature, every man upon this ſcore, by the right he
hath to preſerve mankind in general, may reſtrain,
or where it is neceſſary, deſtroy things roxious
to them, and ſo may bring ſuch evil on any one,
who hath tranſgreſſed that law, as may make
him repent the doing of it, and thereby deter
him, and by his example others, from doing the
like miſchief And in this caſe, and upon this
ground, *every man hath a right to puniſh the offender, and be executioner of the law of nature.*

§ 9 I doubt not but this will ſeem a very
ſtrange doctrine to ſome men : but before they
condemn

condemn it, I defire them to refolve me, by
what right any prince or ftate can put to death,
or *punish an alien*, for any crime he commits in
their country It is certain their laws, by virtue
of any fanction they receive from the promulgated will of the legiflative, reach not a ftranger:
they fpeak not to him, nor, if they did, is he
bound to hearken to them The legiflative authority, by which they are in force over the fubjects of that common-wealth, hath no power
over him Thofe who have the fupreme power
of making laws in *England*, *France* or *Holland*,
are to an *Indian*, but like the reft of the world,
men without authority and therefore, if by the
law of nature every man hath not a power to
punifh offences againft it, as he foberly judges
the cafe to require, I fee not how the magiftrates
of any community can *punish an alien* of another
country, fince, in reference to him, they can
have no more power than what every man naturally may have over another.

§ 10 Befides the crime which confifts in viola-
ting the law, and varying from the right rule of
reafon, whereby a man fo far becomes degenerate,
and declares himfelf to quit the principles of human nature, and to be a noxious creature, there
is commonly *injury* done to fome perfon or other,
and fome other man receives damage by his tranf-
greffion in which cafe he who hath received
any damage, has, befides the right of punifhment
common to him with other men, a particular
right to feek *reparation* from him that has done
it and any other perfon, who finds it juft, may
alfo join with him that is injured, and affift him
in recovering from the offender fo much as may
make fatisfaction for the harm he has fuffered.

§ 11.

§. 11 From thefe *two diftinct rights*, the one of *punifhing* the crime *for reftraint*, and preventing the like offence, which right of punifhing is in every body, the other of taking *reparation*, which belongs only to the injured party, comes it to pafs that the magiftrate, who by being magiftrate hath the common right of punifhing put into his hands, can often, where the public good demands not the execution of the law, *remit* the punifhment of criminal offences by his own authority, but yet cannot *remit* the fatisfaction due to any private man for the damage he has received. That, he who has fuffered the damage has a right to demand in his own name, and he alone can remit the damnified perfon has this power of appropriating to himfelf the goods or fervice of the offender, *by right of felf-prefervation*, as every man has a power to punifh the crime, to prevent its being committed again, *by the right he has of preferving all mankind*, and doing all reafonable things he can in order to that end: and thus it is, that every man, in the ftate of nature, has a power to kill a murderer, both *to deter* others from doing the like injury, which no reparation can compenfate, by the example of the punifhment that attends it from every body, and alfo to fecure men from the attempts of a criminal, who having renounced reafon, the common rule and meafure God hath given to mankind, hath, by the unjuft violence and flaughter he hath committed upon one, declared war againft all mankind, and therefore may be deftroyed as a *lion* or a *tyger*, one of thofe wild favage beafts, with whom men can have no fociety nor fecurity and upon this is grounded that great law of nature, *Whofo fheddeth man's blood, by man fhall his blood be fhed.* And *Cain* was so fully convinced, that every one had a right to destroy such a criminal, that after the murder of his brother, he cries out, *Every one that findeth me, shall slay me*, so plain was it writ in the hearts of all mankind

§ 12 By the same reason may a man in the state of nature *punish the lesser breaches* of that law   It will perhaps be demanded, with death? I answer, each transgression may be *punished* to that *degree*, and with so much *severity*, as will suffice to make it an ill bargain to the offender, give him cause to repent, and terrify others from doing the like   Every offence, that can be committed in the state of nature, may in the state of nature be also punished equally, and as far forth as it may, in a common-wealth . for though it would be besides my present purpose, to enter here into the particulars of the law of nature, or its *measures of punishment*; yet, it is certain there is such a law, and that too, as intelligible and plain to a rational creature, and a studier of that law, as the positive laws of common-wealths, nay, possibly, plainer ; as much as reason is easier to be understood, than the fancies and intricate contrivances of men, following contrary and hidden interests put into words , for so truly are a great part of the *municipal laws* of countries, which are only so far right, as they are founded on the law of nature, by which they are to be regulated and interpreted

§ 13. To this strange doctrine, *viz* 'That *in t'e state of nature every one has the executive power* of the law of nature, I doubt not but it will be objected, that it is unreasonable for men to be judges in their own cases, that self-love will make men partial to themselves and their friends   and on the other side, that ill nature, passion and revenge
venge

venge will carry them too far in punishing others, and hence nothing but confusion and diforder will follow, and that therefore God hath certainly appointed government to reftrain the partiality and violence of men I easily grant, that *civil government* is the proper remedy for the inconveniencies of the flate of nature, which muft certainly be great, where men may be judges in their own cafe, fince it is eafy to be imagined, that he who was fo unjuft as to do his brother an injury, will fcarce be fo juft as to condemn himfelf for it but I fhall defire thofe who make this objection, to remember, that *abfolute monarchs* are but men, and if government is to be the remedy of thofe evils, which neceffarily follow from men's being judges in their own cafes, and the flate of nature is therefore not to be endured, I defire to know what kind of government that is, and how much better it is than the flate of nature, where one man, commanding a multitude, has the liberty to be judge in his own cafe, and may do to all his fubjects whatever he pleafes, without the leaft liberty to any one to queftion or controul thofe who execute his pleafure? and in whatfoever he doth, whether led by reafon, miftake or paffion, muft be fubmitted to? much better it is in the flate of nature, wherein men are not bound to fubmit to the unjuft will of another and if he that judges, judges amifs in his own, or any other cafe, he is anfwerable for it to the reft of mankind.

§. 14 It is often afked as a mighty objection, *where are*, or ever were there any *men in fuch a ftate of nature?* To which it may fuffice as an anfwer at prefent, that fince all princes and rulers of *independent* governments all through the world, are in a ftate of nature, it is plain the world ne-

ver

,er was, nor ever will be, without numbers of
men in that ftate. I have named all governors of
independent communities, whether they are, or
are not, in league with others for it is not every
compact that puts an end to the ftate of nature
between men, but only this one of agreeing together mutually to enter into one community,
and make one body politic, other promiſes and
compacts, men may make with one another, and
yet ftill be in the ftate of nature. The promiſes
and bargains for truck, &c between the two
men in the defert iſland, mentioned by *Garcilaffo
de la Vega*, in his ftory of *Peru*, or between a
Swiſs and an *Indian*, in the woods of *America*,
are binding to them, though they are perfectly in
a ftate of nature, in reference to one another.
for truth and keeping of faith belongs to men, as
men, and not as members of fociety

§. 15. To thoſe that fay, there were never any
men in the ftate of nature, I will not only oppoſe
the authority of the judicious *Hooker, Eccl Pol
lib* 1 *fect* 10 where he fays, *The laws which
have been hitherto mentioned, i e the laws of nature, do bind men abſolutely, even as they are men,
although they have never any ſettled fellowſhip, never any ſolemn agreement among themſelves what to
do, or not to do but foraſmuch as we are not by
ourſelves fufficient to furnish ourſelves with compe-
tent ſtore of things, needful for ſuch a life as our
nature doth deſire, a life fit for the dignity of man ;
therefore to ſupply thoſe defects and imperfections
which are in us, as living fingle and ſolely by ourſelves, we are naturally induced to ſeek communion
and fellowſhip with others this was the cauſe of
men's uniting themſelves at firſt in politic focieties.*
But I moreover affirm, that all men are naturally
in that ftate, and remain fo, till by their own
consents

consents they make themselves members of some politic society, and I doubt not in the sequel of this discourse, to make it very clear.

CHAP III.

Of the State of War

§ 16 THE *state of war* is a state of *enmity* and *destruction* and therefore declaring by word or action, not a passionate and hasty, but a sedate settled design upon another man's life, *puts him in a state of war* with him against whom he has declared such an intention, and so has exposed his life to the other's power to be taken away by him, or any one that joins with him in his defence, and espouses his quarrel; it being reasonable and just, I should have a right to destroy that which threatens me with destruction · for, *by the fundamental law of nature, man being to be preserved* as much as possible, when all cannot be preserved, the safety of the innocent is to be preferred . and one may destroy a man who makes war upon him, or has discovered an enmity to his being, for the same reason that he may kill a *wolf* or a *lion*, because such men are not under the ties of the common law of reason, have no other rule, but that of force and violence, and so may be treated as beasts of prey, those dangerous and noxious creatures, that will be sure to destroy him whenever he falls into their power

§ 17 And hence it is, that he who attempts to get another man into his absolute power, does thereby *put himself into a state of war* with him; it being to be understood as a declaration of a design upon his life . for I have reason to conclude,

clude, that he who would get me into his power
without my consent, would use me as he pleased
when he had got me there, and destroy me too
when he had a fancy to it , for no body can desire to *have me in his absolute power*, unless it be
to compel me by force to that which is against
the right of my freedom, *i e* make me a slave
To be free from such force is the only security
of my preservation, and reason bids me look on
him, as an enemy to my preservation, who would,
take away that *freedom* which is the fence to it:
so that he who makes an *attempt to enslave* me,
thereby puts himself into a state of war with me.
He that, in the state of nature, *would take away
the freedom* that belongs to any one in that state,
must necessarily be supposed to have a design to
take away every thing else, that *freedom* being
the foundation of all the rest , as he that, in the
state of society, would take away the *freedom* belonging to those of that society or common-
wealth, must be supposed to design to take away
from them every thing else, and so be looked on
s in a state of war

§ 18 This makes it lawful for a man to *kill a
thief*, who has not in the least hurt him, nor declared any design upon his life, any farther than,
by the use of force, so to get him in his power,
as to take away his money, or what he pleases,
from him , because using force, where he has no
right, to get me into his power, let his pretence
be what it will, I have no reason to suppose, that
he, who would take *take away my liberty*, would
not, when he had me in his power, take away
every thing else And therefore it is lawful for
me to treat him as one who has *put himself into
a state of war* with me, *i e* kill him if I can ;
for to that hazard does he justly expose himself,
whoever

whoever introduces a ftate of war, and is aggreffor in it.

§ 19. And here we have the plain *difference*
between the ftate of nature and the ftate of war,
which however fome men have confounded, are
as far diftant, as a ftate of peace, good will, mutual affiftance and prefervation, and a ftate of enmity, malice, violence and mutual deftruction,
are one from another Men living together according to reafon, without a common fuperior on
earth, with authority to judge between them, is
properly the ftate of nature But force, or a declared defign of force, upon the perfon of another, where there is no common fuperior on
earth to appeal to for relief, *is the ftate of war*
and it is the want of fuch an appeal gives a man
the right of war even againft an *aggreffor*, tho'
he be in fociety and a fellow fubject Thus a
thief, whom I cannot harm, but by appeal to
the law, for having ftolen all that I am worth,
I may kill, when he fets on me to rob me but of
my horfe or coat, becaufe the law, which was
made for my prefervation, where it cannot inter-
pofe to fecure my life from prefent force, which,
if loft, is capable of no reparation, permits me
my own defence, and the right of war, a liberty
to kill the aggreffor, becaufe the aggreffor allows
not time to appeal to our common judge, nor the
decifion of the law, for remedy in a cafe where
the mifchief may be irreparable Want of a
common judge with authority, puts all men in a
ftate of nature force without right, upon a
man's perfon, makes a ftate of war, both where
there is, and is not, a common judge

§ 20. But when the actual force is over, the
ftate of war ceafes between thofe that are in fociety, and are equally on both fides fubjected to
                                            , the

the fair determination of the law, because then there lies open the remedy of appeal for the paſt injury, and to prevent future harm · but where no ſuch appeal is, as in the ſtate of nature, for want of poſitive laws, and judges with authority to appeal to, the ſtate of war once begun, conti-nues, with a right to the innocent party to de-ſtroy the other whenever he can, until the ag-greſſor offers peace, and deſires reconciliation on ſuch terms as may repair any wrongs he has al-ready done, and ſecure the innocent for the fu-ture, nay, where an appeal to the law, and conſtituted judges, lies open, but the remedy is denied by a manifeſt perverting of juſtice, and a barefaced wreſting of the laws to protect or in-demnify the violence or injuries of ſome men, or party of men, *there* it is hard to imagine any thing but *a ſtate of war* for where-ever violence is uſed, and injury done, though by hands, ap-pointed to adminiſter juſtice, it is ſtill violence and injury, however coloured with the name, pretences, or forms of law, the end whereof be-ing to protect and redreſs the innocent, by an unbiaſſed application of it, to all who are under it, where-ever that is not *bona fide* done, war is made upon the ſufferers, who having no appeal on earth to right them, they are left to the only remedy in ſuch caſes, an appeal to heaven

§ 21 To avoid this *ſtate of war* (wherein there is no appeal but to heaven, and wherein every the leaſt difference is apt to end, where there is no authority to decide between the con-tenders) is one great reaſon of men's putting themſelves into ſociety, and quitting the ſtate of nature for where there is an authority, a power on earth, from which relief can be had by ap-peal, there the continuance of the *ſtate of war* is excluded,

excluded, and the controverfy is decided by that power. Had there been any fuch court, any fuperior jurifdiction on earth, to determine the right between *Jephtha* and the *Ammonites*, they had never come to a *ftate of war* but we fee he was forced to appeal to heaven The Lord the *Judge* (fays he) *be judge this day between the children of* Ifrael *and the children of* Ammon, *Jud* xi 27. and then profecuting, and relying on his *appeal,* he leads out his army to battle. and therefore in fuch controverfies, where the queftion is put, *who fhall be judge?* It cannot be meant, who fhall decide the controverfy ; every one knows what *Jephtha* here tells us, that *the Lord the Judge* fhall judge Where there is no judge on earth, the appeal lies to God in heaven That queftion then cannot mean, who fhall judge, whether another hath put himfelf in a *ftate of war* with me, and whether I may, as *Jephtha* did, *appeal to heaven* in it ? of that I myfelf can only be judge in my own confcience, as I will anfwer it, at the great day, to the fupreme judge of all men.

CHAP IV

OF SLAVERY

§ 22 THE *natural liberty* of man is to be free from any fuperior power on earth, and not to be under the will or legiflative authority of man, but to have only the law of nature for his rule The *liberty of man,* in fociety, is to be under no other legiflative power, but that eftablifhed, by confent, in the common-wealth, nor under the dominion of any will, or reftraint

of

of any law, but what that legiflative fhall enact, according to the truft put in it Freedom then is not what Sir *Robert Filmer* tells us, *Obfervati-ons, A* 55 *a liberty for every one to do what he lifts, to live as he pleafes, and not to be tied by any laws* but *freedom of men under government* is, to have a ftanding rule to live by, common to every one of that fociety, and made by the legiflative power erected in it ; a liberty to follow my own will in all things, where the rule prefcribes not ; and not to be fubject to the inconftant, uncertain, unknown, arbitrary will of another man: as *freedom of nature* is, to be under no other reftraint but the law of nature

§ 23 This *freedom* from abfolute, arbitrary power, is fo neceffary to, and clofely joined with a man's prefervation, that he cannot part with t, but by what forfeits his perfervation and life together for a man, not having the power of his own life, *cannot*, by compact, or his own confent, *enflave himfelf* to any one, nor put himfelf under the abfolute, arbitrary power of another, to take away his life, when he pleafes. No body can give more power than he has himfelf , and he that can-not take away his own life, cannot give another power over it.   Indeed, having by his fault for-fe ted his own life, by fome act that deferves death ; he, to whom he has forfeited it, may (when he has him in his power) delay to take it, and make ufe of him to his own fervice, and he does him no injury by it for, whenever he finds the hardfhip of his flavery outweigh the value of his life, it is in his power, by refifting the will of his mafter, to draw on himfelf the death he defires.

§ 24. This is the perfect condition of *flavery*, which is nothing elfe, but *the ftate of war con-*

I

tinued, between a lawful conqueror and a captive. for, if once compact enter between them, and make an agreement for a limited power on the one fide, and obedience on the other, the *state of war and slavery* ceases as long as the compact endures for, as has been said, no man can, by agreement, pass over to another that which he hath not in himself, a power over his own life.

I confess, we find among the *Jews*, as well as other nations, that men did sell themselves; but, it is plain, this was only to *drudgery*, *not to slavery* for, it is evident, the person fold was not under an absolute, arbitrary, despotical power: for the master could not have power to kill him, at any time, whom, at a certain time, he was obliged to let go free out of his service, and the master of such a servant was so far from having an arbitrary power over his life, that he could not, at pleasure, so much as maim him, but the loss of an eye, or tooth, set him free, *Exod.* xxi.

CHAP V.

Of PROPERTY

§ 25 WHether we consider natural *reason*, which tells us, that men, being once born, have a right to their preservation, and consequently to meat and drink, and such other things is nature affords for their subsistence or *revelation*, which gives us an account of those grants God made of the world to *Adam*, and to *Noah*, as king *David* says *Psal.* cxv 16 *has given the earth to the children of men*, given it to mankind in common But this being supposed, it seems to some a very great difficulty, how any one should ever come to have a *property* in any thing. I will not content myself to answer, that if it be difficult

cult to make out *property*, upon a fuppofition that God gave the world to *Adam*, and his pofterity in common, it is impoffible that any man, but one univerfal monarch, fhould have any *property* upon a fuppofition, that God gave the world to *Adam*, and his heirs in fucceffion, exclufive of all the reft of his pofterity But I fhall endeavour to fhew, how men might come to have a *property* in feveral parts of that which God gave to mankind in common, and that without any exprefs compact of all the commoners

§ 26 God, who hath given the world to men in common, hath alfo given them reafon to make ufe of it to the beft advantage of life, and convenience The earth, and all that is therein, is given to men for the fupport and comfort of their being. And tho' all the fruits it naturally produces, and beafts it feeds, belong to mankind in common, as they are produced by the fpontaneous hand of nature, and no body has originally a private dominion, exclufive of the reft of mankind, in any of them, as they are thus in their natural ftate · yet being given for the ufe of men, there muft of neceffity be *a means to appropriate* them fome way or other, before they can be of any ufe, or at all beneficial to any particular man. The fruit, or venifon, which nourifhes the wild Indian, who knows no inclofure, and is ftill a tenant in common, muft be his, and fo his, *i e.* a part of him, that another can no longer have any right to it, before it can do him any good for the fupport of his life

§ 27. Though the earth, and all inferior creatures, be common to all men, yet every man has a *property* in his own *perfon* this no body has any right to but himfelf The *labour* of his body, and the *work* of his hands, we may fay, are

I 2 properly

properly his Whatfoever then he removes out
of the ftate that nature hath provided, and left it
in, he hath mixed his *labour* with, and joined to it
fomething that is his own, and thereby makes it
his *property*. It being by him removed from the
common ftate nature hath placed it in, it hath by
this *labour* fomething annexed to it, that excludes
the common right of other men for this *labour*
being the unqueftionable property of the labourer,
no man but he can have a right to what that is
once joined to, at leaft where there is enough, and
as good, left in common for others

§ 28 He that is nourifhed by the acorns he
picked up under an oak, or the apples he gathered from the trees in the wood, has certainly
appropriated them to himfelf No body can deny but the nourifhment is his I afk then, when
did they begin to be his? when he digefted? or
when he eat? or when he boiled? or when he
brought them home? or when he picked them
up? and it is plain, if the firft gathering made
them not his, nothing elfe could That *labour*
put a diftinction between them and common.
that added fomething to them more than nature,
the common mother of all, had done; and fo
they became his private right. And will any one
fay, he had no right to thofe acorns or apples, he
thus appropriated, becaufe he had not the confent of all mankind to make them his? Was it a
robbery thus to affume to himfelf what belonged
to all in common? If fuch a confent as that was
neceffary, man had ftarved, notwithftanding the
plenty God had given him We fee in *commons,*
which remain fo by compact, that it is the taking
any part of what is common, and removing it
out of the ftate nature leaves it in, which *begins
the property*; without which the common is of
no

no ufe And the taking of this or that part, does not depend on the exprefs confent of all the commoners Thus the grafs my horfe has bit; the turfs my fervant has cut, and the ore I have digged in any place, where I have a right to them in common with others, become my *property*, without the affignation or confent of any body. The *labour* that was mine, removing them out of that common ftate they were in, hath *fixed* my *property* in them

§ 29 By making an explicit confent of every commoner, neceffary to any one's appropriating to himfelf any part of what is given in common, children or fervants could not cut the meat, which their father or mafter had provided for them in common, without affigning to every one his peculiar part. Though the water running in the fountain be every one's, yet who can doubt, but that in the pitcher is his only who drew it out? His *labour* hath taken it out of the hands of nature, where it was common, and belonged equally to all her children, and *hath* thereby *appropriated* it to himfelf

§ 30 Thus this law of reafon makes the deer that *Indian*'s who hath killed it; it is allowed to be his goods, who hath beftowed his labour upon it, though before it was the common right of every one And amongft thofe who are count-ed the civilized part of mankind, who have made and multiplied pofitive laws to determine *property*, this original law of nature, for the *beginning of property*, in what was before common, ftill takes place; and by virtue thereof, what fifh any cne catches in the ocean, that great and ftill remain-ing common of mankind; or what ambergrife any one takes up here, is by the *labour* that re-moves it out of that common ftate nature left it

I 3 in,

in, *made* his *property*, who takes that pains about
it. And even amongst us, the hare that any one
is hunting, is thought his who purfues her during the chafe for being a beaft that is ftill
looked upon as common, and no man's private
poffeffion, whoever has employed fo much *labour*
about any of that kind, as to find and purfue her,
has thereby removed her from the ftate of nature,
wherein fhe was common, and hath *begun a property*.

§. 31 It will perhaps be objected to this, that
if gathering the acorns, or other fruits of the
earth, *&c* makes a right to them, then any one
may *ingrofs* as much as he will To which I
anfwer, Not fo The fame law of nature, that
does by this means give us property, does alfo
bound that *property* too God has given us all things
richly, 1 Tim vi. 12 is the voice of reafon confirmed by infpiration. But how far has he given
it us? *To enjoy* As much as any one can make
ufe of to any advantage of life before it fpoils,
fo much he may by his labour fix a property
in whatever is beyond this, is more than his
fhare, and belongs to others Nothing was made
by God for man to fpoil or deftroy. And thus,
confidering the plenty of natural provifions there
was a long time in the world, and the few fpen-
ders, and to how fmall a part of that provifion
the induftry of one man could extend itfelf, and
ingrofs it to the prejudice of others, efpecially
keeping within the *bounds*, fet by reafon, of
what might ferve for his *ufe*, there could be then
little room for quarrels or contentions about property fo eftablifhed.

§. 32. But the *chief matter of property* being
now not the fruits of the earth, and the beafts
that fubfift on it, but *the earth itfelf*; as that
which

which takes in and carries with it all the reft, I think it is plain, that *property* in that too is acqui-red as the former. *As much land* as a man tills, plants, improves, cultivates, and can ufe the pro-duct of, fo much is his *property*. He by his la-bour does, as it were, inclofe it from the com-mon. Nor will it invalidate his right, to fay every body elfe has an equal title to it, and therefore he cannot appropriate, he cannot inclofe, with-out the confent of all his fellow-commoners, all mankind. God, when he gave he world in com-mon to all mankind, commanded man alfo to la-bour, and the penury of his condition required it of him. God and his reafon commanded him to fubdue the earth, *i. e.* improve it for the be-nefit of life, and therein lay out fomething upon it that was his own, his labour. He that in obe-dience to this command of God, fubdued, tilled and fowed any part of it, thereby annexed to it fomething that was his *property*, which another had no title to, nor could without injury take from him.

§ 33. Nor was this *appropriation* of any par-cel of *land*, by improving it, any prejudice to any other man, fince there was ftill enough, and as good left, and more than the yet unpro-vided could ufe. So that, in effect, there was never the lefs left for others becaufe of his in-clofure for himfelf: for he that leaves as much as another can make ufe of, does as good as take no-thing at all. No body could think himfelf injured by the drinking of another man, though he took a good draught, who had a whole river of the fame water left him to quench his thirft: and the cafe of land and water, where there is enough of both, is perfectly the fame.

I 4 § 34.

§ 34 God gave the world to men in common, but since he gave it to them for their benefit, and the greatest conveniencies of life they were capable to draw from it, it cannot be supposed he meant it should always remain common and uncultivated He gave it to the use of the industrious and rational, (and *labour* was to be *his title* to it,) not to the fancy or covetousness of the quarrelsome and contentious He that had as good left for his improvement, as was already taken up, needed not complain, ought not to meddle with what was already improved by another's labour if he did, it is plain he defired the benefit of another's pains, which he had no right to, and not the ground which God had given him in common with others to labour on, and whereof there was as good left, as that already possessed, and more than he knew what to do with, or his industry could reach to.

§ 35 It is true, in *land* that is *common* in *England,* or any other country, where there is plenty of people under government, who have money and commerce, no one can inclose or appropriate any part, without the consent of all his fellow-commoners, because this is left common by compact, i e by the law of the land, which is not to be violated And though it be common, in respect of some men, it is not fo to all mankind . but is the joint property of this country, or this parish Besides, the remainder, after fuch inclofure, would not be as good to the rest of the commoners, as the whole was when they could all make ufe of the whole, whereas in the beginning and firft peopling of the great common of the world, it was quite otherwife The law man was under, was rather for appropriating God commanded, and his wants

forced

forced him to *labour* That was his *property* which could not be taken from him where-ever he had fixed it And hence subduing or cultivating the earth, and having dominion, we see are joined together The one gave title to the other. So that God, by commanding to subdue, gave authority so far to *appropriate*. and the condition of human life, which requires labour and materials to work on, necessarily introduces private possessions

§ 36 The *measure of property* nature has well set by the extent of men's *labour and the conveniencies of life*· no man's labour could subdue, or appropriate all, nor could his enjoyment consume more than a small part, so that it was impossible for any man, this way, to intrench upon the right of another, or to acquire to himself a property, to the prejudice of his neighbour, who would still have room for as good, and as large a possession (after the other had taken out his) as before it was appropriated This *measure* did confine every man's *possession* to a very moderate proportion, and such as he might appropriate to himself, without injury to any body, in the first ages of the world, when men were more in danger to be lost, by wandering from their company, in the then vast wilderness of the earth, than to be straitened for want of room to plant in. And the same *measure* may be allowed still without prejudice to any body, as full as the world seems: for supposing a man, or family, in the state they were at first peopling of the world by the children of *Adam*, or *Noah*, let him plant in some inland, vacant places of *America*, we shall find that the *possessions* he could make himself, upon the *measures* we have given, would not be very large, nor, even to this day, prejudice the rest of mankind, or give them reason to complain, or think them-

I 5

selves

felves injured by this man's incroachment, though the race of men have now fpread themfelves to all the corners of the world, and do infinitely exceed the fmall number was at the beginning Nay, the extent of *ground* is of fo little value, *without labour*, that I have heard it affirmed, that in *Spain* itfelf a man may be permitted to plough, fow and reap, without being difturbed, upon land he has no other title to, but only his making ufe of it. But, on the contrary, the inhabitants think themfelves beholden to him, who, by his induftry on neglected, and confequently wafte land, has increafed the flock of corn, which they wanted But be this as it will, which I lay no ftrefs on, this I dare boldly affirm, that the fame *rule of propriety*, *(viz)* that every man fhould have as much as he could make ufe of, would hold, ftill in the world, without ftraitening any body, fince there is land enough in the world to fuffice double the inhabitants, had not the *invention of money*, and the tacit agreement of men to put a value on it, introduced (by confent) larger poffeffions, and a right to them ; which, how it has done, I fhall by and by fhew more at large

§ 37. This is certain, that in the beginning, before the defire of having more than man needed, had altered the intrinfic value of things, which depends only on their ufefulnefs to the life of man, or had *agreed, that a little piece of yellow metal,* which would keep without wafting or decay, fhould be worth a great piece of flefh, or a whole heap of corn, though men had a right to appropriate, by their labour, each one to himfelf, as much of the things of nature, as he could ufe yet this could not be much, nor to the prejudice of others, where the fame plenty was ftill left to thofe who would ufe the fame induftry. To which let me add, that he who appropiates land

and to himself by his labour, does not leſſen, but
ncreaſe the common ſtock of mankind for the
proviſions ſerving to the ſupport of human life,
produced by one acre of incloſed and cultivated
land, are (to ſpeak much within compaſs) ten
times more than thoſe which are yielded by an
acre of land of an equal richneſs lying waſte in
common. And therefore he that incloſes, and has
a greater plenty of the conveniencies of life from
ten acres, than he could have from an hundred
left to nature, may truly be ſaid to give ninety
acres to mankind for his labour now ſupplie
him with proviſions out of ten acres, which were
but the product of an hundred lying in common I
have here rated the improved land very low, in mak
ing its product but as ten to one, when it is much
nearer an hundred to one · for I aſk, whether in
the wild woods and uncultivated waſte of *Am.-
rica,* left to nature, without any improvement,
tillage or huſbandry, a thouſand acres yield the
needy and wretched inhabitants as many conveniencies of life, as ten acres of equally fertile land
do in *Devonſhire,* where they are well cultivated ?

Before the appropriation of land, he who gathered as much of the wild fruit, killed, caught,
or tamed, as many of the beaſts, as he could ,
he that ſo imployed his pains about any of the
ſpontaneous products of nature, as any way to
alter them from the ſtate which nature put them
in, *by* placing any of his *labour* on them, did
thereby *acquire a property in them* but if they
periſhed, in his poſſeſſion, without their due uſe,
if the fruits rotted, or the veniſon putrified, before he could ſpend it, he offended againſt the
common law of nature, and was liable to be
puniſhed, he invaded his neighbour's ſhare, for
he had *no right, further than his uſe* called for
ar

any of them, and they might ferve to afford him conveniencies of life

§ 38. The fame *measures* governed the *posses-or of land* too whatfoever he tilled and reaped, laid up and made ufe of, before it fpoiled, that was his peculiar right, whatfoever he enclofed, and could feed, and make ufe of, the cattle and product was alfo his But if either the grafs of his inclofure rotted on the ground, or the fruit of his planting perifhed without gathering, and lay-ing up, this part of the earth, notwithftanding his inclofure, was ftill to be looked on as wafte, and might be the poffeffion of any other Thus, at the beginning, *Cain* might take as much ground as he could till, and make it his own land, and it leave enough to *Abel*'s fheep to feed on, a few acres would ferve for both their poffeffions. But as families increafed, and induftry inlarged their ftocks, then *poffeffions inlarged* with the need of them, but yet it was commonly *without any fixed property in the ground* they made ufe of, till they incorporated, fettled themfelves together, and built cities, and then, by confent, they came in time, to fet out the *bounds of their diftinct ter-ritories*, and agree on limits between them and their neghbours, and by laws within themfelves, fettled the *properties* of thofe of the fame fociety · or we fee, that in that part of the world which was firft inhabited, and therefore like to be beft peopled, even as low down as *Abraham*'s time, they wandered with their flocks, and their herds, which was their fubftance, freely up and down; and this *Abraham* did, in a country where he was a ftranger Whence it is plain, that at leaft a great part of the *land lay in common*, that the inhabitants valued it not, nor claimed property in any more than they made ufe of But when there

was

was not room enough in the same place, for their
herds to feed together, they by consent, as *Abraham* and *Lot* did, *Gen* xiii. 5. separated and inlarged their pasture, where it best liked them.
And for the same reason *Esau* went from his father, and his brother, and planted in *mount Seir*,
Gen. xxxvi. 6.

§. 39 And thus, without supposing any private
dominion, and property in *Adam*, over all the
world, exclusive of all other men, which can no
way be proved, nor any one's property be made
out from it; but supposing the *world* given, as it
was, to the children of men *in common*, we see
how *labour* could make men distinct titles to several parcels of it, for their private uses; wherein there could be no doubt of right, no room for
quarrel

§ 40 Nor is it so strange, as perhaps before
consideration it may appear, that the *property of
labour* should be able to over-balance the community of land for it is *labour* indeed that *puts
the difference of value* on every thing; and let
any one consider what the difference is between
an acre of land planted with tobacco or sugar,
sown with wheat or barley, and an acre of the
same land lying in common, without any husbandry upon it, and he will find, that the improvement of *labour makes* the far greater part of the
value I think it will be but a very modest computation to say, that of the *products* of the earth
useful to the life of man nine tenths are the *ef-
jects of labour* nay, if we will estimate things as
they come to our use, and cast up the several expences about them, what in them is purely owing to *nature* and what to *labour*, we shall find,
that in most of them ninety-nine hundredths are
wholly to be put on the account of *labour*.

§ 41.

§ 41 There cannot be a clearer demonſtration, of any thing, than ſeveral nations of the *Ameri-ans* aie of this, who are rich in land, and poor in all the comforts of life; whom natuie having furniſhed as liberally as any other people, with the materials of plenty, *i e* a fruitful ſoil, apt to produce in abundance, what might ſerve for food, raiment, and delight, yet for *want of im-proving it by labour,* have not one hundredth part of the conveniencies we enjoy and a king of a large and fruitful territory there, feeds, lodges, and is clad worſe than a day-labourer in *England*

§. 42 To make this a little clearer, let us but trace ſome of the ordinary proviſions of life, through their ſeveral progreſſes, before they come to our uſe, and ſee how much they receive of their *value from human induſtry* Bread, wine and cloth, are things of daily uſe, and great plenty, yet notwithſtanding, acorns, water and leaves, cr ſkins, muſt be our bread, drink and cloathing, did not *labour* furniſh us with theſe more uſeful commodities for whatever *bread* is more worth than acorns, wine than water, and *cloth* or *ſilk*, than leaves, ſkins or moſs, that is wholly *owing to labour* and *induſtry* ; the one of theſe being the food and raiment which unaſſiſted nature furniſhes us with ; the other, proviſions which our induſtry and pains prepare for us, which how much they exceed the other in value, when any one hath computed, he will then ſee how much *labour makes the far greateſt part of the value* of things we enjoy in this world and the ground which produces the materials, is ſcarce to be reckoned in, is any, or at moſt, but a very ſmall part of it, ſo little, that even amongſt us, land that is left wholly to nature, that hath no improvement of paſturage, tillage, or planting,

is called, as indeed it is, *waste*, and we shall
find the benefit of it amount to little more than
nothing

This shews how much numbers of men are to
be preferred to largeness of dominions, and that
the increase of lands, and the right employing of
them, is the great art of government and that
prince, who shall be so wise and godlike, as by
established laws of liberty to secure protection and
encouragement to the honest industry of mankind,
against the oppression of power and narrowness of
party, will quickly be too hard for his neighbours but this by the by To return to the argument in hand,

§ 43 An acre of land, that bears here twenty bushels of wheat, and another in *America*,
which, with the same husbandry, would do the
like, are, without doubt, of the same natural in-
trinsic value: but yet the benefit mankind receives from the one in a year, is worth 5*l* and
from the other possibly not worth a penny, if all
the profit an *Indian* received from it were to be
valued, and sold here, at least, I may truly say,
not one thousandth It is *labour* then which *puts
the greatest part of the value upon land*, without
which it would scarcely be worth any thing · it
is to that we owe the greatest part of all its useful products? for all that the straw, bran, bread,
of that acre of wheat, is more worth than the
product of an acre of as good land, which lies
waste, is all the effect of labour for it is not
barely the plough-man's pains, the reaper's and
and thresher's toil, and the baker's sweat, is to
be counted into the *bread* we eat, the labour of
those who broke the oxen, who digged and
wrought the iron and stones, who felled and
framed the timber employed about the plough,
mill,

mill, oven, or any other utenfils, which are a vaft number, requifite to this corn, from its being feed to be fown to its being made bread, muft all be *charged on* the account of *labour,* and received as an effect of that nature and the earth furnifhed only the almoft worthlefs materials, as in themfelves It would be a ftrange *catalogue of things, that induftry provided and made ufe of, about every loaf of bread,* before it came to our ufe, if we could trace them ; iron, wood, leather, bark, timber, ftone, bricks, coals, lime, cloth, dying drugs, pitch, tar, mafts, ropes, and all the materials made ufe of in the fhip, that brought any of the commodities made ufe of by any of the workmen, to any part of the work , all which it would be almoft impoffible, at leaft too long, to reckon up

§ 44 From all which it is evident, that though the things of nature are given in common, yet man, by being mafter of himfelf, and *proprietor of his own perfon, and the actions or labour of it, had ftill in himfelf the great foundation of property*; and that, which made up the great part of what he applied to the fupport or comfort of his being, when, invention and arts had improved the conveniencies of life, was perfectly his own, and did not belong in common to others

§ 45 Thus *labour,* in the beginning, *gave a right of property,* wherever any one was pleafed to employ it upon what was common, which remained a long while the far greater part, and is yet more than mankind makes ufe of Men, at firft, for the moft part, contented themfelves with what unaffifted nature offered to their neceffities and though afterwards in fome parts of the world, (where the increafe of people and
flock,

stock, with the *use of money*, had made land scarce, and so of some value) the several *communities* settled the bounds of their distinct territories, and by laws within themselves regulated the properties of the private men of their society, and so, *by compact* and agreement, *settled the property* which labour and industry began, and the leagues that have been made between several states and kingdoms, either expresly or tacitly disowning all claim and right to the land in the others possession, have, by common consent given up their pretences to their natural common right, which originally they had to those countries, and so have, by *positive agreement, set-led a property* amongst themselves, in distinct parts and parcels of the earth, yet there are still *great tracts of ground* to be found, which (the inhabitants thereof not having joined with the rest of mankind, in the consent of the use of their common money) *lie waste*, and are more than the people who dwell on it do, or can make use of, and so still lie in common; tho' this can scarce happen amongst that part of mankind that have consented to the use of money

§ 46. The greatest part of *things really useful* to the life of man, and such as the necessity of subsisting made the first commoners of the world look after, as it doth the *Americans* now, *are ge-*nerally things of *short duration*, such as, if they are not consumed by use, will decay and perish of themselves: gold, silver and diamonds, are things that fancy or agreement hath put the value on, more than real use, and the necessary support of life Now of those good things which nature hath provided in common, every one had a right (as hath been said) to as much as he could use,

and

and *property* in all that he could effect with his labour, all that his *induftry* could extend to, to alter from the ftate nature had put it in, was his He that *gathered* a hundred bufhels of acorns or apples, had thereby a *property* in them, they were his goods as foon as gathered He was only to look, that he ufed them before they fpoiled, elfe he took more than his fhare, and robbed others And indeed it was a foolifh thing, as well as difhoneft, to hoard up more than he could make ufe of. If he gave away a part to any body elfe, fo that it perifhed not ufelefly in his poffeffion, thefe he alfo made ufe of And if he alfo bartered away plums, that would be rotted in a week, for nuts that would laft good for his eating a whole year, he did no injury, he wafted not the common ftock; deftroyed no part of the portion of goods that belonged to others, fo long as nothing perifhed ufelefly in his hands. Again, if he would give his nuts for a piece of metal, pleafed with its colour, or exchange his fheep for fhells, or wool for a fparkling pebble or a diamond, and keep thofe by him all his life, he invaded not the right of others, he might heap up as much of thefe durable things as he pleafed; the *exceeding of the bounds of* his *juft property* not lying in the largenefs of his poffef fion, but the perifhing of any thing ufelefly in it

§ 47 And thus *came in the ufe of money,* fome lafting thing that men might keep without fpoiling, and that by mutual confent men would take in exchange for the truly ufeful, but perifhable fupports of life

§ 48. And as different degrees of induftry were apt to give men poffeffions in different pro- portions,

portions, so this *invention of money* gave them the opportunity to continue and enlarge them for supposing an island, separate from all possible commerce with the rest of the world, wherein there were but an hundred families, but there were sheep, horses and cows, with other useful animals, wholsome fruits, and land enough for corn for a hundred thousand times as many, but nothing in the island, either because of its commonness, or perishableness, fit to supply the place of *money*; what reason could any one have there to enlarge his possessions beyond the use of his family, and a plentiful supply to its *consumption*, either in what their own industry produced, or they could barter for like perishable, useful commodities, with others? Where there is not some thing, both lasting and scarce, and so valuable to be hoarded up, there men will be apt to enlarge their *possessions of land*, were it never so rich, never so free for them to take for I ask, what would a man value ten thousand, or an hundred thousand acres of excellent *land*, ready cultivated, and well stocked too with cattle, in the middle of the inland parts of *America*, where he had no hopes of commerce with other parts of the world, to draw *money* to him by the sale of the product? It would not be worth the inclosing, and we should see him give up again to the wild common of nature, whatever was more than would supply the conveniencies of life to be had there for him and his family

§ 49. Thus in the beginning all the world was *America*, and more so than that is now; for no such thing as *money* was any where known. Find out something that hath the *use and value of money* amongst his neighbours, you shall see the

the same man will begin presently to enlarge his possessions

§ 50 But since gold and silver, being little useful to the life of man in proportion to food, raiment, and carriage, has its *value* only from the consent of men, whereof *labour* yet *makes*, in great part, *the measure*, it is plain, that men have agreed to a disproportionate and unequal *possession of the earth*, they having, by a tacit and voluntary consent, found out a way how a man may fairly possess more land than he himself can use the product of, by receiving in exchange for the overplus gold and silver, which may be hoarded up without injury to any one, these metals not spoiling or decaying in the hands of the possessor This partage of things in an inequality of private possessions, men have made practicable out of the bounds of society, and without compact, only by putting a value on gold and silver, and tacitly agreeing in the use of money for in governments, the laws regulate the right of property, and the possession of land is determined by positive constitutions.

§ 51. And thus, I think, it is very easy to conceive, without any difficulty, *how labour could at first begin a title of property* in the common things of nature, and how the spending it upon our uses bounded it So that there could then be no reason of quarrelling about title, nor any doubt about the largeness of possession it gave Right and conveniency went together; for as a man had a right to all he could employ his labour upon, so he had no temptation to labour for more than he could make use of This left no room for controversy about the title, nor for incroachment on the right of others; what portion a man
carved

carved to himself, was eafily feen; and it was ufelefs, as well as difhoneft, to carve himfelf too much, or take more than he needed.

CHAP VI.

Of Paternal Power.

§ 52 IT may perhaps be cenfured as an impertinent criticifm, in a difcourfe of this nature, to find fault with words and names, that have obtained in the world and yet poffibly it may not be amifs to offer new ones, when the old are apt to lead men into miftakes, as this of *paternal power* probably has done, which feems to to place the power of parents over their children wholly in the *father*, as if the *mother* had no fhare in it , whereas, if we confult reafon or revelation, we fhall find, fhe hath an equal title. This may give one reafon to afk, whether this might not be more pioperly called *parental pow-er* ? for whatever obligation nature and the right of generation lays on children, it muft certainly bind them equal to both the concurrent caufes of it And accordingly we fee the pofitive law of God every where joins them together, without diftinction, when it commands the obedience of children, *Honour thy father and thy mother*, Exod. x 12 *Whofoever curfeth his father or his mother*, Lev. xx 9 *Ye fhall fear every man his mother and his father*, Lev xix 3 *Children, y your parents*, &c Eph vi. 1 is the ftile of the Old and New Teftament.

§ 53 Had but this one thing been well confidered, without looking any deeper into the matter, it might perhaps have kept men from

running

running into thofe grofs miftakes, they have made, about this power of parents ; which, however it might, without any great harfhnefs, bear the name of abfolute dominion, and regal authority, when under the title of *paternal power* it feemed appropriated to the father, would yet have founded but oddly, and in the very name fhewn the abfurdity, if this fuppofed abfolute power over children had been called *parental*, and thereby have difcovered, that it belonged to the *mother* too for it will but very ill ferve the turn of thofe men, who contend fo much for the abfolute power and authority of the *fatherhood*, as they call it, that the mother fhould have any fhare in it, and it would have but ill fupported the *monarchy* they contend for, when by the very name it appeared, that that fundamental authority, from whence they would derive their government of a fingle perfon only, was not placed in one, but two perfons jointly But to let this of names pafs.

§. 54 Though I have faid above, *Chap* II. *That all men by nature are equal,* I cannot be fuppofed to underftand all forts of *equality age* or *virtue* may give men a juft precedency . *excellency of parts* and *merit* may place others above the common level · *birth* may fubject fome, and *alliance* or *benefits* others, to pay an obfervance to thofe to whom nature, gratitude, or other refpects, may have made it due and yet all this confifts with the *equality*, which all men are in, in refpect of jurifdiction or dominion one over another, which was the *equality* I there fpoke of, as proper to the bufinefs in hand, being that *equal right*, that every man hath, *to his natural freedom*, without being fubjected to the will or authority of any other man

§. 55.

§ 55. *Children*, I confess, are not born in this full state of *equality*, though they are born to it. Their parents have a sort of rule and jurisdiction over them, when they come into the world, and for some time after, but it is but a temporary one. The bonds of this subjection are like the swaddling clothes they are wrapt up in, and supported by, in the weakness of their infancy age and reason as they grow up, loosen them, till at length they drop quite off, and leave a man at his own free disposal

§ 56 *Adam* was created a perfect man, and his body and mind in full possession of their strength and reason, and so was capable, from the first instant of his being to provide for his own support and preservation, and govern his actions according to the dictates of the law of reason which God had implanted in him. From him the world is peopled with his descendants, who are all born infants, weak and helpless, without knowledge or understanding: but to supply the defects of this imperfect state, till the improvement of growth and age hath removed them, *Adam* and *Eve*, and after them all *parents* were, by the law of nature, *under an obligation to preserve, nourish, and educate the children* they had begotten, not as their own workmanship, but the workmanship of their own maker, the Almighty, to whom they were to be accountable for them

§ 57 The law, that was to govern *Adam*, was the same that was to govern all his posterity, the *law of reason* But his offspring having another way of entrance into the world, different from him, by a natural birth, that produced them ignorant and without the use of *reason*, they were

not

not prefently *under that law* ; for no body can be under a law, which is not promulgated to him, and this law being promulgated or made known by *reafon* only, he that is not come to the ufe of his *reafon*, cannot be faid to be *under this law*, and *Adam's* children, being not prefently as foon as born *under this law of reafon,* were not prefently free . for *law,* in its true notion, *is* not fo much the limitation as *the direction of a free and intelligent agent* to his proper intereft, and prefcribes no farther than is for the general good of thofe under that law . could they be happier without it, the *law,* as an ufclefs thing, would of itfelf vanifh , and that ill deferves the name of confinement which hedges us in only from bogs and precipices. So that, however it may be miftaken, *the end of law is* not to abolifh or reftrain, but *to preferve and enlarge freedom* for in all the ftates of created beings capable of laws, *where there is no law, there is no freedom* for *liberty* is, to be free from reftraint and violence from others , which cannot be, where there is no law but freedom is not, as we are told, *a liberty for every man to do what he lifts* (for who could be free, when every other man's humour might domineer over him ?) but a *liberty* to difpofe, and order as he lifts, his perfon, actions, poffeffions, and his whole property, within the allowance of thofe laws under which he is, and therein not to be fubject to the arbitrary will of another, but freely follow his own

§. 58 The *power,* then, *that parents have* over their children, arifes from that duty which is incumbent on them, to take care of their offspring, during the imperfect ftate of childhood To inform the mind, and govern the actions of their

ye'

yet ignorant non-age, till reason shall take its place, and ease them of that trouble, is what the children want, and the parents are bound to. for God having given man an understanding to direct his actions, has allowed him a freedom of will, and liberty of acting, as properly belonging thereunto, within the bounds of that law he is under But whilst he is in an estate, wherein he has not *understanding* of his own to direct his *will*, he is not to have any *will* of his own to follow · he that *understands* for him, must *will* for him too ; he must prescribe to his will, and regulate his actions , but when he comes to the estate that made his *father a freeman*, the *son is a freeman* too

§ 59 This holds in all the laws a man is under, whether natural or civil Is a man under the law of nature ? *What made him free* of that law ? what gave him a free disposing of his property, according to his own will, within the compass of that law ? I answer, a state of maturity wherein he might be supposed capable to know that law, that so he might keep his actions within the bounds of it When he has acquired that state, he is presumed to know how far that law is to be his guide, and how far he may make use of his *freedom*, and so comes to have it, till then, some body else must guide him, who is presumed to know how far the law allows a liberty If such a state of reason, such an age of discretion *made him free*, the same shall make his son free too Is a man under the law of *England* ? *What made him free* of that law ? that is, to have the liberty to dispose of his actions and possessions according to his own will, within the permission of that law ? A capacity of knowing that law; which is supposed by that law, at the age of one
K   and

and twenty years, and in some cases sooner. If this *made* the father *free*, it shall *make* the son *free* too Till then we see the law allows the son to have no will, but he is to be guided by the will of his father or guardian, who is to understand for him And if the father die, and fail to substitute a deputy in his trust, if he hath not provided a tutor, to govern his son, during his minority, during his want of understanding, the law takes care to do it, some other must govern him, and be a will to him, till he hath *attained to a state of freedom*, and his understanding be fit to take the government of his will But after that, the father and son are equally *free* as much as tutor and pupil after nonage, equally subjects of the same law together, without any dominion left in the father over the life, liberty, or estate of his son, whether they be only in the state and under the law of nature, or under the positive laws of an established government.

§ 60 But if, through defects that may happen out of the ordinary course of nature, any one comes not to such a degree of reason, wherein he might be supposed capable of knowing the law, and so living within the rules of it, he is *never capable of being a free man*, he is never let loose to the disposure of his own will (because he knows no bounds to it, has not understanding, its proper guide) but is continued under the tuition and government of others, all the time his own understanding is uncapable of that charge And so *lunatics and ideots* are never set free from the government of the parents; *children, who are not as yet come unto those years whereat they may have, and innocents which are excluded by a natural defect from ever having*, thirdly, *madmen, which for the present cannot possibly have the use of right reason reafon to guide themfelves, have for their guide, the reafon that guideth other men which are tutors over them, to feek and procure their good for them,* fays Hooker, Eccl Pol *lib.* 1 *fect.* 7 All which feems no more than that duty, which God and nature has laid on man, as well as other creatures, to preferve their offspring, till they can be able to fhift for themfelves, and will fcarce amount to an inftance or proof of *parents* regal authority

§ 61 Thus we are *born free,* as we are born rational , not that we have actually the exercife of either : age, that brings one, brings with it the other too And thus we fee how *natural freedom and fubjection to parents* may confift together, and are both founded on the fame principle A *child* is *free* by his father's title, by his father's underftanding, which is to govern him till he hath it of his own. The *freedom of a man at years of difcretion,* and the *fubjection* of a child *to* his *parents,* whilft yet fhort of that age, are fo confiftent, ard fo diftinguifhable, that the moft blinded contenders for monarchy, *by right of fatherhood,* cannot mifs this *difference;* the moft obftinate cannot but allow their confiftency · for were their doctrine all true, were the right heir of *Adam* now known, and by that title fettled a monarch in his throne, invefted with all the abfolute unlimited power Sir *Robert Filmer* talks of , if he fhould die as foon as his heir were born, muft not the *child,* notwithftanding he were never fo free, never fo much fovereign, be in fubjection to his mother and nurfe, to tutors and governors, all age and education brought him reafon and abilities to govern himfelf and others ? The neceffities of his life, the health of his body, and the information of his mind, would require him

K 2

to be directed by the will of others, and not his
own, and yet will any one think, that this reftraint and fubjection were inconfiftent with, or
fpoiled him of that liberty or fovereignty he had
a right to, or gave away his empire to thofe who
had the government of his nonage? This government over him only prepared him the better
and fooner for it If any body fhould afk me,
when my fon is *of age to be free?* I fhall anfwer,
juft when his monarch is of age to govern *But
at what time,* fays the judicious *Hooker,* Eccl
Pol 1 fcct 6 *a man may be faid to have attained
fo far forth the ufe of reafon, as fufficeth to make
him capable of thofe laws whereby he is then bound
to guide his actions this is a great deal more eafy
for fenfe to difcern, than for any one by fkill and
learning to determine.*

§ 62 Common-wealths themfelves take notice
of, and allow, that there is a *time when men* are
to *begin to act like free men,* and therefore till
that time require not oaths of fealty, or allegiance,
or other public owning of, or fubmiffion to the
government of their countries

§ 63 The *freedom* then of man, and liberty
of acting according to his own will, is *grounded
on his having reafon,* which is able to inftruct
him in that law he is to govern himfelf by, and
make him know how far he is left to the freedom of his own will To turn him loofe to an
unreftrained liberty, before he has reafon to guide
him, is not the allowing him the privilege of his
nature to be free, but to thruft him out amongft
brutes, and abandon him to a ftate as wretched,
and as much beneath that of a man as their's.
This is that which puts the *authority* into the
parents hands to govern the *minority* of their
children God hath made it their bufinefs to
employ

employ this care on their off-spring, and hath placed in them suitable inclinations of tenderness and concern to temper this power, to apply it, as his wisdom designed it, to the children's good, as long as they should need to be under it

§ 64 But what reason can hence advance this care of the *parents* due to their off-spring into an *absolute arbitrary dominion* of the father, whose power reaches no farther, than by such a discipline, as he finds most effectual, to give such strength and health to their bodies, such vigour and rectitude to their minds, as may best fit his children to be most useful to themselves and others, and, if it be necessary to his condition, to make them work, when they are able, for their own subsistence But in this power the *mother* too has her share with the *father*.

§ 65 Nay, this *power* so little belongs to the *father* by any peculiar right of nature, but only as he is guardian of his children, that when he quits his care of them, he loses his power over them, which goes along with their nourishment and education, to which it is inseparably annexed, and it belongs as much to the *foster father* of an exposed child, as to the natural father of another So little power does the bare *act of begetting* give a man over his issue, if all his care ends there, and this be all the title he hath to the name and authority of a father. And what will become of this *paternal power* in that part of the world, where one woman hath more than one husband at a time? or in those parts of *America*, where, when the husband and wife part, which happens frequently, the children are all left to the mother, follow her, and are wholly under her care and provision? If the father die whilst the children are young, do they not natu-

rally

rally every where owe the fame obedience to their *mother*, during their minority, as to their father were he alive? and will any one fay, that the mother hath a legiflative power over her children? that fhe can make ftanding rules, which fhall be of perpetual obligation, by which they ought to regulate all the concerns of their property, and bound their liberty all the courfe of their lives? or can fhe inforce the obfervation of them with capital punifhments? for this is the proper *power of the magiftrate*, of which the father hath not fo much as the fhadow His command over his children is but temporary, and reaches not their life or property it is but a help to the weaknefs and imperfection of their nonage, a difcipline neceffary to their education. and though a *father* may difpofe of his own poffeffions as he pleafes, when his children are out of danger of perifhing for want, yet *his power* extends not to the lives or goods, which either their own induftry, or another's bounty has made their's, nor to their liberty neither, when they are once arrived to the infranchifement of the years of difcretion The *father's empire* then ceafes, and he can from thence forwards no more difpofe of the liberty of his fon, than that of any other man and it muft be far from an abfolute or perpetual jurifdiction, from which a man may withdraw himfelf, having licence from divine authority to *leave father and mother, and cleave to his wife.*

§ 66 But though there be a time when a *child* comes to be as *free* from fubjection to the will and command of his father, as the father himfelf is free from fubjection to the will of any body elfe, and they are each under no other reftraint, but that which is common to them both, whether

whether it be the law of nature, or municipal law of their country, yet this freedom exempts not a son from the *honour* which he ought, by the law of God and nature, *to* pay his *parents* God having made the parents instruments in his great design of continuing the race of mankind, and the occasions of life to their children, as he hath laid on them an obligation to nourish, preserve, and bring up their off-spring, so he has laid on the children a perpetual obligation of *honouring their parents*, which containing in it an inward esteem and reverence to be shewn by all outward expressions, ties up the child from any thing that may ever injure or affront, disturb or endanger, the happiness, or life of those from whom he received his, and engages him in all actions of defence, relief, assistance and comfort of those, by whose means he entered into being, and has been made capable of any enjoyments of life from this obligation to state, no freedom can absolve children But this is very far from giving parents a power of command over their children, or an authority to make laws and dispose as they please of their lives or liberties It is one thing to owe honour, respect, gratitude and assistance, another to require an absolute obedience and submission The *honour due to parents*, a monarch in his throne owes his mother, and yet this lessens not his authority, nor subjects him to her government

§ 67 The subjection of a minor places in the father a temporary government, which terminates with the minority of the child · and the *honour due from a child*, places in the parents a perpetual right to respect, reverence, support and compliance too, more or less, as the father's care, cost, and kindness in his education, has been more or less This ends not with minority,

but

but helds in all parts and conditions of a man's
life   The want of diftinguishing thefe two powers, *viz* that which the father hath in the right
of *tuition*, during minority, and the right of *ho-*
nour all his life, may perhaps have caufed a
great part of the miftakes about this matter   for
to fpeak properly of them, the firft of thefe is
rather the privilege of children, and duty of parents, than any prerogative of paternal power
The nourifhment and education of their children
is a charge fo incumbent on parents for their
children's good, that nothing can abfolve them
from taking care of it   and though the *power of*
commanding and chaftifing them go along with it,
yet God hath woven into the principles of human
nature fuch a tendernefs for their off-fpring, that
there is little fear that parents fhould ufe their
power with too much rigour ; the excefs is feldom on the fevere fide, the ftrong byafs of nature
drawing the other way   And therefore God almighty when he would exprefs his gentle dealing
with the *Ifraelites,* he tells them, that though he
chaftened them, *he chaftened them as a man chaf-*
tens his fon, Deut viii 5   *i e* with tendernefs
and affection, and kept them under no feverer
difcipline than what was abfolutely beft for them,
and had been lefs kindnefs to have flackened
This is that power to which *child en* are commanded *obedience,* that the pains and care of
their parents may not be increafed, or ill rewarded

§ 68. On the other fide, *honour* and *fupport,*
all that which gratitude requires to return for
the benefits received by and from them, is the
indifpenfible duty of the child, and the proper
privilege of the parents   This is intended for
the parents advantage, as the other is for the
child's,

child's, though education, the parents duty, feems to have moft power, becaufe the ignorance and infirmities of childhood ftand in need of reftraint and correction; which is a vifible exercife of rule, and a kind of dominion And that duty which is comprehended in the word *honour*, requires lefs obedience, though the obligation be ftronger on grown, than younger children: for who can think the command, *Children obey your parents*, requires in a man, that has children of his own, the fame fubmiffion to his father, as it does in his yet young children to him, and that by this precept he were bound to obey all his father's commands, if, out of a conceit of authority, he fhould have the indifcretion to treat him ftill as a boy?

§. 69 The firft part then of *paternal power*, or rather duty, which is *education*, belongs to to the father, that it terminates at a certain feafon, when the bufinefs of education is over, it ceafes of itfelf, and is alfo alienable before for a man may put the tuition of his fon in other hands, and he that has made his fon an *apprentice* to another, has difcharged him, during that time, of a great part of his obedience both to himfelf and to his mother But all the *duty of honour*, the other part, remains never the lefs entire to them, nothing can cancel that it is fo infeparable from them both, that the father's authority cannot difpoffefs the mother of this right, nor can any man difcharge his fon from *honouring* her that bore him But both thefe are very far from a power to make laws, and inforcing them with penalties, that may reach eftate, liberty, limbs and life The power of commanding ends with nonage, and though, after that, *honour* and *refpect*, fupport and defence, and whatfoever gra-

titude

titude can oblige a man to, for the higheſt benefits he is naturally capable of, be always due
from a ſon to his parents ; yet all this puts no
ſcepter into the father's hand, no ſovereign power of commanding. He has no dominion over
his ſon's property, or actions ; nor any right,
that his will ſhould preſcribe to his ſon's in all
things, however it may become his ſon in many
things, not very inconvenient to him and his family, to pay a deference to it

§ 70 A man may owe *honour* and reſpect to
an ancient, or wiſe man , defence to his child
or friend , relief and ſupport to the diſtreſſed ,
and gratitude to a benefactor, to ſuch a degree,
that all he he has, all he can do, cannot ſuffici-
ently pay it : but all theſe give no authority, no
right to any one, of making laws over him from
whom they are owing. And it is plain, all this
is due not only to the bare title of father ; not
only becauſe, as has been ſaid, it is owing to the
mother too , but becauſe theſe obligations to parents, and the degrees of what is required of
children, may be varied by the different care and
kindneſs, trouble and expence, which is often
employed upon one child more than another

§ 71. This ſhews the reaſon how it comes to
paſs, that *parents in ſocieties,* where they themſelves are ſubjects, retain a *power over their children,* and have as much right to their ſubjection, as thoſe who are in the ſtate of nature
Which could not poſſibly be, if all political power
were only paternal, and that in truth they were
one and the ſame thing for then, all paternal
power being in the prince, the ſubject could naturally have none of it But theſe two *powers,*
political and *paternal,* are ſo perfectly diſtinct
and ſeparate , are built upon ſo different foundations,

tions, and given to so different ends, that every subject that is a father, has as much a paternal power over his children, as the prince has over his: and every prince, that has parents, owes them as much filial duty and obedience, as the meaneft of his fubjeĉts do to their's, and can therefore contain not any part or degree of that kind of dominion, which a prince or magiftrate has over his fubjeĉt.

§ 72 Through the obligation on the parents to *bring up* their children, and the obligation on children to *honour* their parents, contain all the power on the one hand, and fubmiffion on the other, which are proper to this relation, yet there is *another power* ordinarily *in the father*, whereby he has a tie on the obedience of his children; which tho' it be common to him with other men, yet the occafions of fhewing it, almoft conftantly happening to fatheis in their private familes, and the inftances of it elfewhere being rare, and lefs taken notice of, it paffes in the world for a part of *paternal jurifdiĉtion* And this is the power men generally have to *beftow their eftates* on thofe who pleafe them beft ; the poffeffion of the father being the expeĉtation and inheritance of the children, ordinaiily in certain proportions, according to the law and cuftom of each country ; yet it is commonly in the father's power to beftow it with a more fparing or liberal hand, according as the behaviour of this or that child hath comported with his will and humour

§ 73 This is no fmall tie on the obedience of children and there being always annexed to the enjoyment of land, a fubmiffion to the government of the country, of which that land is a part; it has been commonly fuppofed, that a *father* could *oblige his pofterity to that government*, of which he himfelf was a fubjeĉt, and that his com-
                                                              paĉt

pact held them, whereas, it being only a neceſſary
condition annexed to the land, and the inheritance
of an eſtate which is under that government,
reaches only thoſe who will take it on that condition, and ſo is no natural tie or engagement, but
a voluntary ſubmiſſion for *every man's children*
being by nature as *free* as himſelf, or any of his
anceſtors ever were, may, whilſt they are in that
freedom, chooſe what ſociety they will join themſelves to, what common-wealth they will put
themſelves under. But if they will enjoy the *inheritance* of their anceſtors, they muſt take it on
the ſame terms their anceſtors had it, and ſubmit
to all the conditions annexed to ſuch a poſſeſſion.
By this power indeed fathers oblige their children
to obedience to themſelves, even when they are
paſt minority, and moſt commonly too ſubject
them to this or that political power; but neither
of theſe by any peculiar right of *fatherhood*, but by
the reward they have in their hands to inforce
and recompence ſuch a compliance, and is no
more power than what a *French-man* has over an
Engliſh man, who by the hopes of an eſtate he
will leave him, will certainly have a ſtrong tie
on his obedience: and if, when it is left him,
he will enjoy it, he muſt certainly take it upon
the conditions annexed to the *poſſeſſion of land* in
that country where it lies, whether it be *France*
or *England*.

§ 74. To conclude then, tho' the *father's power* of commanding extends no farther than the
minority of his children, and to a degree only fit
for the diſcipline and government of that age;
and tho' that *honour* and *reſpect*, and all that
which the *Latins* called *piety*, which they indiſ-
penſably owe to their parents all their life-time,
and in all eſtates, with all that ſupport and de--
fence

fence is due to them, gives the father no power of governing, *i e* making laws and enacting penalties on his children , though by all this he has no dominion over the property or actions of his son : yet it is obvious to conceive how eafy it was, in the firft ages of the world, and in places fiill, where the thinnefs of people gives families leave to feparate into unpoffeffed quarters, and they have room to remove or plant themfelves in yet vacant habitations, for the *father of the family* to become the prince of * it , he had been a ruler from the beginning of the infancy of his children : and fince without fome government it would be hard for them to live together, it was likelieft it fhould, by the exprefs or tacit confent of the children when they were grown up, be in the father, where it feemed without any change barely
                                                    to

* It is no improbable opinion therefore, which the arch-philofopher was of, that the chief perfon in every houfhold was always, as it were, a king   fo when numbers of houfholds joined themfelves in civil focieties together, kings were the fiift kind of governors amongft them, which is alfo, as it feemeth, the reafon why the name of fathers continued ftill in them, who, of fathers were made rulers, as alfo the antient cuftom of governors to do as *Melchizedec*, and being kings, to excercife the office of priefts, which fathers did at the firft, grew perhaps by the fame occafion Howbeit, this is not the only kind of regiment that has been received in the woild The inconveniences of one kind have caufed fundry others to be devifed , fo that in a word, all public regiment, of what kind foever, feemeth evidently to have rifen from the deliberate advice, confultation and compofition between men, judging it convenient and behoveful , there being no impoffibilty in nature confidered by itfelf, but that man might have lived without any public regiment, *Hooker s Eccl P lib* 1. *fect.* 10.

to continue, when indeed nothing more was re-quired to it, than the permitting the *father* to ex-ercife alone, in his family, that executive power of the law of nature, which every free man na-turally hath, and by that permiſſion reſigning up to him a monarchical power, whilſt they re-mained in it. But that this was not by any *pater-nal right*, but only by the conſent of his children, is evident from hence, that no body doubts, but if a ſtranger, whom chance or buſineſs had brought to his family, had there killed any of his chil-dren, or committed any other fact, he might con-demn and put him to death, or otherwiſe have puniſhed him, as well as any of his children; which it was impoſſible he ſhould do by virtue of any paternal authority over one who was not his child, but by virtue of that executive power of the law of nature, which, as a man, he had a right to: and he alone could puniſh him and his family, where the reſpect of his children had laid by the exerciſe of ſuch a power, to give way to the dignity and authority they were willing ſhould remain in him, above the reſt of his family

§ 75 Thus it was eaſy, and almoſt natural for children, by a tacit, and ſcarce avoidable con-ſent, to make way for the *father's authority and government* They had been accuſtomed in their childhood to follow his direction, and to refer their little differences to him, and when they were men, who fitter to rule them? Their little pro-perties, and leſs covetouſneſs, ſeldom afforded greater controverſies, and when any ſhould ariſe, where could they have a fitter umpire than he, by whoſe care they had every one been ſuſtained and brought up, and who had a tenderneſs for them all? It is no wonder that they made no dif-ſtinction betwixt minority and full age; nor looked
after

after one and twenty, or any other age that might make them the free difposers of themfelves and foitunes, when they could have no defire to be out of their pupilage · the government they had been under, during it, continued ftill to be more their protection than reftraint, and they could no where find a greater fecurity to their peace, liberties, and fortunes, than in the *rule of a father*

§ 76 Thus the natural *fathers of families,* by an infenfible change, became the *politic monarchs* of them too · and as they chanced to live long, and leave able and worthy heirs, for feveral fuc- ceffions, or otherwife; fo they laid the foundati- ons of hereditary, or elective kingdoms, under feveral conftitutions and mannors, according as chance, contrivance, or occafions happened to mould them But if princes have their titles in their fathers right, and it be a fufficient proof of the natural *right of fathers* to political authority, becaufe they commonly were thofe in whofe hands we find, *de facto,* the exercife of government : I fay, if this argument be good, it will as ftrongly prove, that all princes, nay princes only, ought to be priefts, fince it is as certain, that in the beginning, *the father of the family was prieft, as that he was ruler in his own houfhold.*

CHAP. VII.

Of Political or Civil Society.

§ 77 GOD having made man fuch a crea- ture, that in his own judgment, it was not good for him to be alone, put him un- der ftrong obligations of neceffity, convenience, and inclination to drive him into *fociety,* as well

as

as fitted him with underſtanding and language to continue and enjoy it The *firſt ſociety* was between man and wife, which gave beginning to that between parents and children , to which, in time, that between maſter and ſervant came to be added and though all theſe might, and commonly did meet together, and make up but one family, wherein the maſter or miſtreſs of it had ſome ſort of rule proper to a family , each of theſe, or altogether, came ſhort of *political ſociety*, as we ſhall ſee, if we conſider the different ends, ties, and bounds of each of theſe

§ 78. *Conjugal ſociety* is made by a voluntary compact between man and woman , and tho' it conſiſt chiefly in ſuch a communion and right in one another's bodies as is neceſſary to its chief end, procreation , yet it draws with it mutual ſupport and aſſiſtance, and a communion of intereſts too, as neceſſary not only to unite their care and affection, but alſo neceſſary to their common off-ſpring, who have a right to be nouriſhed, and maintained by them, till they are able to provide for themſelves.

§ 79 For the end of *conjunction, between male and female*, being not barely procreation, but the continuation of the ſpecies ; this conjunction betwixt male and female ought to laſt, even after procreation, ſo long as is neceſſary to the nouriſhment and ſupport of the young ones, who are to be ſuſtained by thoſe that got them, till they are able to ſhift and provide for themſelves This rule, which the infinite wiſe maker hath ſet to the works of his hands, we find the inferior creatures ſteadily obey. In thoſe viviparous animals which feed on graſs, the *conjunction between male and female* laſts no longer than the very act of copulation ; becauſe the teat of the dam being ſufficient

cient to nourish the young, till it be able to feed on grafs, the male only begets, but concerns not himself for the female or young, to whofe fufterance he can contribute nothing But in beafts of prey the *conjunction* lafts longer . becaufe the dim not being able well to fubfift herfelf, and nourish her numerous off-fpring by her own prey alone, a more laborious, as well as more dangerous way of living, than by feeding on grafs, the affiftance of the male is neceffary to the maintenance of their common family, which cannot fubfift till they are able to prey for themfelves, but by the joint care of male and female The fame is to be obferved in all birds, (except fome domeftic ones, where plenty of food excufes the cock from feeding, and taking care of the young brood) whofe young needing food in the neft, the cock and hen continue mates, till the young are able to ufe their wing, and provide for themfelves

§ 80 And herein I think lies the chief, if not the only reafon, *why the male and female in mankind are tied to a longer conjunction* than other creatures, *viz* becaufe the female is capable of conceiving, and *de facto* is commonly with child again, and brings forth too a new birth, long before the former is out of a dependency for fupport on his parents help, and able to fhift for himfelf, and has all the affiftance is due to him from his parents . whereby the father, who is bound to take care for thofe he hath begot, is under an obligation to continue in conjugal fociety with the fame woman longer than other creatures, whofe young being able to fubfift of themfelves, before the time of procreation returns again, the conjugal bond diffolves of itfelf, and they are at liberty, till *Hymen* at his ufual anniverfary

niverfary feafon fummons them again to chufe new mates Wherein one cannot but admire the wifdom of the great Creator, who having given to man forefight, and an ability to lay up for the future, as well as to fupply the prefent neceffity, hath made it neceffary, that *fociety of man and wife fhou'd be more lafting*, than of male and female amongft other creatures , that fo their induftry might be encouraged, and their intereft better united, to make provifion and lay up goods for their common iffue, which uncertain mixture, or eafy and frequent folutions of conjugal fociety would mightily difturb

§ 81 But tho' thefe are ties upon *mankind,* which make the *conjugal bonds* more firm and lafting in man, than the other fpecies of animals , yet it would give one reafon to enquire, why this *compact,* where procreation and education are fecured, and inheritance taken care for, may not be made determinable, either by confent, or at a certain time, or upon certain conditions, as well as any other voluntary compacts, there being no neceffity in the nature of the thing, nor to the ends of it, that it fhould always be for life ; I mean, to fuch as are under no reftraint of any pofitive law, which ordains all fuch contracts to be perpetual

§ 82 But the hufband and wife, though they have but one common concern, yet having different underftandings, will unavoidably fometimes have different wills too , it therefore being neceffary that the laft determination, i e the rule, fhould be placed fomewhere , it naturally falls to the man's fhare, as the abler and the ftronger. But this reaching but to the things of their common intereft and property, leaves the wife in the full and free poffeffion of what by contract is her

peculiar

peculiar right, and gives the husband no more power over her life than she has over his, the *power of the husband* being so far from that of an absolute monarch, that the *wife* has in many cases a liberty to separate from him, where natural right, or their contract allows it, whether that contract be made by themselves in the state of nature, or by the customs or laws of the country they live in, and the children upon such separation fall to the father or mother's lot, as such contract does determine.

§ 83 For all the ends of *marriage* being to be obtained under politic government, as well as in the state of nature, the civil magistrate doth not abridge the right or power of either naturally necessary to those ends, *viz* procreation and mutual support and assistance whilst they are together; but only decides any controversy that may arise between man and wife about them. If it were otherwise, and that absolute *sovereignty* and power of life and death naturally belonged to the husband, and were *necessary to the society between man and wife,* there could be no matrimony in any of those countries where the husband is allowed no such absolute authority. But the ends of matrimony requiring no such power in the husband, the condition of *conjugal society* put it not in him, it being not at all necessary to that state. *Conjugal society* could subsist and attain its ends without it, nay, community of goods, and the power over them, mutual assistance and maintenance, and other things belonging to *conjugal society,* might be varied and regulated by that contract which unites man and wife in that society, as far as may consist with procreation and the bringing up of children till they could shift

for

for themselves ; nothing being neceffary to any fociety, that is not neceffary to the ends for which it is made

§ 84. The *fociety betwixt parents and children,* and the diftinct rights and powers belonging refpectively to them, I have treated of fo largely, in the foregoing chapter, that I fhall not here need to fay any thing of it And I think it is plain, that it is far different from a politic fociety.

§ 85. *Mafter* and *fervant* are names as old as hiftory, but given to thofe of far different condition ; for a freeman makes himfelf a fervant to another, by felling him, for a certain time, the fervice he undertakes to do, in exchange for wages he is to receive · and though this commonly puts him into the family of his mafter, and under the ordinary difcipline thereof ; yet it gives the mafter but a temporary power over him, and no greater than what is contained in the *contract* between them. But there is another fort of fervants, which by a peculiar name we call *flaves,* who being captives taken in a juft war, are, by the right of nature fubjected to the abfolute dominion and arbitrary power, of their mafters Thefe men having, as I fay, forfeited their lives, and with it their liberties, and loft their eftates, and being in the *ftate of flavery,* not capable of any property, cannot in that ftate be confidered as any part of *civil fociety,* the chief end whereof is the prefervation of property

§ 86 Let us therefore confider a *mafter of a family* with all thefe fubordinate relations of *wife, children, fervants,* and *flaves,* united under the domeftic rule of a family ; which, what refemblance foever it may have in its order, offices, and number too, with a little common-wealth, yet is very far from it, both in its conftitution,
power

power and end · or if it muſt be thought a monarchy, and the *paterfamilias* the abſolute monarch
in it, abſolute monarchy will have but a very
flattered and ſhort power, when it is plain, by
what has been ſaid before, that the *maſter of the
family* has a very diſtinct and differently limited
power, both as to time and extent, over thoſe
ſeveral perſons that are in it, for excepting the
ſlave (and the family is as much a family, and his
power as *paterfamilias* as great, whether there be
any ſlaves in his family or no) he has no legiſlative power of life and death over any of them,
and none too but what a *miſtreſs of a family* may
have as well as he.   And he certainly can have
no abſolute power over the whole *family*, who
has but a very limited one over every individual
in it   But how a *family*, or any other ſociety of
men, differ from that which is properly *political
ſociety*, we ſhall beſt ſee, by conſidering wherein
political ſociety itſelf conſiſts

§ 87 Man being born, as has been proved,
with a title to perfect freedom, and an uncon-
trouled enjoyment of all the rights and privileges
of the law of nature, equally with any other
man, or number of men in the world, hath by
nature a power, not only to preſerve his property,
that is, his life, liberty and eſtate, againſt the
rjuries and attempts of other men , but to judge
of, and puniſh the breaches of that law in others,
as he is perſuaded the offence deſerves, even with
death itſelf, in crimes where the heinouſneſs of
the fact, in his opinion, requires it   But becauſe
no *political ſociety* can be, nor ſubſiſt, without
having in itſelf the power to preſerve the property, and in order thereunto, puniſh the offences of
all thoſe of that ſociety , there, and there only
is *political ſociety*, where every one of the members

bers hath quitted this natural power, refigned it up into the hands of the community in all cafes that exclude him not from appealing for protection to the law eftablifhed by it   And thus all private judgment of every particular member being ex- cluded, the community comes to be umpire, by fettled ftanding rules, indifferent, and the fame to all parties, and by men having authority from the community, for the execution of thofe rules, decides all the differences that may happen be- tween any members of that fociety concerning any matter of right, and punifhes thofe offences which any member hath committed againft the fociety, with fuch penalties as the law has efta- blifhed whereby it is eafy to difcern, who are, and who are not, in *political fociety* together Thofe who are united into one body, and have a common eftablifhed law and judicature to appeal to, with authority to decide controverfies between them, and punifh offenders, are in *civil fociety* one with another : but thofe who have no fuch common people, I mean on earth, are ftill in the ftate of nature, each being, where there is no other judge for himfelf, and executioner ; which is, as I have before fhewed it, the perfect *ftate of nature*

§ 88 And thus the common-wealth comes by a power to fet down what punifhment fhall be- long to the feveral tranfgreffions which they think worthy of it, committed amongft the members of that fociety, (which is the *power of making laws)* as well as it has the power to punifh any injury done unto any of its members, by any one that is not of it, (which is the *power of war and peace,*) and all this for the prefervation of the property of all the members of that fociety, as far as is poffible. But though every man who
has

has entered into civil society, and is become a member of any common-wealth, has thereby quitted his power to punish offences, against the law of *nature*, in prosecution of his own private judgment, yet with the judgment of offences, which he has given up to the legislative in all cases, where he can appeal to the magistrate, he has given a right to the common-wealth to employ his force, for the execution of the judgments of the common-wealth, whenever he shall be called to it; which indeed are his own judgments, they being made by himself, or his representative And herein we have the original of the *legislative* and *executive power* of civil society, which is to judge by standing laws, how far offences are to be punished, when committed within the common-wealth; and also to determine, by occasional judgments founded on the present circumstances of the fact, how far injuries from without are to be vindicated, and in both these to employ all the force of all the members, when there shall be need

§ 89. Where-ever therefore any number of men are so united into one society, as to quit every one his executive power of the law of nature, and to resign it to the public, there, and there only, is a *political, or civil society* And this is done, where-ever any number of men, in the state of nature, enter into society to make one people, one body politic, under one supreme government; or else when any one joins himself to, and incorporates with any government already made: for hereby he authorizes the society, or which is all one, the legislative thereof, to make laws for him, as the public good of the society shall require; to the execution whereof, his own assistance (as to his own decrees) is due And

this

this *puts men* out of a state of nature *into* that of a *common-wealth,* by setting up a judge on earth, with authority to determine all the controversies, and redress the injuries that may happen to any member of the common-wealth, which judge is the legislative, or magistrates appointed by it And where-ever there are any number of men, however associated, that have no such decisive power to appeal to, there they are still in the *state of nature*

§ 90 Hence it is evident, that *absolute monarchy,* which by some men is counted the only government in the world, is indeed *inconsistent with civil society,* and so can be no form of civil-government at all · for the *end of civil society,* being to avoid, and remedy those inconveniencies of the state of nature, which necessarily follow from every man's being judge in his own case, by setting up a known authority, to which every one of that society may appeal upon any injury received, or controversy that may arise, and which every one of the * society ought to obey, where-ever any persons are, who have not such an authority to appeal to, for the decision of any difference between them, there those persons are still *in the state of nature,* and so is every *absolute prince,* in respect of those who are under his *dominion*

§ 91 For he being supposed to have all, both legislative and executive power in himself alone,

---

* The public power of all society is above every soul contained in the same society, and the principal use of that power is, to give laws unto all that are under it, which laws in such cases we must obey, unless there be reason shewed which may necessarily inforce, that the law of reason, or of God, doth enjoin the contrary, *Hook Eccl Pol l 1 sect* 16.

there is no judge to be found, no appeal lies open
to any one, who may fairly, and indifferently,
and with authority decide, and from whose
decision relief and redress may be expected of
any injury or inconveniency, that may be suffered
from the prince, or by his order · so that such a
man, however intitled, *Czar* or *Grand Seignior*,
or how you please, is as much *in the state of nature*, with all under his dominion, as he is with
the rest of mankind · for where-ever any two
men are, who have no standing rule, and common
judge to appeal to on earth, for the determination
of controversies of right betwixt them, there they
are still *in the state of* * *nature*, and under all the
incon-

---

* To take away all such mutual grievances, injuries
and wrongs, *i e* such as attend men in the state of
nature, there was no way but only by growing into
composition and agreement amongst themselves, by
ordaining some kind of government public, and by
yielding themselves subject thereunto, that unto whom
they granted authority to rule and govern, by them
the peace, tranquillity and happy estate of the rest
might be procured. Men always knew that where
force and injury was offered, they might be defenders
of themselves, they knew that however men may seek
their own commodity, yet if this were done with injury unto others, it was not to be suffered, but by
all men, and all good means to be withstood. Final-
ly, they knew that no man might in reason take upon
him to determine his own right, and according to his
own determination proceed in maintenance thereof,
in as much as every man is towards himself, and them
whom he greatly affects, partial, and therefore that
strifes and troubles would be endless, except they gave
their common consent, all to be ordered by some,
whom they should agree upon, without which consent
L   there

inconveniencies of it, with only this woful difference to the fubject, or rather flave of an abfolute prince that whereas, in the ordinary ftate
of nature, he has a liberty to judge of his right,
and according to the beft of his power, to maintain it, now, whenever his property is invaded
by the will and order of his monarch, he has not
only no appeal, as thofe in fociety ought
to have, but as if he were degraded from the
common ftate of rational creatures, is denied a
liberty to judge of, or to defend his right, and
fo is expofed to all the mifery and inconveniencies,
that a man can fear from one, who being in the
unreftrained ftate of nature, is yet corrupted with
flattery, and armed with power.

§ 92 For he that thinks *abfolute power purifies
men's blood*, and corrects the bafenefs of human
nature, need read but the hiftory of this, or any
other age, to be convinced of the contrary He
that would have been infolent and injurious in
the woods of *America*, would not probably be
much better in a throne, where perhaps learning
and religion fhall be found out to juftify all that
he fhall do to his fubjects, and the fword prefently filence all thofe that dare queftion it for what
the *protection of abfolute monarchy* is, what kind
of fathers of their countries it makes princes to
be, and to what a degree of happinefs and fecurity it carries civil fociety, where this fort of government is grown to perfection, he that will
look into the late relation of *Ceylon*, may eafily
fee

---

there would be no reafon that one man fhould take
upon him to be lord or judge over another, *Hooker's
Eccl. Pol. l 1 fect 10*

§ 93 In *absolute monarchies* indeed, as well as other governments of the world, the subjects have an appeal to the law, and judges to decide any controversies, and restrain any violence that may happen betwixt the subjects themselves, one amongst another   This every one thinks neces-sary, and believes he deserves to be thought a de-clared enemy to society and mankind, who should go about to take it away.   But whether this be from a true love of mankind and society, and such a charity as we owe all one to another, there is reason to doubt   for this is no more than what every man, who loves his own power, profit, or greatness, may and naturally must do, keep those animals from hurting, or destroying one another, who labour and drudge only for his pleasure and advantage, and so are taken care of, not out of any love the master has for them, but love of himself, and the profit they bring him : for if it be asked, what security, *what fence* is there, in such a state, *against the violence and op-pression of this absolute ruler ?* the very question can scarce be borne   They are ready to tell you, that it deserves death only to ask after safety. Betwixt subject and subject, they will grant, there must be measures, laws and judges, for their mu-tual peace and security   but as for the *ruler,* he ought to be *absolute,* and is above all such cir-cumstances, because he has power to do more hurt and wrong, it is right when he does it.   To ask how you may be guarded from harm, or in-jury, on that side where the strongest hand is to do it, is presently the voice of faction and rebel-lion · as if when men quitting the state of nature entered into society, they agreed that all of them but one, should be under the restraint of laws,

but

but that he fhould ftill retain all the liberty of the ftate of nature, increafed with power, and made licentious by impunity This is to think, that men are fo foolifh, that they take care to avoid what mifchiefs may be done them by pole-*cats*, or *foxes*, but are content, nay, think it fafety, to be devoured by *lions*

§ 94 But whatever flatterers may talk to a-mufe people's underftandings, it hinders not men from feeling , and when they perceive, that any man, in what ftation foever, is out of the bounds of the civil fociety which they are of, and that they have no appeal on earth againft any harm they may receive from him, they are apt to think themfelves in the ftate of nature, in refpect of him whom they find to be fo, and to take care, as foon as they can, to have that *fafety and fecu-rity in civil fociety,* for which it was fiift inftituted, and for which only they entered into it.   And therefore, though perhaps at firft, (as fhall be fhewed more at large hereafter in the following part of this difcourfe) fome one good and excel-lent man having got a pre-eminency amongft the reft, had this deference paid to his goodnefs and virtue, as to a kind of natural authority, that the chief rule, with arbitration of their differences, by a tacit confent devolved into his hands, with-out any other caution, but the affurance they had of his uprightnefs and wifdom , yet when time, giving authority, and (as fome men would per-fuade us) facrednefs of cuftoms, which the negli-gent, and urforeicerg innocence of the firft ages began, had brought in fucceffors of another ftamp, the people finding their properties not fe-cure under the government, as then it was, (whereas government has no other end but the
preſervation

prefervation of * property) could never be fafe nor at reft, *nor think themfelves in civil fociety,* till the legiflature was placed in collective bodies of men, call them fenate, parliament, or what you pleafe By which means every fingle perfon became fubject, equally with other the meaneft men, to thofe laws, which he himfelf, as part of the legiflative, had eftablifhed; nor could any one, by his own authority, avoid the force of the law, when once made, nor by any pretence of fuperiority, plead exemption, thereby to licenfe his own, or the mifcarriages of any of his dependents † *No man in civil fociety can be exempted from the laws of it:* for if any man may do what he thinks fit, and there be no appeal on earth, for redrefs or fecurity againft any harm he fhall do, I afk, whether he be not perfectly ftill in the ftate of nature, and fo can be *no part or member of that civil fociety;* unlefs any one will fay, the ftate of nature and civil fociety are one

L 3 and

---

* At the firft, when fome certain kind of regiment was once appointed, it may be that nothing was then farther thought upon for the manner of governing, but all permitted unto their wifdom and difcretion, which were to rule, till by experience they found this for all parts very inconvenient, fo as the thing which they had devifed for a remedy, did indeed but increafe the fore, which it fhould have cured They faw, that *to live by one man's will, became the caufe of all men's mifery* This conftrained them to come unto laws, wherein all men might fee their duty beforehand, and know the penalties of tranfgreffing them *Hooker's Eccl Pol b 1 fect 10*

† Civil law being the act of the whole body politic, doth therefore over-rule each feveral part of the fame body. *Hooker, ibid*

and the fame thing, which I have never yet
found any one fo great a patron of anarchy as to
affirm

CHAP   VIII.

Of the Beginning of Political Societies

§ 95   MEN being, as has been faid, by nature, all free, equal, and independent, no one can be put out of this eftate, and
fubjected to the political power of another, without his own confent   The only way whereby
any one divefts himfelf of his natural liberty, and
puts on the *bonds of civil fociety,* is by agreeing
with other men to join and unite into a community, for their comfortable, fafe, and peaceable
living one amongft another, in a fecure enjoyment of their properties, and a greater fecurity
againft any, that are not of it.   This any number of men may do, becaufe it injures not the
freedom of the reft, they are left as they were
in the liberty of the ftate of nature   When any
number of men have fo *confented to make one
community or government,* they are thereby prefently incorporated, and make *one body politic,*
wherein the *majority* hath a right to act and conclude the reft -

§ 96   For when any number of men have, by
the confent of every individual, made a *community,* they have thereby made that *community* one
body, with a power to act as one body, which is
only by the will and determination of the *majority*   for that which acts any community, being
only the confent of the individuals of it, and it
being neceffary to that which is one body to move
one way, it is neceffary the body fhould move
that

that way whither the greater force carries it, which is the *consent of the majority* or else it is impossible it should act or continue one body, *one community*, which the consent of every individual that united into it, agreed that it should ; and so every one is bound by that consent to be concluded by the *majority*. And therefore we see, that in assemblies, impowered to act by positive laws, where no number is set by that positive law which impowers them, the *act of the majority* passes for the act of the whole, and of course determines, as having, by the law of nature and reason, the power of the whole

§ 97 And thus every man, by consenting with others to make one body politic under one government, puts himself under an obligation, to every one of that society, to submit to the determination of the *majority*, and to be concluded by it , or else this *original compact*, whereby he with others incorporates into *one society*, would signify nothing, and be no compact, if he be left free, and under no other ties than he was in before in the state of nature For what appearance would there be of any compact ? what new engagement if he were no farther tied by any decrees of the society, than he himself thought fit, and did actually consent to ? This would be still as great a liberty, as he himself had before his compact, or any one else in the state of nature hath, who may submit himself, and consent to any acts of it if he thinks fit.

§ 98. For if *the consent of the majority* shall not, in reason, be received as *the act of the whole*, and conclude every individual ; nothing but the consent of every individual can make any thing to be the act of the whole. but such a consent is next to impossible ever to be had, if we con-

L 4   sider

fider the infirmities of health, and avocations of
bufinefs, which in a number, though much lefs
than that of a common-wealth, will neceffarily
keep many away from the public affembly To
which if we add the variety of opinions, and
contrariety of interefts, which unavoidably happen in all collections of men, the coming into
fociety upon fuch terms would be only like *Cato's*
coming into the theatre, only to go out again.
Such a conflitution as this would make the mighty *Leviathan* of a fhorter duration, than the fee-
bleft creatures, and not let it outlaft the day it
was born in which cannot be fuppofed, till we
can think, that rational creatures fhould defire
and conflitute focieties only to be diffolved : for
where the *majority* cannot conclude the reft, there
they cannot act as one body, and confequently
will be immediately diffolved again

§. 99 Whofoever therefore out of a ftate of
nature unite into a *community*, muft be underftood
to give up all the power, neceffary to the ends
for which they unite into fociety, to the *majority*
of the community, unlefs they exprefly agreed
in any number greater than the majority. And
this is done by barely agreeing to *unite into one
political fociety*, which is *all the compact* that is,
or needs be, between the individuals, that enter
into, or make up a *common-wealth* And thus
that, which begins and actually *conflitutes any political fociety*, is nothing but the confent of any
number of freemen capable of a majority to unite
and incorporate into fuch a fociety And this is
that, and that only, which did, or could give beginning to any *lawful government* in the world

§. 100 To this I find two objections made.

Firft, *That there are no inflances to be found
in flory, of a company of men independent, and*
equal

equal one amongft another, that met together, and in this way began and fet up a government.

Secondly, *It is impoffible of right, that men fhould do fo, becaufe all men being born under government, they are to fubmit to that, and are not at liberty to begin a new one*

§ 101 To the firft there is this to anfwer, That it is not at all to be wondered, that *hiftory* gives us but a very little account of *men, that lived together in the ftate of nature* The inconveniencies of that condition, and the love and want of fociety, no fooner brought any number of them together, but they prefently united and incorporated, if they defigned to continue together. And if we may not fuppofe *m n* ever to have been *in the ftate of nature*, becaufe we hear not much of them in fuch a ftate, we may as well fuppofe the armies of *Salmanaffer* or *Xerxes* were never children, becaufe we hear little of them, till they were men, and imbodied in armies Government is every where antecedent to records, and letters feldom come in amongft a people, till a long continuation of civil fociety has, by other more neceffary arts, provided for their fafety, eafe, and plenty and then they begin to look after the hiftory of their founders, and fearch into their *original*, when they have out lived the memory of it for it is with *commonwealths* as with particular perfons, they are commonly *ignorant of their own births and infancies :* and if they know any thing of their or al, they are beholden for it, to the accidental records that others have kept of it And thofe that we have of the beginning of any polities in the world, excepting that of the *Jews*, where God himfelf immediately interpofed, and which fa-

vours

vours not at all paternal dominion, are all either plain instances of such a beginning as I have mentioned, or at least have manifest footsteps of it

§ 102 He must shew a strange inclination to deny evident matter of fact, when it agrees not with his hypothesis, who will not allow, that the *beginning* of *Rome* and *Venice* were by the uniting together of several men free and independent one of another, amongst whom there was no natural superiority or subjection. And if *Josephus Acosta's* word may be taken, he tells us, that in many parts of *America* there was no government at all *There are great and apparent conjectures,* says he, *that these men,* speaking of those of Peru, *for a long time had neither kings nor common-wealths, but lived in troops, as they do this day in* Florida, *the* Cheriquanas, *those of* Brasil, *and many other nations, which have no certain kings, but as occasion is offered, in peace or war, they choose their captains as they please,* l 1 c 25 If it be said, that every man there was born subject to his father, or the head of his family, that the subjection due from a child to a father took not away his freedom of uniting into what political society he thought fit, has been already proved But be that as it will, these men, it is evident, were actually *free*; and whatever superiority some politicians now would place in any of them, they themselves claimed it not, but by consent were all *equal,* till by the same consent they set rulers' over themselves So that their *politic societies* all *began* from a voluntary union, and the mutual agreement of men freely acting in the choice of their governors, and forms of government.

§. 103 And I hope those who went away from *Sparta* with *Phalantus,* mentioned by *Justin,*

l. 111.

l. iii. c 4 will be allowed to have been *freemen independent* one of another, and to have set up a government over themselves, by their own consent Thus I have given several examples, out of history, of *people free and in the state of nature,* that being met together incorporated and *began a common-wealth.* And if the want of such instances be an argument to prove that *government* were not, nor could not be so *begun,* I suppose the contenders for paternal empire were better let it alone, than urge it against natural liberty for if they can give so many instances, out of history, of *governments begun* upon paternal right, I think (though at best an argument from what has been, to what should of right be, has no great force) one might, without any great danger, yield them the cause But if I might advise them in the case, they would do well not to search too much into the *original of governments,* as they have begun *de facto,* left they should find, at the foundation of the most of them, something very little favourable to the design they promote, and such a power as they contend for.

§ 104. But to conclude, reason being plain on our side, that men are naturally free, and the examples of history shewing, that the *governments* of the world, that were begun in peace, had their beginning laid on that foundation, and were *made by the consent of the people,* there can be little room for doubt, either where the right is, or what has been the opinion, or practice of mankind, about the *first erecting of governments*

§ 105 I will not deny, that if we look back as far as history will direct us, towards the original of common-wealths, we shall generally find them under the government and administration of one man. And I am also apt to believe, that where

where a family was numerous enough to subsist
by itself and continued entire together, without mixing with others, as it often happens,
where there is much land, and few people, the
government commonly began in the father: for
the father having, by the law of nature, the
same power with every man else to punish, as
he thought fit, any offences against that law,
might thereby punish his transgressing children,
even when they are men, and out of their pupilage, and they were very likely to submit to
his punishment, and all join with him against
the offender, in their turns, giving him thereby
power to execute his sentence against any transgression, and so in effect make him the law-maker,
and governor over all that remained in conjunction with his family   He was fittest to be trusted, paternal affection secured their property and
interest under his care, and the custom of obeying him, in their childhood, made it easier to
submit to him, rather than to any other.   If
therefore they must have one to rule them, as
government is hardly to be avoided amongst men
that live together, who so likely to be the man
as he that was their common father, unless negligence, cruelty, or any other defect of mind or
body made him unfit for it? But when either the
father died, and left his next heir, for want of
age, wisdom, courage, or any other quality, less
fit for rule, or where several families met, and
consented to continue together, there, it is not
to be doubted, but they used their natural freedom, to set up him, whom they judged the ablest
and most likely, to rule well over them   Conformable hereunto we find the people of *America*,
who (living out of the reach of the conquering
swords, and spreading domination of the two
great

great empires of *Peru* and *Mexico)* enjoyed their
own natural freedom, though, *cæteris paribus,*
they commonly prefer the heir of their deceafed
king, yet if they find him any way weak, or uncapable, they pafs him by, and fet up the flouteft
and braveft man for their ruler.

§ 106. Thus, though looking back as far as
records give us any account of peopling the world,
and the hiftory of nations, we commonly find the
government to be in one hand , yet it deftroys not
that which I affirm, *viz* that the *beginning of politic fociety* depends upon the confent of the individuals, to join into, and make one fociety , who
when they are thus incorporated, might fet up
what form of government they thought fit. But
this having given occafion to men to miftake, and
think, that by nature government was monarchical, and belonged to the father, it may not be
amifs here to confider, why people in the beginning generally pitched upon this form, which
though perhaps the father's pre-eminency might,
in the firft inftitution of fome common-wealths,
give a rife to, and place in the beginning, in one
hand ; yet it is plain that the reafon, that continued the form of *government in a fingle perfon,*
was not any regard, or refpect to paternal authority , fince all petty *monarchies,* that is, almoft all
monarchies, near their original, have been commonly, at leaft upon occafion, *elective*

§ 107. Firft then, in the beginning of things,
the father's government of the childhood of thofe
fprung from him, having accuftomed them to the
rule of man, and taught them that where it was
exercifed with care and fkill, with affection and
love to thofe under it, it was fufficient to procure
and preferve to men all the political happinefs
they fought for in fociety. It was no wonder that
they

they fhould pitch upon, and naturally run into
that form of government, which from their infancy they had all been accuftomed to, and
which, by experience, they had found both eafy
and fafe   To which, if we add, that *monarchy*
being fimple, and moft obvious to men, whom
neither experience had inftructed in forms of government, nor the ambition or infolence of empire had taught to beware of the incroachments
of prerogative, or the inconveniencies of abfolute
power, which monarchy in fucceffion was apt to
lav claim to, and bring upon them ; it was not
at all ftrange, that they fhould not much trouble
themfelves to think of methods of reftraining any
exorbitances of thofe to whom they had given
the authority over them, and of balancing the
power of government, by placing feveral parts of
it in different hands.   They had neither felt the
oppreffion of tyrannical dominion, nor did the
fafhion of the age, nor their poffeffions, or way
of living, (which afforded little matter for covetoufnefs or ambition) give them any reafon to ap-
prehend or provide againft it , and therefore it
is no wonder they put themfelves into fuch a
frame of government, as was not only, as I faid,
moft obvious and fimple, but alfo beft fuited to
their prefent ftate and condition , which ftood
more in need of defence againft foreign invafi-
ons and injuries, than of multiplicity of laws
The equality of a fimple poor way of living, con-
fining their defires within the narrow bounds of
each man's fmall property, made few controverfies, and fo no need of many laws to decide them,
or variety of officers to fuperintend the procefs,
or look after the execution of juftice, where there
were but few trefpaffes, and few offenders Since
then thofe, who liked one another fo well as to

join

join into fociety, cannot but be fuppofed to have fome acquaintance and friendfhip together, and fome truft one in another, they could not but have greater apprehenfions of others, than of one another. and therefore their firft care and thought cannot but be fuppofed to be, how to fecure themfelves againft foreign force It was natural for them to put themfelves under a *frame of government* which might beft ferve to that end, and chufe the wifeft and braveft man to conduct them in their wars, and lead them out againft their enemies, and in this chiefly be their *ruler.*

§ 108 Thus we fee, that the *kings* of the *Indians* in *America,* which is ftill a pattern of the firft ages in *Afia* and *Europe,* whilft the inhabitants were but too few for the country, and want of people and money gave men no temptation to enlarge ther poffeffions of land, or conteft for wider extent of ground, are little more than *generals of their armies,* and though they command abfolutely in war, yet at home and in time of peace they exercife very little dominion, and have but very modeiate fovereignty, the iefolutions of peace and war being ordinarily either in the people, or in a council. Tho' the war itfelf, which admits not of plurality of governors, naturally devolves the command into the *king's fole authority*

§ 109. And thus in *Ifrael* itfelf, the *chief bufinefs of their judges,* and *firft kings,* feems to have been *to be captains in war,* and leaders of their armies, which (befides what is fignified by *going out and in before the people,* which was, to march forth to war, and home again in the heads of their forces) appears plainly in the ftory of *Jephtha* The *Ammonites* making war upon *Ifrael,*

Ifrael, the *Gileadites* in fear fend to *Jephtha*, a baftard of their family whom they caft off, and article with him, if he will affift them againft the *Ammonites*, to make him a ruler; which they do in thefe words, *And the people made him head and captain over them*, Judg. xi. 11. which was, as it feems, all one as to be *judge* *And he judged If-rael*, Judg xii. 7. that is, was their *captain-gene-ral fix years*. So when *Jotham* upbraids the *She-chemites* with their obligation they had to *Gideon*, who had been their *judge* and ruler, he tells them, *He fought for you, and adventured his life far, and delivered you out of the hands of Midian* Judg. ix 17 Nothing mentioned of him, but what he did as a *general ·* and indeed that is all is found in his hiftory, or in any of the reft of the judges And *Abimelech* particularly is called *king*, though at moft he was but their *general* And when, being weary of the ill conduct of *Samuel*'s fons, the children of *Ifrael* defired a *king, like all the nations to judge them, and go out before them, and to fight their battles*, 1 Sam viii 20 God granting their defire, fays to *Samuel, I will fend thee a man, and thou fhall anoint him to be captain over my people Ifrael, that he may fave my people out of the hands of the Philiftines*, ix 16 As if the only *bufinefs of a king* had been to lead out their armies, and fight in their defence; and ac-cordingly at his inauguration pouring a vial of oil upon him, declares to *Saul*, that *the Lord had anointed him to be captain over his inheritance*, x. 1. And therefore thofe who after *Saul*'s being fo-lemnly chofen and faluted *king* by the *tribes* at *Mifpah*, were unwilling to have him their king, made no other objection but this, *How fhall this man fave us?* v 27 as if they fhould have faid, this man is unfit to be our *king*, not having fkill
                                                    and

and conduct enough in war, to be able to defend us. And when God resolved to transfer the government to *David*, it is in these words, *But now thy kingdom shall not continue. the Lord hath sought him a man after his own heart, and the Lord hath commanded him to be captain over his people,* xiii. 14 As if the whole kingly authority were nothing else but to be their *general* · and therefore the *tribes* who had stuck to *Saul*'s family, and opposed *David*'s reign, when they came to *Hebron* with terms of submission to him, they tell him, amongst other arguments they had to submit to him as to their king, that he was in effect their *king* in *Saul*'s time, and therefore they had no reason but to receive him as their *king* now. *Also* (say they) *in time past, when Saul was king over us, thou wast he that leddest out and broughtest in Israel, and the Lord said unto thee, Thou shalt feed my people Israel, and thou shalt be a captain over Israel.*

§ 110 Thus, whether *a family* by degrees *grew up into a common-wealth*, and the fatherly authority being continued on to the elder son, every one in his turn growing up under it, tacitly submitted to it, and the easiness and equality of it not offending any one, every one acquiesced, till time seemed to have confirmed it, and settled a right of succession by prescription: or whether several families, or the descendants of several families, whom chance, neighbourhood, or business brought together, uniting into society, the need of a general, whose conduct might defend them against their enemies in war, and the great confidence the innocence and sincerity of that poor but virtuous age, (such as are almost all those which begin governments, that ever come to last in the world) gave men one of another, made the first beginners

beginners of common-wealths generally put the rule into one man's hand, without any other expreſs limitation or reſtraint, but what the nature of the thing, and the end of government required. which ever of thoſe it was at firſt put the rule into the hands of a ſingle perſon, certain it is no body was intruſted with it but for the public good and ſafety, and to thoſe ends, in the infancies of common-wealths, thoſe who had it commonly uſed it. And unleſs they had done ſo, young ſocieties could not have ſubſiſted, without ſuch nurſing fathers tender and careful of the public weal, all governments would have ſunk under the weakneſs and infirmities of their infancy, and the prince and the people had ſoon periſhed together

§ 111. But though the *golden age* (before vain ambition, and *amor ſceleratus habendi*, evil concupiſcence, had corrupted men's minds into a miſtake of true power and honour) had more virtue, and conſequently better governors, as well as leſs vicious ſubjects; and there was then *no ſtretching prerogative* on the one ſide, to oppreſs the people, *nor* conſequently on the other, any *diſpute about privilege*, to leſſen or reſtrain the power of the magiſtrate, and ſo no conteſt betwixt rulers and people about governors or government: yet, when ambition and luxury in future ages * would
retain

---

* At firſt, when ſome certain kind of regiment was once approved, it may be nothing was then farther thought upon for the manner of governing, but all permitted unto their wiſdom and diſcretion which were to rule, till by experience they found this for all parts very inconvenient, ſo as the thing which they had deviſed for remedy, did indeed but increaſe the ſore which it ſhould have cured. They ſaw, that to live by one
man's

retain and increase the power, without doing the
business for which it was given; and aided by
flattery, taught princes to have distinct and separate interests from their people, men found it
necessary to examine more carefully *the original
and rights of gov'rnment*; and to find out ways to
restrain the exorbitances, and *prevent the abuses* of
that power, which they having it trusted into another's hands only for their own good, they found
was made use of to hurt them.

§ 112. Thus we may see how probable it is,
that people that were naturally free, and by their
own consent either submitted to the government
of their father, or united together out of different families to make a government, should generally put the *rule into one man's hands*, and chuse
to be under the conduct of *a single person*, without so much as by express conditions limiting or
regulating his power, which they thought safe
enough in his honesty and prudence; though they
never dreamed of monarchy being *Jure Divino*,
which we never heard of among mankind, till it
was revealed to us by the divinity of this last
age; nor ever allowed paternal power to have a
right to dominion, or to be the foundation of all
government. And thus much may suffice to shew,
that as far as we have any light from history, we
have reason to conclude, that all peaceful beginnings of *government* have been *laid in the consent
of the people*. I say *peaceful*, because I shall have
occasion in another place to speak of conquest,
which

---

man's will, became the cause of all men's misery. This
constrained them to come unto laws wherein all men
might see their duty before hand, and know the penalties of transgressing them. *Hooker's Eccl. Pol. l. i.
sect.* 10.

which some esteem a way of beginning of governments

The other objection I find urged against the beginnings of polities, in the way I have mentioned, is this, viz.

§ 113 *That all men being born under government, some or other, it is impossible any of them should ever be free, and at liberty to unite together, and begin a new one, or ever be able to erect a lawful government.*

If this argument be good; I ask, how came so many lawful monarchies into the world ? for if any body, upon this supposition, can shew me any one man in any age of the world *free* to to begin a lawful monarchy, I will be bound to shew him ten other *free men* at liberty, at the same time to unite and begin a new government under a regal, or any other form ; it being demonstration, that if any one, *born under the dominion* of another, may be so *free* as to have a right to command others in a new and distinct empire, every one that is *born under the dominion* of another may be so free too, and may become a ruler, or subject, of a distinct separate government And so by this their own principle, either all men, however *born*, are *free*, or else there is but one lawful prince, one lawful government in the world And then they have nothing to do, but barely to shew us which that is ; which when they have done, I doubt not but all mankind will easily agree to pay obedience to him

§ 114. Though it be a sufficient answer to their objection, to shew that it involves them in the same difficulties that it doth those they use it against ; yet I shall endeavour to discover the weakness of this argument a little farther

All

All men, say they, *are born under government, and therefore they cannot be at liberty to begin a new one* Every one is born a *subject* to *his father, or his prince, and is therefore under the perpetual tie of subjection and allegiance* It is plain mankind never owned nor confidered any fuch natural *subjection that they were born in,* to one or to the other that tied them, without their own confents, to a fubjection to them and their heirs.

§ 115 For there are no examples fo frequent in hiftory, both facred and profane, as thofe of men withdrawing themfelves and their obedience, from the jurifdiction they were born under, and the family or community they were bred up in, and *fetting up new governments* in other places , from whence fprang all that number of petty common-wealths, in the beginning of ages, and which always multiplied, as long as there was room enough, till the ftronger, or more fortunate, fwallowed the weaker , and thofe great ones again breaking to pieces, diffolved into leffer dominions. All which are fo many teftimonies againft paternal fovereignty, and plainly prove, that it was not the natural right of the *father* defcending to his heirs, that made governments in the beginning, fince it was impoffible, upon that ground, there fhould have been fo many little kingdoms ; all muft have been but only one univerfal monarchy, if men had not been at *liberty to feparate* themfelves from their familes, and the government, be it what it will, that was fet up in it, and go and make diftinct common-wealths and other governments, as they thought fit

§ 116 This has been the practice of the world from its firft beginning to this day , nor is it now any more hindrance to the freedom of mankind, that they are *born under conft, tuted and . . . ti—*

SICO

lities, that have eftablifhed laws, and fet forms of government, than if they were born in the woods, amongft the unconfined inhabitants, that run loofe in them   for thofe, who would perfuade us, that *by being born under any government, we are natu- rally fubjects to it,* and have no more any title or pretence to the freedom of the ftate of nature, have no other reafon (bating that of paternal power, which we have already anfwered) to pro- duce for it, but only, becaufe our fathers or pro- genitors paffed away their natural liberties, and thereby bound up themfelves and their pofterity to a perpetual fubjection to the government, which they themfelves fubmitted to   It is true, that whatever engagements or promifes any one has made for himfelf, he is under the obligation of them, but *cannot,* by any *compact* whatfoever, *bind his children or pofterity*   for his fon, when a man, being altogether as free as the father, any *act of the father can no more give away the liberty of the fon,* than it can of any body elfe   he may indeed annex fuch conditions to the land, he en- joyed as a fubject of any common-wealth, as may oblige his fon to be of that community, if he will enjoy thofe poffeffions which were his father's, becaufe that eftate being his father's property, he may difpofe, or fettle it, as he pleafes

§. 117 And this has generally given the occa- fion to miftake in this matter, becaufe common- wealths not permitting any part of their domini- ons to be difmembered, nor to be enjoyed by any but thofe of their community, the fon cannot or- dinarly enjoy the poffeffions of his father, but under the fame terms his father did, by becoming a member of the fociety, whereby he puts him- felf prefently under the government he finds there eftablifhed, as much as any other fubject of that common-wealth.

common-wealth. And thus *the confent of freemen, born under government*, which only *makes them members of it*, being given feparately in their turns, as each comes to be of age, and not in a multitude together, people take no notice of it, and thinking it not done at all, or not neceffary, conclude they are naturally fubjects as they are men.

§ 118 But it is plain, *governments* themfelves underftand it otherwife, they claim *no power over the fon, becaufe of that they had over the father*, nor look on children as being their fubjects, by their fathers being fo If a fubject of *England* have a child, by an *Englifh* woman in *France*, whofe fubject is he? Not the king of *England's*, for he muft have leave to be admitted to the privileges of it nor the king of *France's*, for how then has his father a liberty to bring him away, and breed him as he pleafes? and who ever was judged as a *traytor* or *deferter*, if he left, or warred againft a country, for being barely born in it of parents that were aliens there? It is plain then, by the practice of governments themfelves, as well as by the law of right reafon, that *a child is born a fubject of no country or government* He is under his father's tuition and authority, till he comes to age of difcretion; and then he is a freeman, at liberty what government he will put himfelf under, what body politic he will unite himfelf to. for if an *Englifhman's* fon, born in *France*, be at liberty, and may do fo, it is evident there is no tie upon him by his fathers being a fubject of this kingdom; nor is he bound up by any compact of his anceftors And why then hath not his fon, by the fame reafon, the fame liberty, though he be born any where elfe? Since the power that a father hath naturally over his chil-

dren,

dren, is the fame, where-ever they be born, and the ties of natural obligations, are not bounded by the pofitive limits of kingdoms and common-wealths

§. 119 *Every man* being, as has been fhewed, *naturally free,* and nothing being able to put him into fubjection to any earthly power, but only his own *confent*, it is to be confidered, what fhall be underftood to be a *fufficient declaration* of a man's *confent, to make him fubject* to the laws of any government There is a common diftinction of an exprefs and a tacit confent, which will con-cern our prefent cafe   No body doubts but an exprefs *confent*, of any man entering into any fo-ciety, makes him a perfect member of that foci-ety, a fubject of that government The difficulty is, what ought to be looked upon as a *tacit con-fent,* and how far it binds, *i. e* how far any one fhall be looked on to have confented, and thereby fubmited to any goverrment, where he has made no expreffiors of it at all.   And to this I fav, that every man, that hath any poffeffions, or en-joyment, of any part of the dominions of any government, doth thereby give his *tacit confent,* and is as far forth obliged to obedience to the laws of that government, during fuch enjoyment, as any one under it, whether this his poffeffion be of land, to him and his heirs for ever, or a lodging only for a week, or whether it be barely travelling freely on the highway, and in effect, it reaches as far as the very being of any one within the territories of that government

§ 120 To underftand this better, it is fit to confider, that every man, when he at firft incor-porates himfelf into any common-wealth, he, by his uniting himfelf thereunto, annexed alfo, and fubmits to the community, thofe poffeffions, which
he

he has, or shall acquire, that do not already belong to any other government. for it would be
a direct contradiction, for any one to enter into
society with others for the securing and regulating of property, and yet to suppose his land,
whose property is to be regulated by the laws of
the society, should be exempt from the jurisdiction of that government, to which he himself, the
proprietor of the land, is a subject By the same act
therefore, whereby any one unites his person which
was before free, to any common-wealth, by the
same he unites his possessions, which were before
free, to it also, and they become, both of them,
person and possession, subject to the government
and dominion of that common-wealth, as long as
it hath a being Whoever therefore, from thenceforth, by inheritance, purchase, permission, or
otherways *enjoys any part of the land*, so annexed
to, and under the government *of that common-
wealth, must take it with the condition* it is under;
that is, *of submitting to the government of the
common-wealth*, under whose jurisdiction it is, as
far forth as any subject of it.

§ 121 But since the government has a direct
jurisdiction only over the land, and reaches the
possessor of it, (before he has actually incorporated himself in the society) only as he dwells upon, and enjoys that, the obligation any one is
under, by virtue of such enjoyment, to *submit to
the government*, *begins and ends with the enjoyment*;
so that whenever the owner, who has given nothing but such a *tacit consent* to the government,
will, by donation, sale, or otherwise, quit the
said possession, he is at liberty to go and incorporate himself into any other common-wealth; or
to agree with others to begin a new one, *in vacuis
locis*, in any part of the world, they can find free

M   and

and unpoffeffed : whereas he, that has once, **by**
actual agreement, and any *expr fs* declaration,
given his *confent* to be of any common-wealth,
is perpetually and indifpenfibly obliged to be,
and remain unalterably a fubject to it, and can
never be again in the liberty of the ftate of nature , unlefs by any calamity, the government
he was under comes to be diffolved ; or elſe by
fome public act cuts him off from being any longer a member of it

§ 122 But fubmitting to the laws of any country, living quietly, and enjoying privileges and
protection under them, *makes not a man a member of*
that fociety this is only a local protection and
homage due to and from all thofe, who, not being
in a ftate of war, come within the territories belonging to any government, to all parts whereof
the force of its laws extends But this no more
makes a man a member of that fociety, a perpetual
fubject of that common-wealth, than it would
make a man a fubject to another, in whofe family he found it convenient to abide for fome time ;
though, whilfl he continued in it, he were obliged to comply with the laws, and fubmit to the
government he found there. And thus we fee,
that *foreigners*, by living all their lives under another government, and enjoying the privileges and
protection of it, though they are bound, even in
confcience, to fubmit to its adminiftration, as far
forth as any denion , yet do not thereby come
to be *fubj* ºs *or members of that common-wealth*
Nothing can make any man fo, but his actually
entering into it by pofitive engagement, and exprefs
promife and compact This is that, which I
think concerning the beginning of political focieties and that *confent which makes any one a mem-*
ber of any common wealth

C H A P.

CHAP. IX.

Of the Ends of Political Society, and Government.

§ 123. IF man in the state of nature be so free, as has been said, if he be absolute lord of his own person and possessions, equal to the greatest, and subject to no body, why will he part with his freedom? why will he give up this empire, and subject himself to the dominion and controul of any other power? To which it is obvious to answer, that though in the state of nature he hath such a right, yet the enjoyment of it is very uncertain, and constantly exposed to the invasion of others. for all being kings as much as he, every man his equal, and the greater part no strict observers of equity and justice, the enjoyment of the property he has in this state is very unsafe, very unsecure. This makes him willing to quit a condition, which, however free, is full of fears and continual dangers and it is not without reason, that he seeks out, and is willing to join in society with others, who are already united, or have a mind to unite, for the mutual *preservation* of their lives, liberties and estates, which I call by the general name, *property*.

§ 124 The great and *chief end*, therefore, of men's uniting into common-wealths, and putting themselves under government, *is the preservation of their property* To which in the state of nature there are many things wanting

First, There wants an *established*, settled, known *law*, received and allowed by common consent to be the standard of right and wrong,

and

and the common meafure to decide all controverfies between them   for though the law of
nature be plain and intelligible to all rational
creatures , yet men being biaffed by their intereft,
as well as ignorant for want of ftudy of it, are
not apt to allow of it as a law binding to them in
the application of it to their particular cafes.

§ 125 Secondly, In the ftate of nature there
wants *a known and indifferent judge,* with authority to determine all differences according to the
eftablifhed law , for every one in that ftate being
both judge and executioner of the law of nature,
men being partial to themfelves, paffion and revenge is very apt to carry them too far, and with
too much heat, in their own cafes , as well as
negligence, and unconcernednefs, to make them
too remifs in other men's

§ 126 *Thirdly,* In the ftate of nature there
often wants *power* to back and fupport the fen-
tence when right, and to *give* it due *execution.*
They who by any injuftice offended, will feldom
fail, where they are able, by force to make good
their injuftice , fuch refiftance many times makes
the punifhment dangerous, and frequently deftructive, to thofe who attempt it

§. 127 Thus mankind, notwithftanding all the
privileges of the ftate of nature, being but in an
ill condition, while they remain in it, are quickly
driven into fociety   Hence it comes to pafs, that
we feldom find any number of men live any time
together in this ftate   The inconveniencies that
they are therein expofed to , by the irregular and
uncertain exercife of the power every man has of
punifhing the tranfgreffions of other , make them
take fanctuary under the eftablifhed laws of
government, and therein feek *the prefervation of
their property*   It is this makes them fo willingly
give

give up every one his single power of punishing, to be exercised by such alone, as shall be appointed to it amongst them; and by such rules as the community, or those authorized by them to that purpose, shall agree on. And in this we have the original *right and rise of both the legislative and executive power*, as well as of the governments and societies themselves.

§ 128 For in the state of nature, to omit the liberty he has of innocent delights, a man has two powers.

The first is to do whatsoever he thinks fit for the preservation of himself, and others within the permission of the *law of nature* by which law, common to them all, he and all the rest of *mankind are one community*, make up one society, distinct from all other creatures. And were it not for the corruption and vitiousness of degenerate men, there would be no need of any other; no necessity that men should separate from this great and natural community, and by positive agreements combine into smaller and divided associations.

The other power a man has in the state of nature, is the *power to punish the crimes* committed against that law. Both these he gives up, when he joins in a private, if I may so call it, or particular politic society, and incorporates into any common-wealth, separate from the rest of mankind.

§ 129 The first *power*, viz *of doing whatsoever he thought for the preservation of himself*, and the rest of mankind, *he gives up* to be regulated by laws made by the society, so far forth as the preservation of himself, and the rest of that society shall require, which laws of the society in many things confine the liberty he had by the law of nature.

§ 130.

§ 130 *Secondly,* The *power of punishing he
wholly gives up,* and engages his natural force,
(which he might before employ in the execution
of the law of nature, by his own single authority, as he thought fit) to assist the executive power
of the society, as the law thereof shall require.
for being now in a new state, wherein he is to
enjoy many conveniencies, from the labour, affist-
ance, and society of others in the same community, as well as protection from its whole
strength, he is to part also with as much of his
natural liberty, in providing for himself, as the
good, prosperity, and safety of the society shall
require, which is not only necessary, but just,
since the other members of the society do the
like.

§ 131 But though men, when they enter into society, give up the equality, liberty, and executive power they had in the state of nature, into
the hands of the society, to be so far disposed of
by the legislative, as the good of the society shall
require, yet it being only with an intention in
every one the better to preserve himself, his liberty and property, (for no rational creature can
be supposed to change his condition with an intention to be worse) the power of the society, or *legislative* constituted by them, can *never be supposed to extend farther, than the common good*, but
is obliged to secure every one's property, by providing against those three defects above mentioned,
that made the state of nature so unsafe and unea-
sy And so whoever has the legislative or supreme power of any common-wealth, is bound
to govern by established *standing laws,* promulgated and known to the people, and not by extemporary decrees ; by *indifferent* and upright *judges,*
who are to decide controversies by those laws ; and

to

to employ the force of the community at home, *only in the execution of such laws*, or abroad, to prevent or redress foreign injuries, and secure the community from inroads and invasion. And all this to be directed to no other end, but the *peace, safety*, and *public good* of the people.

CHAP. X.

Of the Forms of a Common-wealth.

§ 132 THE majority having, as has been shewed, upon men's first uniting into society, the whole power of the community naturally in them, may employ all that power in making laws for the community from time to time, and executing those laws by officers of their own appointing, and then the *form* of the government is a perfect *democracy*; or else may put the power of making laws into the hands of a few select men, and their heirs or successors, and then it is an *oligarchy*; or else into the hands of one man, and then it is a *monarchy*; if to him and his heirs, it is an *hereditary monarchy*; if to him only for life, but upon his death the power only of nominating a successor to return to them, an *elective monarchy*. And so accordingly of these the community may make compounded and mixed forms of government, as they think good. And if the legislative power be at first given by the majority to one or more persons only for their lives, or any limited time, and then the supreme power to revert to them again, when it is so reverted, the community may dispose of it again anew into what hands they please, and so constitute a new form of government; for the *form of government depending upon the placing the supreme power*, which is *the legislative*, it being

M 4 impossible

impoſſible to conceive that an inferior power ſhould preſcribe to a ſuperior, or any but the ſupreme make laws, according as the power of making laws is placed, ſuch is the *form of the common-wealth*

§. 133 By *common-wealth*, I muſt be underſtood all along to mean not a democracy, or any form of government, but *any independent commun.ty*, which the *Latines* ſignified by the word *ci-vitas*, to which the word which beſt anſwers in our language, is *common-wealth*, and moſt properly expreſſes ſuch a ſociety of men, which community or city in *Engliſh* does not, for there may be ſubordinate communities in a government, and city amongſt us has a quite different notion from common-wealth and therefore, to avoid ambiguity, I crave leave to uſe the word *common-wealth* in that ſenſe, in which I find it uſed by king *James the firſt* , and I take it to be its genuine ſignification , which if any body diſlike, I conſent with him to change it for a better.

CHAP. XI.

Of the Extent of the Legiſlative Power.

§. 134. THE great end of men's entering into ſociety, being the enjoyment of their properties in peace and ſafety, and the great inſtrument and means of that being the laws eſtabliſhed in that ſociety, the *firſt and fundamental poſitive law* of all common-wealths *is the eſtabliſhing of the legiſlative* power; as the *firſt and fundamental natural law*, which is to govern even the legiſlative itſelf, *is the preſervation of the ſociety*, and (as far as will conſiſt with the public good) of every perſon in it   This
legiſlative

legiflative is not only *the fupreme power* of the common-wealth, but facred and unalterable in the hands where the community have once placed it ; nor can any edict of any body elfe, in what form foever conceived, or by what power foever backed, have the force and obligation of a *law*, which has not its *fanction from* that *legiflative* which the public has chofen and appointed for without this the law could not have that, which is abfolutely neceffary to its being a *law*, * *the confent of the fo-ciety*, over whom no body can have a power to make laws, but by their own confent, and by authority received from them ; and therefore all the *obedience*, which by the moft folemn ties any one can be obliged *to* pay, ultimately terminates in this *fupreme power*, and is directed by thofe laws

M 5 which

---

* The lawful power of making laws to command whole politic focieties of men, belonging fo properly unto the fame intire focieties, that for any prince or potentate o' what kind foever upon earth, to exercife the fame of himfelf, and not by exprefs commiffion immediately and perfonally received from God, or elfe by authority derived at the firft from their confent, upon whofe perfons they impofe laws, it is no better than mere tyranny Laws they are not therefore which public approbation hath not made fo *Hooker's Eccl Pol l* i. *fct* 10 Of this point therefore we are to note, that fith men naturally have no full and perfect power to command whole politic multitudes of men, therefore utterly without our confent, we could in fuch fort be at no man's commandment living And to be commanded we do confent, when that fociety, whereof we be a part, hath at any time before conferred, without revoking the fame after by the like univerfal agreement

Laws therefore human, of what kind fo ever, are available by confent *Ibid.*

which it enacts. nor can any oaths to any foreign power whatfoever, or any domeftic fubordinate power, difcharge any member of the fociety from his *obedience to the legiflative,* acting purfuant to their truft, nor oblige him to any obedience contrary to the laws fo enacted, or farther than they do allow; it being ridiculous to imagine one can be tied ultimately to *obey* any *power* in the fociety, which is not the *fupreme*

§ 135 Though the *legiflative,* whether placed in one or more, whether it be always in being, or only by intervals, though it be the *fupreme* power in every common-wealth, yet,

Firft, It is *not,* nor can poffibly be ab olutely *arbitrary* over the lives and fortunes of the people: for it being but the joint power of every member of the fociety given up to that perfon, or affembly, which is legiflator, it can be no more than thofe perfons had in a ftate of nature before they entered into fociety, and gave up to the community. for nobody can tranffer to another more power than he has in himfelf, and nobody has an abfolute arbitrary power over himfelf, or over any other, to deftroy his own life, or take away the life or property of another A man, as has been proved, cannot fubject himfelf to the arbitrary power of another, and having in the ftate of nature no arbitrary power over the life, liberty, or poffeffion of another, but only fo much as the law of nature gave him for the prefervation of himfelf, and the reft of mankind; this is all he doth, or can give up to the common-wealth, and by it to the *legiflative power,* fo that the legiflative can have no more than this. Their power, in the utmoft bounds of it, is *limited to the public good* of the fociety It is a power, that hath no other end but prefervation, and therefore

can never * have a right to deftroy, enflave, or
defignedly to impoverifh the fubjects. The obligations of the law of nature ceafe not in fociety,
but only in many cafes are drawn clofer, and
have by human laws known penalties annexed to
them, to inforce their obfervation Thus the
law of nature ftands as an eternal rule to all men,
legiflators as well as others The *rules* that they
make for other men's actions, muft, as well as
their own and other men's actions, be conformable to the law of nature, *i e* to the will of
God, of which that is a declaration, and the
*fundamental law of nature being the prefervation
of mankind*, no human fanction can be good, or
valid againft it

§ 136.

---

* Two foundations there are which bear up public
focieties, the one a natural inclination, whereby all
men defire fociable life and fellowfhip, the other an
order, exprefly or fecretly agreed upon, touching the
manner of their union in living together the latter is
that which we call the law of a common weal, the
very foul of a politic body, the parts whereof are by
law animated, held together, and fet on work in fuch
actions as the common good requireth Laws politic,
ordained for external order and regiment amongft
men, are never framed as they fhould be, unlefs prefuming the will of man to be inwardly obftinate, rebellious, and averfe from all obedience to the facred
laws of his nature, in a word unlefs prefuming man
to be, in regard of his depraved mind, little better
than a wild beaft, they do accordingly provide, not
withftanding, fo to frame his outward actions, that
they be no hinderance unto the common good, for
which focieties are inftituted Unlefs they do this,
they are not perfect. *Hooker's Eccl. Pol l 1 fect 10.*

§. 136. *Secondly,* * The *legiflative,* or fupreme authority, cannot affume to its felf a power to rule by extemporary arbitrary decrees, but *is bound to difpenfe juftice,* and decide the rights of the fubject *by promulgated ftanding laws, and known authorized judges* for the law of nature being unwritten, and fo no where to be found but in the minds of men, they who through paffion or intereft fhall mifcite, or mifapply it, cannot fo eafily be convinced of their miftake where there is no eftablifhed judge and fo it ferves not, as it ought, to determine the rights, and hence the properties of thofe that live under it, efpecially where every one is judge, interpreter, and executioner of it too, and that in his own cafe and he that has right on his fide, having ordinarily but his own fingle ftrength, hath not force enough to defend himfelf from injuries, or to punifh delinquents To avoid thefe inconveniencies, which diforder men's properties in the ftate of nature, men unite into focieties, that they may have the united ftrength of the whole fociety to fecure and defend their properties, and may have ftanding rules to bound it, by which every one may know what is his To this end
it

---

* Human laws are meafures in refpect of men whofe actions they muft direct, howbeit fuch meafures they are as have alfo their higher rules to be meafured by, which rules are two, the law of God, and the law of nature, fo that laws human muft be made according to the general laws of nature, and without contradiction to any pofitive law of fcripture, otherwife they are ill made *Hooker's Eccl Pol l* iii *fect* 9.

To conftrain men to any thing inconvenient doth feem unreafonable *Ibid lib* 1. *fect* 10 it is that men give up all their natural power to the society which they enter into, and the community put the legislative power into such hands as they think fit, with this trust, that they shall be governed by *declared laws*, or else their peace, quiet, and property will still be at the same uncertainty, as it was in the state of nature.

§. 137 Absolute arbitrary power, or governing without *settled standing laws*, can neither of them consist with the ends of society and government, which men would not quit the freedom of the state of nature for, and tie themselves up under, were it not to preserve their lives, liberties and fortunes, and by *stated rules* of right and property to secure their peace and quiet It cannot be supposed that they should intend, had they a power so to do, to give to any one, or more, an *absolute arbitrary power* over their persons and estates, and put a force into the magistrate's hard to execute his unlimited will arbitrarily upon them This were to put themselves into a worse condition than the state of nature, wherein they had a liberty to defend their right against the injuries of others, and were upon equal terms of force to maintain it, whether invaded by a single man, or many in combination. Whereas by supposing they have given up themselves to the *absolute arbitrary power* and will of a legislator, they have disarmed themselves, and armed him, to make a prey of them when he pleases; he being in a much worse condition, who is exposed to the arbitrary power of one man, who has the command of 100,000, than he that is exposed to the arbitrary power of 100,000 single men, no body being secure, that his will, who has such a command, is better than that of other men, though his force be 100,000 times stronger.

ftronger. And therefore, whatever form the common-wealth is under, the ruling power ought to govern by *declared* and *received laws*, and not by extemporary dictates and undetermined refolutions. for then mankind will be in a far worfe condition than in the ftate of nature, if they fhall have armed one, or a few men with the joint power of a multitude, to force them to obey at pleafure the exorbitant and unlimited decrees of their fuddcn thoughts, or unreftrained, and till that moment unknown wills, without having any meafures fet down which may guide and juftify their actions. for all the power the government has, being only for the good of the fociety, as it ought not to be *arbitrary* and at pleafure, fo it ought to be exerciſed by *eſtabliſhed and promulgated laws*, that both the people may know their duty, and be fafe and fecure within the limits of the law, and the rulers too kept within their bounds, and not be tempted, by the power they have in their hands, to employ it to fuch purpoſes, and by fuch meafures, as they would not have known, and own not willingly.

§ 138 *Thirdly*, The *fupreme power cannot take* from any man any part of his *property* without his own confent for the prefervation of property being the end of government, and that for which men enter into fociety, it neceſſarily fuppoſes and requires, that the people fhould *have property*, without which they muſt be fuppofed to loſe that, by entering into fociety, which was the end for which they entered into it, too grofs an abfurdity for any man to own Men therefore *in fociety having property*, they have fuch a right to the goods, which by the law of the community are their's, that no body hath a right to take their fubftance or any part of it from them, without their

 own

own confent without this they have no *property*
at all; for I have truly no *property* in that, which
another can by right take from me, when he
pleafe, againft my confent Hence it is a miftake to think, that the *fupreme or legiflative power* of any common-wealth, can do what it will,
and difpofe of the eftates of the fubject *arbitrarily*,
or take any part of them at pleafure This
is not much to be feared in governments where
the *legiflative* confifts, wholly or in part, in affemblies which are variable, whofe members, upon the diffolution of the affembly, are fubjects
under the common laws of their country, equally
with the reft. But in governments, where the
legiflative is in one lafting affembly always in being, or in one man, as in abfolute monarchies,
there is danger ftill, that they will think themfelves to have a diftinct intereft from the reft of the
community, and fo will be apt to increafe their
own riches and power, by taking what they think
fit from the people for a man's property is not
at all fecure, though there be good and equitable
laws to fet the bounds of it between him and his
fellow-fubjects, if he who commands thofe fubjects have power to take from any private man,
what part he pleafes of his *property*, and ufe and
difpofe of it as he thinks good

§ 139 But *government*, into whatfoever hands
it is put, being, as I have before fhewed, intruft-
ed with this condition, and *for this end*, that men
might have and fecure their *properties*, the prince,
or fenate, however it may have power to make
laws, for the regulating of *property* between the
fubjects one amongft another, yet can never have
a power to take to themfelves the whole, or any
part of the fubjects *property*, without their own
confent. for this would be in effect to leave them

no

no *property* at all. And to let us fee, that even *abfolute power*, where it is neceffary, is *not arbitrary* by being abfolute, but is ftill limited by that reafon, and confined to thofe ends, which required it in fome cafes to be abfolute, we need look no farther than the common practice of martial difcipline : for the prefervation of the army, and in it of the whole common-wealth, requires an *abfolute obedience* to the command of every fuperior officer, and it is juftly death to difobey or difpute the moft dangerous or unreafonable of them, but yet we fee, that neither the ferjeant, that could command a foldier to march up to the mouth of a cannon, or ftand in a breach, where he is almoft fure to perifh, can command that foldier to give him one penny of his money, nor the *general*, that can condemn him to death for deferting his poft, or for not obeying the moft defperate orders, can yet, with all his *abfolute power* of life and death, difpofe of one farthing of that foldier's eftate, or feize one jot of his goods, whom yet he can command any thing, and hang for the leaft difobedience; becaufe fuch a blind obedience is neceffary to that end, for which the commander has his power, *viz* the prefervation of the reft; but the difpofing of his goods has nothing to do with it

§ 140 It is true, governments cannot be fupported without great charge, and it is fit every one who enjoy his fhare of the protection, fhould pay out of his eftate his proportion for the maintenance of it. But ftill it muft be with his own confent, *i e* the confent of the majority, giving it either by themfelves, or their reprefentatives, chofen by them : for if any one fhall claim a *power to lay* and levy *taxes* on the people, by his own

own authority, and without such consent of the people, he thereby invades the *fundamental law of property*, and subverts the end of government: for what property have I in that, which another may by right take, when he pleases, to himself?

§ 141 *Fourthly*, The *legislative cannot transfer the power of making laws* to any other hands for it being but a delegated power from the people, they who have it cannot pass it over to others. The people alone can appoint the form of the common-wealth, which is by constituting the legislative, and appointing in whose hands that shall be. And when the people have said, We will submit to rules, and be governed by *laws* made by such men, and in such forms, no body else can say, other men shall make *laws* for them; nor can the people be bound by any *laws*, but such as are enacted by those whom they have chosen, and authorized to make *laws* for them. The power of the *legislative*, being derived from the people by a positive voluntary grant and institution, can be no other than what that positive grant conveyed, which being only to make *laws*, and not to make *legislators*, the *legislative* can have no power to transfer their authority of making laws, and place it in other hands.

§ 142 These are *bounds* which the trust, that is put in them by the society, and the law of God and nature, have *set to the legislative* power of every common-wealth, in all forms of government.

First, they are to govern by *promulgated esta-blished laws*, not to be varied in particular cases, but to have one rule for rich and poor, for the favourite at court, and the country man at plough.

Secondly,

Secondly These *laws* also ought to be defigned *for* no other end ultimately, but *the good
of the people*

Thirdly, They muft *not raife taxes* on the
*property of the people, without the confent of the
people*, given by themſelves, or their deputies
And this properly concerns only ſuch governments where the *legiſlative* is always in being, or,
at leaſt where the people have not reſerved any
part of the legiſlative to deputies, to be from
time to time chofen by themſelves

Fourthly, The *leg flative* neither muft *nor can
transfer the power of making laws* to any body
elfe, or place it any where, but where the people have

C H A P XII

*Of the Legiſlative, Executive, and Federative
Power of the Common-wealth.*

§ 143 THE *legiſlative* power is that, which
has a right *to direct how the force
of the common-wealth* fhall be employed for preferving the community and the members of it.
But becauſe thoſe laws which are conftantly to
be executed, and whoſe force is always to continue, may be made in a little time; therefore
there is no need, that the *legiſlative* fhould be
always in being, not having always bufinefs to
do And becauſe it may be too great a temptation to human frailty, apt to grafp at power, for
the fame perfons, who have the power of making
laws, to have alfo in their hands the power to
execute them, whereby they may exempt themſelves

felves from obedience to the laws they make, and
fuit the law, both in its making, and execution,
to their own private advantage, and thereby come
to have a diftinct intereft from the reft of the
community, contrary to the end of fociety and
government: therefore in well-ordered common-
wealths, where the good of the whole is fo confider'd, as it ought, the *legiflative* power is put
into the hands of divers perfons, who duly affembled, have by themfelves, or jointly with
others, a power to make laws, which when they
have done, being feparated again, they are themfelves fubject to the laws they have made, which
is a new and near tie upon them, to take care,
that they make them for the public good

§ 144 But becaufe the laws, that are at once,
and in a fhort time made, have a conftant and
lafting force, and need a *perpetual execution*, or
an attendance thereunto; therefore it is neceffary
there fhould be a *power always in being,* which
fhould fee to the *execution* of the laws that are
made, and remain in force   And thus the *legiflative* and *executive power* come often to be fepa-
raced

§ 145 There is another *power* in every common-wealth, which one may call *natural,* becaufe
it is that which anfwers to the power every man
naturally had before he entered into fociety: for
though in a common-wealth the members of it are
diftinct perfons ftill in reference to one another,
and as fuch are governed by the laws of the fociety; yet in reference to the reft of mankind,
they make one body, which is, as every member
of it before was, ftill in the ftate of nature with
the reft of mankind   Hence it is, that the controverfies that happen between any man of the fociety with thofe that are out of it, are managed
by

by the public ; and an injury done to a member
of their body, engages the whole in the reparation of it So that under this confideration, the
whole community is one body in the ftate of nature, in refpect of all other ftates or perfons out
of its community

§ 146. This therefore contains the power of
war and peace, leagues and alliances, and all the
tranfactions, with all perfons and communities without the common-wealth, and may be
called *federative*, if any one pleafes So the
thing be underftood, I am indifferent as to the
name

§ 147 Thefe two powers, *executive* and *federative*, though they be really diftinct in themfelves, yet one comprehending the *execution* of
the municipal laws of the fociety *within* itfelf,
upon all that are parts of it , the other the management of the *fecurity and intereft of the public without*, with all thofe that may receive benefit or damage from, yet they are always almoft
united And though this *federative power* in the
well or ill management of it be of great moment
to the common-wealth, yet it is much lefs capable to be directed by antecedent, ftanding, pofitive
laws, than the *executive* , and fo muft neceffarily
be left to the prudence and wifdom of thofe,
whofe hands it is in, to be managed for the public good · for the *laws* that concern fubjects one
amongft another, being to direct their actions,
may well enough *precede* them But what is to
be done in reference to *foreigners*, depending
much upon their actions, and the variation of
defigns and interefts, muft be *left* in great part *to*
the *prudence* of thofe, who have this power committed to them, to be managed by the beft of
their

their skill, for the advantage of the common-wealth.

§ 148 Though, as I said, the *executive* and *federative power* of every community be really distinct in themselves, yet they are hardly to be separated, and placed at the same time, in the hands of distinct persons: for both of them re-quiring the force of the society for their exercise, it is almost impracticable to place the force of the common wealth in distinct, and not subordinate hands, or that the *executive* and *federative power* should be *placed* in persons, that might act sepa-rately, whereby the force of the public would be under different commands which would be apt some time or other to cause disorder and ruin

---

C H A P. XIII.

Of the Subordination of the Powers of the Common-wealth.

§ 149 THOUGH in a constituted common-wealth, standing upon its own ba-sis, and acting according to its own nature, that is, acting for the preservation of the community, there can be but *one supreme power*, which is *the legislative*, to which all the rest are and must be subordinate, yet the legislative being only a fidu-ciary power to act for certain ends, there remains still *in the people a supreme power to remove or alter the legislative*, when they find the *legislative* act contrary to the trust reposed in them. for all *power given with trust* for the attaining an *end*, being limited by that end, whenever that *end* is manifestly neglected, or opposed, the *trust* must necessarily be *forfeited*, and the power devolve into the hands of those that gave it, who may

place

place it anew where they shall think best for their safety and security. And thus the *community* perpetually *retains a supreme power* of saving themselves from the attempts and designs of any body, even of their legislators, whenever they shall be so foolish, or so wicked, as to lay and carry on designs against the liberties and properties of the subject. for no man or society of men, having a power to deliver up their *preservation*, or consequently the means of it, to the absolute will and arbitrary dominion of another, whenever any one shall go about to bring them into such a slavish condition, they will always have a right to preserve, what they have not a power to part with, and to rid themselves of those, who invade this fundamental, sacred, and unalterable law of *self-preservation*, for which they entered into society. And thus the *community* may be said in this respect to be *always the supreme power*, but not as considered under any form of government, because this power of the people can never take place till the government be dissolved.

§ 150. In all cases, whilst the government subsists, the *legislative is the supreme power*. for what can give laws to another, must needs be superior to him, and since the legislative is no otherwise legislative of the society, but by the right it has to make laws for all the parts, and for every member of the society, prescribing rules to their actions, and giving power of execution, where they are transgressed, the *legislative* must needs be the *supreme*, and all other powers, in any members or parts of the society, derived from and subordinate to it.

§ 151. In some common wealths, where the *legislative* is not always in being, and the *executive* is vested in a single person, who has also a share
in

in the legiflative, there that fingle perfon in a very tolerable fenfe may alfo be called *supreme:* not that he has in himfelf all the fupreme power, which is that of law making; but becaufe he has in him the *fupreme execution,* from whom all inferior magiftrates derive all their feveral fubordinate powers, or at leaft the greateft part of them having alfo no legiflative fuperior to him, there being no law to be made without his confent, which cannot be expected fhould ever fubject him to the other part of the legiflative, *he is* properly enough in this fenfe *supreme* But yet it is to be obferved, that tho' *oaths of allegiance* and fealty are taken to him, it is not to him as fupreme legiflator, but as *fupreme executor* of the law, made by a joint power of him with others ; *allegiance* being nothing but an *obedience according to law,* which when he violates, he has no right to obedience, nor can claim it otherwife than as the public perfon vefted with the power of the law, and fo is to be confidered as the image, phantom, or reprefentative of the common-wealth, acted by the will of the fociety, declared in its laws, and thus he has no will, no power, but that of the law But when he quits this reprefentation, this public will, and acts by his own private will, he degrades himfelf, and is but a fingle private perfon without power, and without will, that has any right to *obedience,* the members owing no *obedience* but to the public will of the fociety.

§ 152 The *executive power,* placed any where but in a perfon that has alfo a fhare in the legiflative, is vifibly fubordinate and accountable to it, and may be at pleafure changed and difplaced, fo that it is not the *fupreme executive power,* that is exempt from *fubordination,* but the *fupreme executive*

cutive

cutive power vested in one, who having a share
in the legislative, has no distinct superior legislative
to be subordinate and accountable to, farther than
he himself shall join and consent; so that he is
no more subordinate than he himself shall think
fit, which one may certainly conclude will be
but very little Of other *ministerial and subordinate powers* in a common-wealth, we need not
speak, they being so multiplied with infinite variety, in the different customs and constitutions
of distinct common-wealths, that it is impossible
to give a particular account of them all. Only
thus much, which is necessary to our present purpose, we may take notice of concerning them, that
they have no manner of authority, any of them,
beyond what is by positive grant and commission
delegated to them, and are all of them accountable to some other power in the commonwealth

§. 153 It is not necessary, no, nor so much as
convenient, that the *legislative* should be *always
in being*, but absolutely necessary that the executive power should, because there is not always
need of new laws to be made, but always need
of execution of the laws that are made When
the *legislative* hath put the *execution* of the
laws, they make, into other hands, they have
a power still to resume it out of those hands,
when they find cause, and to punish for any
mal-administration against the laws. The same
holds also in regard of the *federative* power, that
and the *executive* being both *ministerial* and *subordinate to the legislative*, which, as has been shewed,
in a constituted common-wealth is the supreme
The *legislative* also in this case being supposed to
consist of several persons, (for if it be a single
person, it cannot but be always in being, and so
will, as supreme, naturally have the supreme
executive

executive power, together with the legiflative) may *affemble, and exercife their legiflature*, at the times that either their original conftitution, or their own adjournment, appoints, or when they pleafe; if neither of thefe hath appointed any time, or there be no other way prefcribed to convoke them · for the fupreme power being placed in them by the people, it is always in them, and they may exercife it when they pleafe, unlefs by their original conftitution they are limited to certain feafons, or by an act of their fupreme power they have adjourned to a certain time, and when that time comes, they have a right to *affemble* and act again.

§ 154. If the *legiflative*, or any part of it, be made up of *reprefentatives* chofen for that time by the people, which afterwards return into the ordinary ftate of fubjects, and have no fhare in the legiflature but upon a new choice, this power of chufing muft alfo be exercifed by the people, either at certain appointed feafons, or elfe when they are fummoned to it; and in this latter cafe, the power of convoking the legiflative is ordinarily placed in the executive, and has one of thefe two limitations in refpect of time that either the original conftitution requires their *affembling* and *acting* at certain intervals, and then the executive power does nothing but minifterially iffue directions for their electing and affembling, according to due form; or elfe it is left to his prudence to call them by new elections, when the occafions or exigencies of the public require the amendment of old, or making of new laws, or the redrefs or prevention of any inconveniencies, that lie on, or threaten the people.

§. 155. It may be demanded here, What if the executive power, being poffeffed of the force

N

of the common-wealth, fhall make ufe of that force to hinder the *meeting* and *acting of the legiflative*, when the original conftitution, or the public exigencies require it ? I fay, ufing force upon the people without authority, and contrary to the truft put in him that does fo, is a ftate of war with the people, who have a right to *reinftate* their *legiflative in the exercife* of their power : for having erected a legiflative, with an intent they fhould exercife the power of making laws, either at certain fet times, or when there is need of it, when they are hindered by any force from what is fo neceffary to the fociety, and wherein the fafety and prefervation of the people confifts, the people have a right to remove it by force. In all ftates and conditions, the true remedy of *force* without authority, is to oppofe *force* to it. The ufe of *force* without authority, always puts him that ufes it into a *ftate of war*, as the aggreffor, and renders him liable to be treated accordingly.

§ 156 The *power of affembling and difmiffing the legiflative,* placed in the executive, gives not the executive a fuperiority over it, but is a fiduciary truft placed in him, for the fafety of the people, in a cafe where the uncertainty and variablenefs of human affairs could not bear a fteady fixed rule · for it not being poffible, that the firft framers of the government fhould, by any forefight, be fo much mafters of future events, as to be able to prefix fo juft periods of return and duration to the *affemblies of the legiflative,* in all times to come, that might exactly anfwer all the exigencies of the common-wealth , the beft remedy could be found for this defect, was to truft this to the prudence of one who was always to be prefent, and whofe bufinefs it was to watch over

the

the public good. Constant *frequent meetings of the legislative*, and long continuations of their assemblies, without necessary occasion, could not but be burdensome to the people, and must necessarily in time produce more dangerous inconveniencies, and yet the quick turn of affairs might be sometimes such as to need their present help: any delay of their *convening* might endanger the public, and sometimes too their business might be so great, that the limited time of their sitting might be too short for their work, and rob the public of that benefit which could be had only from their mature deliberation. What then could be done in this case to prevent the community from being exposed some time or other to eminent hazard, on one side or the other, by fixed intervals and periods, set to the *meeting and acting of the legislative*, but to intrust it to the prudence of some, who being present, and acquainted with the state of public affairs, might make use of this prerogative for the public good ? and where else could this be so well placed as in his hands, who was intrusted with the execution of the laws for the same end ? Thus supposing the regulation of times for the *assembling and sitting of the legislative*, not settled by the original constitution, it naturally fell into the hands of the executive, not as an arbitrary power depending on his good pleasure, but with this trust always to have it exercised only for the public weal, as the occurrences of times and change of affairs might require. Whether *settled periods of their convening,* or *a liberty* left to the prince for *convoking the legislative*, or perhaps a mixture of both, hath the least inconvenience attending it, it is not my business here to inquire, but only to shew, that though the executive power may have the prero-

gative

gative of *convoking* and *diffolving* fuch *conventions of the legiflative,* yet is not thereby fuperior to it

§ 157. Things of this world are in fo conftant a flux, that nothing remains long in the fame ftate. Thus people, riches, trade, power, change their ftations, flourifhing mighty cities come to ruin, and prove in times negle&ted defolate corners, whilft other unfrequented places grow into populous countries, filled with wealth and inhabitants. But things not always changing equally, and private intereft often keeping up cuftoms and privileges, when the reafons of them are ceafed, it often comes to pafs, that in governments, where part of the legiflative confifts of *reprefentatives* chofen by the people, that in tra&t of time this *reprefentation* becomes very *unequal* and difproportionate to the reafons it was at firft eftablifhed upon. To what grofs abfurdities the following of cuftom, when reafon has left it, may lead, we may be fatisfied, when we fee the bare name of a town, of which there remains not fo much as the ruins, where fcarce fo much houfing as a fheepcote, or more inhabitants than a fhepherd is to be found, fends *as many reprefentatives* to the grand affembly of law-makers, as a whole county numerous in people, and powerful in riches. This ftrangers ftand amazed at, and every one muft confefs needs a remedy, tho' moft think it hard to find one, becaufe the conftitution of the legiflative being the original and fupreme a&t of the fociety, antecedent to all pofitive laws in it, and depending wholly on the people, no inferior power can alter it. And therefore the *people,* when the *legiflative* is once conftituted, having, in fuch a government as we have been fpeaking of, no power to a&t as

long

long as the government ſtands; this inconvenience is thought incapable of remedy

§. 158 *Salus populi ſuprema lex*, is certainly ſo juſt and fundamental a rule, that he, who ſincerely follows it, cannot dangerouſly err If therefore the executive, who has the power of convoking the legiſlative, obſerving rather the true proportion, than faſhion of *repreſentation*, regulates, not by old cuſtom, but true reaſon, the *number of members*, in all places that have a right to be diſtinctly repreſented, which no part of the people however incorporated can pretend to, but in proportion to the aſſiſtance which it affords to the public, it cannot be judged to have ſet up a new legiſlative, but to have reſtored the old and true one, and to have rectified the diſorders which ſucceſſion of time had inſenſibly, as well as inevitably introduced: For it being the intereſt as well as intention of the people, to have a fair and *equal repreſentative*; whoever brings it neareſt to that, is an undoubted friend to, and eſtabliſher of the government, and cannot miſs the conſent and approbation of the community; *prerogative* being nothing but a power, in the hands of the prince, to provide for the public good, in ſuch caſes, which depending upon unforeſeen and uncertain occurrences, certain and unalterable laws could not ſafely direct, whatſoever ſhall be done manifeſtly for the good of the people, and the eſtabliſhing the government upon its true foundations, is, and always will be, juſt *prerogative* The power of erecting new corporations, and therewith *new repreſentatives*, carries with it a ſuppoſition, that in time the *meaſures of repreſentation* might vary, and thoſe places have a juſt right to be repreſented which before had none, and by the ſame reaſon, thoſe ceaſe to have a right

and be too inconfiderable for fuch a privilege,
which before had it. 'Tis not a change from
the prefent ftate, which perhaps corruption or
decay has introduced, that makes an inroad upon
the government, but the tendency of it to injure
or opprefs the people, and to fet up one part or
party, with a diftinction from, and an unequal
fubjection of the reft Whatfoever cannot but
be acknowledged to be of advantage to the fociety, and people in general, upon juft and lafting
meafures, will always, when done, juftify itfelf,
and whenever the people fhall chufe their *reprefentatives upon* juft and undeniably *equal meafures,*
fuitable to the original frame of the government,
it cannot be doubted to be the will and act of
the fociety, whoever permitted or caufed them fo
to do

CHAP. XIV.

Of PREROGATIVE.

§. 159 WHERE the legiflative and executive power are in diftinct hands,
(as they are in all moderated monarchies, and
well-framed governments) there the good of the
fociety requires, that feveral things fhould be left
to the difcretion of him that has the executive
power for the legiflators not being able to fore-
fee, and provide by laws, for all that may be ufeful
to the community, the executor of the laws,
having the power in his hands, has by the common law of nature a right to make ufe of it for
the good of the fociety, in many cafes, where
the municipal law has given no direction, till the
legiflative can conveniently be affembled to provide for it. Many things there are, which the
law

law can by no means provide for; and those must necessarily be left to the discretion of him that has the executive power in his hands, to be ordered by him as the public good and advantage shall require. nay, it is fit that the laws themselves should in some cases give way to the executive power, or rather to this fundamental law of nature and government, *viz* That as much as may be, *all* the members of the society are to be preserved for since many accidents may happen, wherein a strict and rigid observation of the laws may do harm, (as not to pull down an innocent man's house to stop the fire, when the next to it is burning) and a man may come sometimes within the reach of the law, which makes no distinction of persons, by an action that may deserve reward and pardon, 'tis fit the ruler should have a power, in many cases, to mitigate the severity of the law, and pardon some offenders. for the *end of government* being *the preservation of all*, as much as may be, even the guilty are to be spared, where it can prove no prejudice to the innocent.

§ 160 This power to act according to discretion, for the public good, without the prescription of the law, and sometimes even against it, *is* that which is called *prerogative* for since in some governments the law-making power is not always in being, and is usually too numerous, and so too slow, for the dispatch requisite to execution, and because also it is impossible to foresee, and so by laws to provide for, all accidents and necessities that may concern the public, or to make such laws as will do no harm, if they are executed with an inflexible rigour, on all occasions, and upon all persons that may come in their way, therefore there is a latitude left to

N 4

the

the executive power, to do many things of choice which the laws do not prescibe.

§ 161. This power, whilst employed for the benefit of the community, and suitably to the trust and ends of the government, *is undoubted prerogative*, and never is questioned · for the people are very seldom or never scrupulous or nice in the point, they are far from examining *prerogative*, whilst it is in any tolerable degree employed for the use it was meant, that is, for the good of the people, and not manifestly against it : but if there comes to be a *question* between the executive power and the people, about a thing claimed as a *prerogative*, the tendency of the exercise of such *prerogative* to the good or hurt of the people, will easily decide that question

§. 162 It is easy to conceive, that in the infancy of governments, when common-wealths differed little from families in number of people, they differed from them too but little in number of laws : and the governors being as the fathers of them, watching over them for their good, the government was almost all *prerogative*. A few established laws served the turn, and the discretion and care of the ruler supplied the rest. But when mistake or flattery prevailed with weak princes to make use of this power for private ends of their own, and not for the public good, the people were fain by express laws to get prerogative determined in those points wherein they found disadvantage from it and thus declared *limitations of prerogative* were by the people found necessary in cases which they and their anceftors had left, in the utmost latitude, to the wisdom of those princes who made no other but a right use of it, that is, for the good of their people.

§. 163.

§. 163 And therefore they have a very wrong notion of government, who fay, that the people have *incroached upon the prerogative*, when they have got any part of it to be defined by pofitive laws for in fo doing they have not pulled from the prince any thing that of right belonged to him, but only declared, that that power which they indefinitely left in his or his anceftors hands, to be exercifed for their good, was not a thing which they intended him when he ufed it other-wife · for the end of government being the good of the community, whatfoevei alterations are made in it, tending to that end, cannot be an *in-croachment* upon any body, fince no body in go-vernment can have a right tending to any other end · and thofe only are *incroachments* which prejudice or hinder the public good Thofe who fay otherwife, fpeak as if the prince had a dif-tinct and feparate intereft from the good of the community, and was not made for it; the root and fource from which fpring almoft all thofe evils and diforders which happen in kingly go-vernments. And indeed, if that be fo, the peo-ple under his government are not a fociety of rational creatures, entered into a community for their mutual good; they are not fuch as have fet rulers over themfelves, to guard, and promote that good; but are to be looked on as an herd of inferior creatures under the dominion of a mafter, who keeps them and works them for his own pleafure or profit. If men were fo void of rea-fon, and brutifh, as to enter into fociety upon fuch terms, *prerogative* might indeed be, what fome men would have it, an arbitrary power to do things hurtful to the people.

§ 164 But fince a rational creature cannot be fuppofed, when free, to put himfelf into fubjec-

N 5

tion to another, for his own harm, (though, where he finds a good and wife ruler, he may not perhaps think it either neceffary or ufeful to fet precife bounds to his power in all things) *prerogative* can be nothing but the people's permitting their rulers to do feveral things, of their own free choice, where the law was filent, and fometimes too againft the direct letter of the law, for the public good; and their acquiefcing in it when fo done for as a good prince, who is mindful of the truft put into his hands, and careful of the good of his people, cannot have too much *prerogative*, that is, power to do good; fo a weak and ill prince, who would claim that power which his predeceffors exercifed without the direction of the law, as a prerogative belonging to him by right of his office, which he may exercife at his pleafure, to make or promote an intereft diftinct from that of the public, gives the people an occafion to claim their right, and limit that power, which, whilft it was exercifed for their good, they were content fhould be tacitly allowed

§ 165 And therefore he that will look into the *hiftory of England*, will find, that *prerogative* was always *largeft* in the hands of our wifeft and beft princes, becaufe the people, obferving the whole tendency of their actions to be the public good, contefted not what was done without law to that end or, if any human frailty or miftake (for princes are but men, made as others) appeared in fome fmall declinations from that end, yet 'twas vifible, the main of their conduct tended to nothing but the care of the public. The people therefore, finding reafon to be fatisfied with thefe princes, whenever they acted without, or contrary

contrary to the letter of the law, acquiefced in what they did, and, without the leaft complaint, let them inlarge their *prerogative* as they pleafed, judging rightly, that they did nothing herein to the prejudice of their laws, fince they acted conformable to the foundation and end of all laws, the public good.

§ 166 Such god-like princes indeed had fome title to arbitrary power by that argument, that would prove abfolute monarchy the beft government, as that which God himfelf governs the univerfe by, becaufe fuch kings partake of his wifdom and goodnefs. Upon this is founded that faying, That the reigns of good princes have been always moft dangerous to the liberties of their people · for when their fuccesfors, managing the government with different thoughts, would draw the actions of thofe good rulers into precedent, and make them the ftandard of their *prerogative*, as if what had been done only for the good of the people was a right in them to do, for the harm of the people, if they fo pleafed; it has often occafioned conteft, and fometimes public diforders, before the people could recover their original right, and get that to be declared not to be *prerogative*, which truly was never fo; fince it is impoffible that any body in the fociety fhould ever have a right to do the people harm; though it be very poffible, and reafonable, that the people fhould not go about to fet any bounds to the *prerogative* of thofe kings, or rulers, who themfelves tranfgreffed not the bounds of the public good for *prerogative is nothing but the power of doing public good without a rule*

§. 167 The power of *calling parliaments* in *England*, as to precife time, place, and duration, is certainly a *prerogative* of the king, but ftill
with

with this truſt, that it ſhall be made uſe of for the good of the nation, as the exigencies of the times, and variety of occaſions, ſhall require: for it being impoſſible to foreſee which ſhould always be the fitteſt place for them to aſſemble in, and what the beſt ſeaſon; the choice of theſe was left with the executive power, as might be moſt ſubſervient to the public good, and beſt ſuit the ends of parliaments.

§. 168. The old queſtion will be aſked in this matter of *prerogative,* But *who ſhall be judge* when this power is made a right uſe of? I anſwer. between an executive power in being, with ſuch a prerogative, and a legiſlative that depends upon his will for their convening, there can be no *judge on earth*; as there can be none between the legiſlative and the people, ſhould either the executive, or the legiſlative, when they have got the power in their hands, deſign, or go about to enſlave or deſtroy them. The people have no other remedy in this, as in all other caſes where they have no judge on earth, but to *appeal to heaven:* for the rulers, in ſuch attempts, exerciſing a power the people never put into their hands, (who can never be ſuppoſed to conſent that any body ſhould rule over them for their harm) do that which they have not a right to do. And where the body of the people, or any ſingle man, is deprived of their right, or is under the exerciſe of a power without right, and have no appeal on earth, then they have a liberty to appeal to heaven, whenever they judge the cauſe of ſufficient moment And therefore, though the *people cannot* be *judge,* ſo as to have, by the conſtitution of that ſociety, any ſuperior power, to determine and give effective ſentence in the caſe; yet they have, by a law antecedent and pa a-

mount

mount to all positive laws of men, reserved that
ultimate determination to themselves which belongs to all mankind, where there lies no appeal
on earth, *viz.* to judge, whether they have just
cause to make their appeal to heaven.   And this
judgment they cannot part with, it being out of
a man's power so to submit himself to another,
as to give him a liberty to destroy him ; God and
nature never allowing a man so to abandon himself, as to neglect his own preservation : and since
he cannot take away his own life, neither can he
give another power to take it   Nor let any one
think, this lays a perpetual foundation for disorder ; for this operates not, till the inconveniency
is so great, that the majority feel it, and are weary of it, and find a necessity to have it amended.
But this the executive power, or wise princes,
never need come in the danger of · and it is the
thing, of all others, they have most need to avoid,
as of all others the most perilous.

C H A P. XV.

Of *Paternal, Political, and Despotical Power*, con-
sidered together.

§ 169. THOUGH I have had occasion to
speak of these separately before,
yet the the great mistakes of late about government, having, as I suppose, arisen from confound-
ing these distinct powers one with another, it may
not, perhaps, be amiss, to consider them here
together.

§ 170 First, then, *Paternal* or *parental power*
is nothing but that which parents have over their
children, to govern them for the child 's good,
till they come to the use of reason, c   of

knowledge, wherein they may be fuppofed capable to underftand that rule, whether it be the law
of nature, of the municipal law of their country,
they are to govern themfelves by : capable, I fay,
to know it, as well as feveral others, who live
as freemen under that law. The affection and
tendernefs which God hath planted in the breaft
of parents towards their children, makes it evident, that this is not intended to be a fevere arbitrary government, but only for the help, in-
ftruction, and prefervation of their offspring. But
happen it as it will, there is, as I have proved,
no reafon why it fhould be thought to extend to
life and death, at any time, over their children,
more than over any body elfe ; neither can there
be any pretence why this *parental power* fhould
keep the child, when grown to a man, in fubjection to the will of his parents, any farther than
having received life and education from his parents, obliges him to refpect, honour, gratitude,
affiftance and fupport, all his life, to both father
and mother   And thus, 'tis true, the *paternal* is
a natural *government*, but not at all extending itfelf to the ends and jurifdictions of that which is
political   The *power of the father doth not reach*
at all to the *property* of the child, which is only
in his own difpofing.

§. 171. *Secondly, Political power* is that power,
which every man having in the ftate of nature,
has given up into the hands of the fociety, and
therein to the governors, whom the fociety hath
fet over itfelf, with this exprefs or tacit truft, that
it fhall be employed for their good, and the prefervation of their property   now this *power,*
which every man has *in the ftate of nature*, and
which he parts with to the fociety in all fuch cafes
where the fociety can fecure him, is to ufe fuch
means,

means, for the preferving of his own property, as he thinks good, and nature allows him, and to punifh the breach of the law of nature in others, fo as (according to the beft of his reafon) may moft conduce to the prefervation of himfelf, and the reft of mankind. So that the *end and meafure of this power,* when in every man's hands in the ftate of nature, being the prefervation of all his fociety, that is, all mankind in general, it can have no other *end or meafure,* when in the hands of the magiftrate, but to preferve the members of that fociety in their lives, liberties, and poffeffions, and fo cannot be an abfolute, arbitrary power over their lives and fortunes, which are as much as poffible to be preferved; but a *power to make laws,* and annex fuch *penalties* to them, as may tend to the prefervation of the whole, by cutting off thofe parts, and and thofe only, which are fo corrupt, that they threaten the found and healthy, without which no feverity is lawful. And this *power has its original only from compact* and agreement, and the mutual confent of thofe who make up the community.

§. 172. *Thirdly Defpotical power* is an abfolute, arbitrary power one man has over another, to take away his life, whenever he pleafes. This is a power, which neither nature gives, for it has made no fuch diftinction between one man and another; nor compact can convey for man not having fuch an arbitrary power over his own life, cannot give another man fuch a power over it; but it is the *effect only of forfeiture,* which the aggreffor makes of his own life, when he puts himfelf into the ftate of war with another. for having quitted reafon, which God hath given to be the rule betwixt man and man, and the common bond whereby human kind is united into one

fellowfhip

fellowſhip and ſociety, and having renounced the
way of peace which that teaches, and made uſe
of the force of war, to compaſs his unjuſt ends
upon another, where he has no right; and ſo re-
volting from his own kind to that of beaſts, by
making force, which is their's, to be his rule of
right, he renders himſelf liable to be deſtroyed
by the injured perſon, and the reſt of mankind,
that will join with him in the execution of juſtice, as any other wild beaſt, or noxious brute,
with whom mankind can have neither ſociety nor
ſecurity * And thus *captives*, taken in a juſt and
lawful war, and ſuch only, are *ſubject to a deſpotical power*, which, as it ariſes not from compact,
ſo neither is it capable of any, but is the ſtate of
war continued for what compact can be made
with a man that is not maſter of his own life?
what condition can he perform? and if he be
once allowed to be maſter of his own life, the
deſpotical, arbitrary power of his maſter ceaſes.
He that is maſter of himſelf, and his own life, has
a right too to the means of preſerving it, ſo that
as ſoon as compact enters, ſlavery ceaſes, and he ſo
far quits his abſolute power, and puts an end to
the ſtate of war, who enters into conditions with
his captive.

§ 173. *Nature gives* the firſt of theſe, *viz.
paternal power to parents* for the benefit of their
children during their minority, to ſupply their
want of ability, and underſtanding how to manage their property (By *property* I muſt be underſtood here, as in other places, to mean that
property which men have in their perſons as well
as goods.) *Voluntary agreement gives* the ſecond,
viz.

---

* A other copy corrected by Mr Locke, has it thus,.
Noxious brute that is deſtructive to their being

viz *political power to governors* for the benefit of their fubjects, to fecure them in the poffeffion and ufe of their properties And *forfeiture gives* the third *defpotical power to lords* for their own benefit, over thofe who are ftript of all property.

§ 174 He, that fhall confider the diftinct rife and extent, and the different ends of thefe feveral powers, will plainly fee, that *paternal power* comes as far fhort of that of the *magiftrate*, as *defpotical* exceeds it; and that *abfolute dominion*, however placed, is fo far from being one kind of civil fociety, that it is as inconfiftent with it, as flavery is with property *Paternal power* is only where minority makes the child incapable to manage his property; *political*, where men have property in their own difpofal; and *defpotical*, over fuch as have no property at ll

---

CHAP. XVI.

Of CONQUEST.

§ 175 THough governments can originally have no other rife than that before mentioned, nor *polities be founded on* any thing but *the confent of the people*, yet fuch have been the diforders ambition has filled the world with, that in the noife of war, which makes fo great a part of the hiftory of mankind, *this confent is* little taken notice of and therefore many have miftaken the force of arms for the confent of the people, and reckon conqueft as one of the originals of government. But *conqueft* is as far from fetting up any government, as demolifhing an houfe is from building a new one in the place. Indeed, it often makes way for a new frame of

a common-a common-wealth, by deftroying the former, but, without the confent of the people, can never erect a new one

§ 176 That the *aggreffor*, who puts himfelf into the ftate of war with another, and *unjuftly invades* another man's right, *can*, by fuch unjuft war, *never* come to *have a right over the conquered*, will be eafily agreed by all men, who will not think, that robbers and pyrates have a right of empire over whomfoever they have force enough to mafter; or that men are bound by promifes, which unlawful force extorts from them Should a robber break into my houfe, and with a dagger at my throat make me feal deeds to convey my eftate to him, would th s give him any title? Juft fuch a title, by his fword, has an *unjuft conqueror*, who forces me into fubmiffion The injury and the crime is equal, whether committed by the wearer of a crown, or fome petty villain. The title of the offender, and the number of his followers, make no difference in the offence, unlefs it be to aggravate it. The only difference is, great robbers punifh little ones to keep them in their obedience, but the great ones are rewarded with laurels and triumphs, becaufe they are too big for the weak hands of juftice in this world, and have the power in their own poffeffion, which fhould punifh offenders. What is my remedy againft a robber, that fo broke into my houfe? *Appeal* to the law for juftice But perhaps juftice is denied, or I am crippled and cannot ftir, robbed and have not the means to do it. If God has taken away all means of feeking remedy, there is nothing left but patience But my fon, when able, may feek the relief of the law, which I am denied. he or his fon may renew his *appeal*, till he recover his right But the

conquered,

conquered, or their children, have no court, no arbitrator on earth to appeal to Then they may *appeal*, as *Jephtha* did, *to heaven*, and repeat their *appeal* till they have recover the native right of their anceftors, which was, to have fuch a legiflative over them, as the majority fhould approve, and freely acquiefce in If it be objected, This would caufe endlefs trouble , I anfwer, no more than juftice does, where fhe lies open to all that appeal to her. He that troubles his neighbour without a caufe, is punifhed for it by the juftice of the court he appeals to and he that *appeals to heaven* muft be fure he has right on his fide ; and a right too that is worth the trouble and coft of the appeal, as he will anfwer at a tribunal that cannot be deceived, and will be fure to retribute to every one according to the mifchiefs he hath created to his fellow fubjects; that is, any part of mankind · from whence it is plain, that he that *conquers in an unjuft war can thereby have no title to the fubjection and obedience of the conquered*

§. 177 But fuppofing victory favours the right fide, let us confider a *conqueror in a lawful war*, and fee what power he gets, and over whom

Firft, It is plain he *gets no power by his conqueft over thofe that conquered with him* They that fought on his fide cannot fuffer by the conqueft, but muft at leaft be as much freemen as they were before And moft commonly they ferve upon terms, and on condition to fhare with their leader, and enjoy a part of the fpoil, and other advantages that attend the conquering fword , or at leaft have a part of the fubdued country beftowed upon them. And *the conquering people are not*, I hope, *to be flaves by conqueft*, and wear their laurels only to fhew they are facrifices to

their

their leaders triumph. They that found abfolute monarchy upon the title of the fword, make their heroes, who are the founders of fuch monarchies, arrant *Draw can-firs*, and forget they had any officers and foldiers that fought on their fide in the battles they won, or affifted them in the fubduing, or, fhared in poffeffing, the countries they maftered. We are told by fome, that the *Englifh* monarchy is founded in the *Norman* conqueft, and that our princes have thereby a title to abfolute dominion. which if it were true, (as by hiftory it appears otherwife) and that *William* had a right to make war on this ifland, yet his dominion by conqueft could reach no farther than to the *Saxons* and *Britons*, that were then inhabitants of this country The *Normans* that came with him, and helped to conquer, and all defcended frcm them, are freemen, and no fubjects by conqueft ; let that give what dominion it will And if I, or any body elfe, fhall claim freedom, as derived from them, it will be very hard to prove the contrary : and it is plain, the law, that has made no diftinction between the one and the other, intends not there fhould be any difference in their freedom or privileges

§. 178. But fuppofing, which feldom happens, that the conquerors and conquered never incorporate into one people, under the fame laws and freedom ; let us fee next *what power a lawful conqueror has over the fubdued ·* and that I fay is purely defpotical He has an abfolute power over the lives of thofe who by an unjuft war have forfeited them, but not over the lives or fortunes of thofe who engaged not in the war, nor over the poffeffions even of thofe who were actually engaged in it.

§. 179.

§ 179. *Secondly*, I say then the *conqueror* gets no power but only over those who have actually affifted, concurred, or confented to that unjuft force that is ufed againft him. for the people having given to their governors no power to do an unjuft thing, fuch as is to make an unjuft war, (for they never had fuch a power in themfelves) they ought not to be charged as guilty of the violence and unjuftice that is committed in an unjuft war, any farther than they actually abet it; no more than they are to be thought guilty of any violence or oppreffion their governors fhould ufe upon the people themfelves, or any part of their fellow fubjects, they having impowered them no more to the one than to the other Conquerors, it is true, feldom trouble themfelves to make the diftinction, but they willingly permit the confufion of war to fweep all together but yet this alters not the right; for the conquerors power over the lives of the conquered, being only becaufe they have ufed force to do, or maintain an injuftice, he can have that power only over thofe who have concurred in that force; all the reft are innocent; and he has no more title over the people of that country, who have done him no injury, and fo have made no forfeiture of their lives, than he has over any other, who, without any injuries or provocations, have lived upon fair terms with him

§ 180 *Thirdly*, The *power a conqueror gets over thofe he overcomes in a juft war, is perfectly defpotical* he has an abfolute power over the lives of thofe, who, by putting themfelves in a ftate of war, have forfeited them; but he has not thereby a right and title to their poffeffions. This I doubt not, but at firft fight will feem a ftrange doctrine, it being fo quite contrary to
the

the practice of the world, there being nothing more familiar in speaking of the dominion of countries, than to say such an one conquered it ; as if conquest, without any more ado, conveyed a right of possession But when we consider, that the practice of the strong and powerful, how universal soever it may be, is seldom the rule of right, however it be one part of the subjection of the conquered, not to argue against the conditions cut out to them by the conquering sword.

§ 181. Though in all war there be usually a complication of force and damage, and the ag-gressor seldom fails to harm the estate, when he uses force against the persons of those he makes war upon , yet it is the use of force only that puts a man into the state of war for whether by force he begins the injury, or else having quietly, and by fraud, done the injury, he refuses to make re-paration, ard by force maintains it, (which is the same thing, as at first to have done it by force) it is the unjust use of force that makes the war for he that breaks open my house, and violently turns me out of doors , or having peaceably got in, by force keeps me out, does in effect the same thing , supposing we are in such a state, that we have no common judge on earth, whom I may appeal to, and to whom we are both obliged to submit for of such I am now speaking. It is the *unjust use of force* then, that *puts a man into the state of war* with another , ard thereby he that is guilty of it makes a forfeiture of his life for quitting reason, which is the rule given between man and man, and using force, the way of beasts, he becomes liable to be destroyed by him he uses force against, as any savage ravenous beast, that is dangerous to his being

§. 182

§ 182. But becaufe the mifcarriages of the father are no faults of the children, and they may
be rational and peaceable, notwithftanding the
brutifhnefs and injuftice of the father; the father, by his mifcarriages and violence, can forfeit
but his own life, but involves not his children in
his guilt or deftruction His goods, which nature, that willeth the prefervation of all mankind
as much as is poffible, hath made to belong to the
children to keep them from perifhing, do ftill
continue to belong to his children for fuppofing
them not to have joined in the war, either thro'
infancy, abfence, or choice, they have done nothing to forfeit them: *nor has the conqueror any
right* to take them away, by the bare title of having fubdued him that by force attempted his deftruction; though perhaps he may have fome
right to them, to repair the damages he has fuftained by the war, and the defence of his own
right, which how far it reaches to the poffeffions
of the conquered, we fhall fee by and by. So
that he that *by conqueft has a right over a man's
perfon* to deftroy him if he pleafes, has *not* thereby a right over *his eftate* to poffefs and enjoy it:
for it is the brutal force the aggreffor has ufed,
that gives his adverfary a right to take away his
life, and deftroy him if he pleafes, as a noxious
creature; but it is damage fuftained that alone
gives him title to another man's goods · for
though I may kill a thief that fets on me in the
highway, yet I may not (which feems lefs) take
away his money, and let him go · this would be
robbery on my fide His force, and the ftate of
war he put himfelf in, made him forfeit his life,
but gave me no title to his goods. The *right
then of conqueft extends only to the lives* of thofe
who joined in the war, *not to their eftates,* but
only

only in order to make reparation for the damages received, and the charges of the war, and that too with refervation of the right of the innocent wife and children.

§. 183 Let the *conqueror* have as much juftice on his fide, as could be fuppofed, he *has* no *right* to feize more than the vanquifhed could forfeit : his life is at the victor's mercy ; and his fervice and goods he may appropriate, to make himfelf reparation ; but he cannot take the goods of his wife and children, they too had a title to the goods he enjoyed, and their fhares in the eftate he poffeffed . for example, I in the ftate of nature (and all common-wealths are in the ftate of nature one with another) have injured another man, and refufing to give fatisfaction, it comes to a ftate of war, wherein my defending by force what I had gotten unjuftly, makes me the aggreffor I am conquered : my life, it is true, as forfeit, is at mercy, but not my wife's and children's. They made not the war, nor affifted in it I could not forfeit their lives, they were not mine to forfeit My wife had a fhare in my eftate, that neither could I forfeit And my children alfo, being born of me, had a right to be maintained out of my labour or fubftance Here then is the cafe the conqueror has a title to reparation for damages received, and the children have a title to their father's eftate for their fubfiftence for as to the wife's fhare, whether her own labour, or compact, gave her a title to it, it is plain, her hufbard could not forfeit what was her's What muft be done in the cafe ? I anfwer ; the fundamental law of nature being, that all, as much as may be, fhould be preferved, it follows, that if there be not enough fully to fatisfy both, viz. for the *conqueror's loffes*, and

children's

childien's maintenance, he that hath, and to
fpare, muſt remit fomething of his full ſatisfac-
tion, and give way to the preſſing and preferable
title of thoſe who are in danger to periſh without it

§ 184. But ſuppoſing the *charge* and *damages
of the war* are to be made up to the conqueror, to the utmoſt farthing; and that the
children of the vanquiſhed, ſpoiled of all their
father's goods, are to be left to ſtarve and periſh;
yet the ſatisfying of what ſhall, on this ſcore,
be due to the conqueror, will ſcarce give him a
title to any country he ſhall conquer for the damages of war can ſcarce amount to the value of any
conſiderable tract of land, in any part of the
world, where all the land is poſſeſſed, and none
lies waſte And if I have not taken away the
conqueror's land, which, being vanquiſhed, it is
impoſſible I ſhould; ſcarce any other ſpoil I have
done him can amount to the value of mine, ſuppoſing it equally cultivated, and of an extent any
way coming near what I had over-run of his.
The deſtruction of a year's product or two (for
it ſeldom reaches four or five) is the utmoſt ſpoil
that uſually can be done for as to money, and
ſuch riches and treaſure taken away, theſe are
none of nature's goods, they have but a fantaſti-
cal imaginary value: nature has put no ſuch upon
them they are of no more account by her ſtan-
dard, than the wampompeke of the *Americans*
to an *European* prince, or the ſilver money of
Europe would have been formerly to an *American.*
And five years product is not worth the perpetual
inheritance, of land, where all is poſſeſſed, and
none remains waſte, to be taken up by him that
is diſſeized · which will be eaſily granted, if one
do but take away the imaginary value of money,

.O

the

the difproportion being more than between five and five hundred, though, at the fame time, half a year's product is more worth than the inheritance, where there being more land than the inhabitants poffefs and make ufe of, any one has liberty to make ufe of the wafte but thefe conquerors take little care to poffefs themfelves of the *lands of the vanquifhed* No damage therefore, that men in the ftate of nature (as all princes and governments are in reference to one another) fuffer from one another, can give a conqueror power to difpoffefs the pofterity of the vanquifhed, and turn them out of that inheritance, which ought to be the poffeffion of them and their defcendants to all generations The conqueror indeed will be apt to think himfelf mafter and it is the very condition of the fubdued not to be able to difpute their right But if that be all, it gives no other title than what bare force gives to the ftronger over the weaker · and, by this reafon, he that is ftrongeft will have a right to whatever he pleafes to feize on

§ 185 Over thofe then that joined with him in the war, and over thofe of the fubdued country that oppofed him not, and the pofterity even of thofe that did, the conqueror, even in a juft war, hath, by his conqueft, no *right of dominion* they are free from any fubjection to him, and if their former government be diffolved, they are at liberty to begin and erect another to themfelves

§ 186 The conqueror, it is true, ufually, by the force he has over them, compels them, with a fword at their breafts, to ftoop to his conditions, and fubmit to fuch a government as he pleafes to afford them, but the inquiry is, what right he has to do fo? If it be faid, they fubmit by their own confent, then *l* is allows their own *confent* to be *neceffary to give the conqueror a title to*

rule

rule over them It remains only to be considered, whether *promises extorted by force*, without right, can be thought consent, and *how far they bind* To which I shall say, they *bind not at all*; because whatsoever another gets from me by force, I still retain the right of, and he is obliged presently to restore He that forces my horse from me, ought presently to restore him, and I have still a right to retake him By the same reason, he that *forced a promise* from me, ought presently to restore it, *i e* quit me of the obligation of it , or I may resume it myself, *i e* chuse whether I will perform it for the law of nature laying an obligation on me only by the rules she prescribes, cannot oblige me by the violation of her rules such is the extorting any thing from me by force Nor does it at all alter the case to say, *I gave my promise*, no more than it excuses the force, and passes the right, when I put my hand in my pocket, and deliver my purse myself to a thief, who demands it with a pistol at my breast.

§ 187. From all which it follows, that the *government of a conqueror*, imposed by force on the subdued, against whom he had no right of war, or who joined not in the war against him, where he had right, *has no obligation* upon them

§ 188 But let us suppose, that all the men of that community, being all members of the same body politic, may be taken to have joined in that unjust war wherein they are subdued, and so their lives are at the mercy of the conqueror

§ 189 I say, this concerns not their children who are in their minority for since a father hath not, in himself, a power over the life or liberty of his child, no act of his can possibly forfeit it So that the children, whatever may have happened to the fathers, are freemen, and the absolute

O 2   power

power of the *conqueror* reaches no farther than the persons of the men that were subdued by him, and dies with them and should he govern them as slaves, subjected to his absolute arbitrary power, he *has* no *such right of dominion over their children* He can have no power over them but by their own consent, whatever he may drive them to say or do ; and he has no lawful authority, whilst force, and not choice, compels them to submission.

§ 190 Every man is born with a double right. *first,* a *right of freedom to his person,* which no other man has a power over, but the free disposal of it lies in himself Secondly, a *right,* before any other man, *to inherit* with his brethren his *father's goods.*

§. 191 By the first of these, a man is *naturally free* from subjection to any government, tho' he be born in a place under its jurisdiction , but if he disclaim the lawful government of the country he was born in, he must also quit the right that belonged to him by the laws of it, and the possessessions there descending to him from his ancestors, if it were a government made by their consent

§ 192 By the second, the *inhabitants* of any country, who are descended, and derive a title to their estates from those who are subdued, and had a government forced upon them against their free consents, *retain a right to the possession of their ancestors,* though they consent not freely to the government, whose hard conditions were by force imposed on the possessors of that country . for the first *conqueror never having had a title to the land* of that country, the people who are the descendants of, or claim under those who were forced to submit to the yoke of a government by constraint, ftraint, have always a right to fhake it off, and free themfelves from the ufurpation or tyranny which the fword hath brought in upon them, till their rulers put them under fuch a frame of government as they willingly and of choice confent' to Who doubts but the Grecian chriftians, defcendants of the antient poffeffors of that country, may juftly caft off the Turkifh yoke, which they have fo long groaned under, whenever they have an opportunity to do it? For no government can have a right to obedience from a people who have not freely confented to it, which they can never be fuppofed to do, till either they are put in a full ftate of liberty to chufe their government and governors, or at leaft till they have fuch ftanding laws, to which they have by themfelves or their reprefentatives given their free confent, and alfo till they are allowed their due property, which is fo to be proprietors of what they have, that no body can take away any part of it without their own confent, without which, men under any government are not in the ftate of freemen, but are direct flaves under the force of war.

§. 193. But granting that the *conqueror* in a juft war has a right to the eftates, as well as power over the perfons of the conquered; which, it is plain, he *hath* not nothing of *abfolute power* will follow from hence, in the continuance of the government, becaufe the defcendants of thefe being all freemen, if he grants them eftates and poffeffions to inhabit his country, (without which it would be worth nothing) whatfoever he grants them, they have, fo far as it is granted, *property* in. The nature whereof is, that *without a man's own confent* it *cannot be taken from him.*

§. 194.

§ 194 Their *perfons* are *free* by a native
right, and their *properties*, be they more or lefs,
are *their own, and at their own difpofe*, and not
at his ; or elfe it is no *property* Suppofing the
conqueror gives to one man a thoufand acres, to
him and his heirs for ever , to another he lets
a thoufand acres for his life, under the rent of 50 l.
or 500 l *per ann* has not the one of thefe a right
to his thoufand acres for ever, and the other, during his life, paying the faid rent ? and hath not
the tenant for life a *property* in all that he gets
over and above his rent, by his labour and induftry during the faid term, fuppofing it be double
the rent ? Can any one fay, the king, or conqueror, after his grant, may by his power of conqueror take away all, or part of the land from
the heirs of one, or from the other during his life,
he paying the rent ? or can he take away from
either the goods or money they have got upon the
faid land, at his pleafure ? If he can, then all free
and voluntary *contracts* ceafe, and are void in the
world ; there needs nothing to diffolve them at
any time, but power enough . and all the *grants*
and *promifes* of *men in power* are but mockery and
collufion . for can there be any thing more ridiculous than to fay, I give you and your's this for
ever, and that in the fureft and moft folemn way
of conveyance that can be devifed ; and yet it is
to be underftood, that I have right, if I pleafe,
to take it away from you again to morrow ?

§. 195. I will not difpute now whether princes are exempt from the laws of their country ,
but this I am fure, they owe fubjection to the
laws of God and nature No body, no power, can
exempt them from the obligations of that eternal
law. Thofe are fo great, and fo ftrong, in the cafe
of *promifes*, that omnipotency itfelf can be tied by
them,

them *Grants, promises,* and *oaths,* are *bonds* that hold the Almighty whatever some flatterers say to princes of the world, who all together, with all their people joined to them, are, in comparison of the great God, but as a drop of the bucket, or a dust on the balance, inconsiderable, nothing'

§ 196 The short of the *case in conquest* is this: the conqueror, if he have a just cause, has a despotical right over the persons of all, that actually aided, and concurred in the war against him, and a right to make up his damage and cost out of their labour and estates, so he injure not the right of any other Over the rest of the people, if there were any that consented not to the war, and over the children of the captives themselves, or the possessions of either, he has no power, and so can have, *by virtue of conquest, no lawful title* himself *to dominion* over them, or derive it to his posterity, but is an aggressor, if he attempts upon their properties, and thereby puts himself in a state of war against them, and has no better a right of principality, he, nor any of his successors, than *Hingar,* or *Hubba,* the Danes, had here in *England;* or *Spartacus,* had he conquered *Italy,* would have had; which is to have their yoke cast off, as soon as God shall give those under their subjection courage and opportunity to do it Thus, notwithstanding whatever title the kings of *Assyria* had over *Judah,* by the sword, God assisted *Hezekiah,* to throw off the dominion of that conquering empire *And the Lord was with Hezekiah, and he prospered; wherefore he went forth, and he rebelled against the king of Assyria, and served him not,* 2 Kings xviii. 7 Whence it is plain, that shaking off a power, which force, and not right, hath set over any one, though it hath the name of *rebellion,* yet is no offence be-

for

fore God, but is that which he allows and coun-
tenances, though even promises and covenants,
when obtained by force, have intervened   for it is
very probable, to any one that reads the story
of *Ahaz* and *Hezekiah* attentively, that the *Af-*
fyrians fubdued *Ahaz*, and depofed him, and made
Hezekiah king in his father's life-time , and that
Hezekiah by agreement had done him homage,
and paid him tribute all this time.

CHAP XVII.

Of USURPATION.

§ 197 AS conqueft may be called a foreign
ufurpation, fo ufurpation is a kind
of domeftic conqueft, with this difference, that
an ufurper can never have right on his fide, it
being no *ufurpation*, but where one has got into
the *poffeffion of what another has right to*. This,
fo far as it is *ufurpation*, is a change only of perfons, but not of the forms and rules of the government   for if the ufurper extend his power
beyond what of right belonged to the lawful
princes, or governors of the common-wealth, it
is *tyranny* added to *ufurpation*

§ 198 In all lawful governments, the defignation of the perfons, who are to bear rule, is as
natural and neceffary a part as the form of the
government itfelf, and is that which had its
eftablifhment originally from the people ; the
anarchy being much alike, to have no form of
government at all , or to agree, that it fhall be
monarchical, but to appoint no way to defign the
perfon that fhall have the power, and be the
monarch   Hence all common-wealths, with the
form of government eftablifhed, have rules alfo
of appointing thofe who are to have any fhare in
the

the public authority, and fettled methods of conveying the right to them: for the anarchy is much alike, to have no form of government at all; or to agree that it fhall be monarchical, but to appoint no way to know or defign the perfon that fhall have the power, and be the monarch. Whoever gets into the exercife of any part of the power, by other ways than what the laws of the community have prefcribed, hath no right to be obeyed, though the form of the commonwealth be ftill preferved; fince he is not the perfon the laws have appointed, and confequently not the perfon the people have confented to. Nor can fuch an *ufurper*, or any deriving from him, ever have a title, till the people are both at liberty to confent, and have actually confented to allow, and confirm in him the power he hath till then ufurped.

CHAP. XVIII.

Of TYRANNY.

§. 199. AS ufurpation is the exercife of power, which another hath a right to, fo *tyranny is the exercife of power beyond right,* which no body can have a right to And this is making ufe of the power any one has in his hands, not for the good of thofe who are under it, but for his own private feparate advantage. When the governor, however intitled, makes not the law, but his will, the rule; and his commands and actions are not directed to the prefervation of the properties of his people, but the fatisfaction of his own ambition, revenge, covetoufnefs, or any other irregular paffion

§ 200 If one can doubt this to be truth, or reafon, becaufe it comes from the obfcure hand

of

of a subject, I hope the authority of a king will make it pass with him. King *James* the first, in his speech to the parliament, 1603, tells them thus, *I will ever prefer the weal of the public, and of the whole common-wealth, in making of good laws and constitutions, to any particular and private ends of mine, thinking ever the wealth and weal of the commonwealth to be my greatest weal and worldly felicity; a point wherein a lawful king doth directly differ from a tyrant for I do acknowledge, that the special and greatest point of difference that is between a rightful king and an usurping tyrant, is this, that whereas the proud and ambitious tyrant doth think his kingdom and people are only ordained for satisfaction of his desires and unreasonable appetites, the righteous and just king doth by the contrary acknowledge himself to be ordained for the procuring of the wealth and property of his people.* And again, in his speech to the parliament, 1609, he hath these words, *The king binds himself by a double oath, to the observation of the fundamental laws of his kingdom; tacitly, as by being a king, and so bound to protect as well the people, as the laws of his kingdom, and expresly, by his oath at his coronation, so as every just king, in a settled kingdom, is bound to observe that paction made to his people, by his laws, in framing his government agreeable thereunto, according to that paction which God made with* Noah, *after the deluge Hereafter, seed-time and harvest, and cold and heat, and summer and winter, and day and night, shall not cease while the earth remaineth And therefore a king governing in a settled kingdom, leaves to be a king, and degenerates into a tyrant, as soon as he leaves off to rule according to his laws* And a little after, *Therefore all kings that are not tyrants, or perjured, will be glad*

*to bound themselves within the limits of their laws ;
and they that perfuade them the contrary, are vipers,
and pefts both againft them and the commonwealth.*
Thus that learned king, who well underftood the
notion of things, makes the difference betwixt a
king and a *tyrant* to confift only in this, that one
makes the laws the bounds of his power, and the
good of the public, the end of his government ;
the other makes all give way to his own will and
appetite.

§ 201 It is a miftake, to think this fault is
proper only to monarchies, other forms of government are liable to it, as well as that for
wherever the power, that is put in any hands for
the government of the people, and the prefervation of their properties, is applied to other
ends, and made ufe of to impoverifh, haraf, or
fubdue them to the arbitrary and irregular commands of thofe that have it , there it prefently
becomes *tyranny*, whether thofe that thus ufe it are
one or many. Thus we read of the thirty tyrants
at *Athens*, as well as one at *Syracufe*, and the intolerable dominion of the *Decemviri* at *Rome* was
nothing better.

§ 202 *Where-ever law ends, tyranny begins*, if
the law be tranfgreffed to another's harm, and
whofoever in authority exceeds the power given
him by law, and makes ufe of the force he has
under his command, to compafs that upon the
fubject, which the law allows not, ceafes in that
to be a magiftrate , and, acting without authority,
may be oppofed, as any other man, who by force
invades the right of another   This is acknowledged in fubordinate magiftrates   He that hath
authority to feize my perfon in the ftreet, may
be oppofed as a thief, and a robber, if he endeavours to break into my houfe to execute a
writ,

writ, notwithstanding that I know he has such a
warrant, and such a legal authority, as will impower him to arrest me abroad. And why this
should not hold in the highest, as well as in the
most inferior magistrate, I would gladly be in-
formed Is it reasonable, that the eldest brother,
because he has the greatest part of his father's
estate, should thereby have a right to take away
any of his younger brothers portions? or that a
rich man, who possessed a whole country, should
from thence have a right to seize, when he
pleased, the cottage and garden of his poor
neighbour? The being rightfully possessed of
great power and riches, exceedingly beyond the
greatest part of the sons of *Adam*, is so far from
being an excuse, much less a reason, for rapine
and oppression, which the endamaging another
without authority is, that it is a great aggravation
of it. for the exceeding the bounds of authority
is no more a right in a great, than in a petty
officer, no more justifiable in a king than a con-
stable, but is so much the worse in him, in that
he has more trust put in him, has already a much
greater share than the rest of his brethren, and is
supposed, from the advantages of his education,
employment, and counsellors, to be more knowing in the measures of right and wrong

§ 203 May the *command's* then *of a prince be
opposed?* may he be resisted as often as any one
shall find himself aggrieved, and but imagine he
has not right done him? This will unhinge and
overturn all polities, and, instead of government
and order, leave nothing but anarchy and confusion

§ 204 To this I answer, that *force* is to be
opposed to nothing, but to unjust and unlawful
force; whoever makes any opposition in any other
case,

cafe, draws on himfelf a juft condemnation both from God and man, and fo no fuch danger or confufion will follow, as is often fuggefted. for,

§. 205. *Firft*, As, in fome countries, the perfon of the prince by the law is facred, and fo, whatever he commands or does, his perfon is ftill free from all queftion or violence, not liable to force, or any judicial cenfure or condemnation But yet oppofition may be made to the illegal acts of any inferior officer, or other commiffioned by him; unlefs he will, by actually putting himfelf into a ftate of war with his people, diffolve the government, and leave them to that defence which belongs to every one in the ftate of nature · for of fuch things who can tell what the end will be ? and a neighbour kingdom has fhewed the world an odd example. In all other cafes the *facrednefs* of the *perfon exempts him from all inconveniencies*, whereby he is fecure, whilft the government ftands, from all violence and harm whatfoever, than which there cannot be a wifer conftitution for the harm he can do in his own perfon not being likely to happen often, nor to extend itfelf far; nor being able by his fingle ftrength to fubvert the laws, nor opprefs the body of the people, fhould any prince have fo much weaknefs, and ill nature as to be willing to do it, the inconveniency of fome particular mifchiefs, that may happen fometimes, when a heady prince comes to the throne, are well recompenfed by the peace of the public, and fecurity of the government, in the perfon of the chief magiftrate, thus fet out of the reach of danger it being fafer for the body, that fome few private men fhould be fometimes in danger to fuffer, than

that

that the head of the republic fhould be eafily, and upon flight occafions, expofed

§ 206. *Secondly,* But this privilege, belonging only to the king's perfon, hinders not, but they may be queftioned, oppofed, and refifted, who ufe unjuft force, though they pretend a commiffion from him, which the law authorizes not, as is plain in the cafe of him that has the king's writ to arreft a man, which is a full commiffion from the king; and yet he that has it cannot break open a man's houfe to do it, nor execute this command of the king upon certain days, nor in certain places, though this commiffion have no fuch exception in it, but they are the limitations of the law, which if any one tranfgrefs, the king's commiffion excufes him not for the king's authority being given him only by the law, he cannot impower any one to act againft the law, or juftify him, by his commiffion, in fo doing; the *commiffion,* or *command of any magiftrate, where he has no authority,* being as *void* and infignificant, as that of any private man, the difference between the one and the other, being that the magiftrate has fome authority fo far, and to fuch ends, and the private man has none at all. for it is not the *commiffion,* but the *authority,* that gives the right of acting · and *againft the laws there can be no authority* But, notwithftanding fuch refiftance, the king's perfon and authority are ftill both fecured, and fo *no danger to governor or government.*

§ 207 *Thirdly,* Suppofing a government wherein the perfon of the chief magiftrate is not thus facred; yet this *doctrine* of the lawfulnefs of *refifting* all unlawful exercifes of his power, *will not upon every flight occafion irdanger* him, *or imbroil the government* for where the injured party

party may be relieved, and his damages repaired by appeal to the law, there can be no pretence for force, which is only to be ufed where a man is intercepted from appealing to the law : for nothing is to be accounted hoftile force, but where it leaves not the remedy of fuch an appeal; and it is fuch *force* alone, that *puts* him that ufes it *into a ftate of war*, and makes it lawful to refift him. A man with a fword in his hand demands my purfe in the high-way, when perhaps I have not twelve pence in my pocket. this man I may lawfully kill. To another I deliver 100l. to hold only whilft I alight, which he refufes to reftore me, when I am got up again, but draws his fword to defend the poffeffion of it by force, if I endeavour to retake it. The mifchief this man does me is a hundred, or poffibly a thoufand times more than the other perhaps intended me (whom I killed before he really did me any), and yet I might lawfully kill the one, and cannot fo much as hurt the other lawfully. The reafon whereof is plain; becaufe the one ufing *force*, which threatned my life, I could not have *time to appeal* to the law to fecure it. and when it was gore, it was too late to appeal. The law could not reftore life to my dead carcafs the lofs was irreparable, which to prevent, the law of nature gave me a right to *deftroy* him, who had put himfelf into a ftate of war with me, and threatned my deftruction. But in the other cafe, my life not being in danger, I may have the *benefit of appealing* to the law, and have reparation for my 100l that way

§. 208 *Fourthly*, But if the unlawful acts done by the magiftrate be maintained (by the power he has got), and the remedy which is due by law, be by the fame power obftructed, yet the *right of refifting*, even in fuch manifeft acts of tyranny, *will not* fuddenly, or on flight occafions, *difturb the government :* for if it reach no farther than fome private men's cafes, though they have a right to defend themfelves, and to recover by force what by unlawful force is taken from them; yet the right to do fo will not eafily engage them in a conteft, wherein they are fure to perifh; it being as impoffible for one, or a few oppreffed men to *difturb the government*, where the body of the people do not think themfelves concerned in it, as for a raving mad-man, or heady mal content to overturn a well-fettled ftate; the people being as little apt to follow the one, as the other.

§ 209. But if either thefe illegal acts have extended to the majority of the people, or if the mifchief and oppreffion has lighted only on fome few, but in fuch cafes, as the precedent, and confequences feem to threaten all; and they are perfuaded in their confciences, that their laws, and with them their eftates, liberties, and lives are in danger, and perhaps their religion too; how they will be hindered from refifting illegal force, ufed againft them, I cannot tell   This is an *inconvenience*, I confefs, *that attends all governments* whatfoever, when the governors have brought it to this pafs, to be generally fufpected of their people, the moft dangerous ftate which they can poffibly put themfelves in; wherein they are the lefs to be pitied, becaufe it is fo eafy to be avoided; it being as impoffible for a governor, if he really means the good of his people, and the prefervation of them, and their laws together, not to make them fee and feel it, as it is for the father of a family, not to let his children fee he loves, and takes care of them

§ 210.

§. 210. But if all the world shall obferve pretences of one kind, and actions of another; arts ufed to elude the law, and the truft of prerogative (which is an arbitrary power in fome things left in the prince's hand to do good, not harm to the people) employed contrary to the end for which it was given. if the people fhall find the minifters and fubordinate magiftrates chofen fuitable to fuch ends, and favoured, or laid by, proportionably as they promote or oppofe them. if they fee feveral experiments made of arbitrary power, and that religion underhand favoured, (though publicly proclaimed againft) which is readieft to introduce it, and the operators in it fupported, as much as may be, and when that cannot be done, yet approved ftill, and liked the better: if a *long train of actions fhew the councils* all tending that way; how can a man any more hinder himfelf from being perfuaded in his own mind, which way things are going, or from cafting about how to fave himfelf, than he could from believing the captain of the fhip he was in, was carrying him, and the reft of the company, to *Algiers*, when he found him always fteering that courfe, though crofs winds, leaks in his fhip, and want of men and provifions did often force him to turn his courfe another way for fome time, which he fteadily returned to again, as foon as the wind, weather, and other circumftances would let him?

CHAP.

CHAP. XIX

Of the Diffolution of Government.

§. 211 HE that will with any clearnefs fpeak
of the *diffolution of government*,
ought in the firft place to diftinguifh between the
diffolution of the fociety and the *diffolution of the government* That which makes the community,
and brings men out of the loofe ftate of nature,
into *one politi. fociety*, is the agreement which
every one has with the reft to incorporate, and
act as one body, and fo be one diftinct common-
wealth. The ufual, and almoft only way
whereby *this union is diffolved*, is the inroad of
foreign force making a conqueft upon them · for
in that cafe, (not being able to maintain and fupport themfelves, as *one intire* and *independent body*) the union belonging to that body which con-
fifted therein, muft neceffarily ceafe, and fo every
one return to the ftate he was in before, with a
liberty to fhift for himfelf, and provide for his
own fafety, as he thinks fit, in fome other
fociety. Whenever the *fociety is diffolved*, it is
certain the government of that fociety cannot
remain. Thus conquerors fwords often cut up
governments by the roots, and mangle focieties
to pieces, feparating the fubdued or fcattered
multitude from the protection of, and dependence
on, that fociety which ought to have preferved
them from violence The world is too well inftructed in, and too forward to allow of, this
way of diffolving governments, to need any more
to be faid of it ; and there wants not much argument to prove, that where the *fociety is diffolved,*

folved, the government cannot remain , that being as impoffible, as for the frame of an houfe to
fubfift when the materials of it are fcattered and
diffipated by a whirl-wind, or jumbled into a
confufed heap by an earth-quake.

§. 212 Befides this over-turning from without, *governments are diffolved from within*,

Firft, When the *legiflative* is *altered* Civil
fociety being a ftate of peace, amorgft thofe
who are of it, from whom the ftate of war is
excluded by the umpirage, which they have provided in their legiflative, for the ending all
differences that may arife amongft any of them,
it is in their *legiflative*, that the members of a
common-wealth are united, and combined together into one coherent living body. This *is the
foul that gives form, life, and unity*, to the common-wealth: fiom hence the feveral members
have their mutual influence, fympathy, and connexion and therefore, when the *legiflative* is
Broken, or *diffolved*, diffolution and death follows:
for the *effence and union of the fociety* confifting in
having one will, the legiflative, when once eftablifhed by the majority, has the declaring, and
as it were keeping of that will The *conftitution
of the legiflative* is the firft and fundamental act
of fociety, whereby provifion is made for the
continuation of their union, under the direction of
perfons, and bonds of laws, made by perfons
authorized thereunto, by the confent and appointment of the people, without which no one
man, or number of men, amongft them, can
have authority of making laws that fhall be
binding to the reft. When any one, or more,
fhall take upon them to make laws, whom the
people have not appointed fo to do, they make
laws without authority, which the people are
not

not therefore bound to obey; by which means they come again to be out of fubjection, and may conftitute to themfelves a *new legiflative,* as they think beft, being in full liberty to refift the force of thofe, who without authority would impofe any thing upon them. Every one is at the difpofure of his own will, when thofe who had, by the delegation of the fociety, the declaring of the public will, are excluded from it, and others ufurp the place, who have no fuch authority or delegation

§ 213 This being ufually brought about by fuch in the commonwealth who mifufe the power they have, it is hard to confider it aright, and know at whofe door to lay it, without knowing the form of government in which it happens. Let us fuppofe then the legiflative placed in the concurrence of three diftinct perfons

1. A fingle hereditary perfon, having the conftant, fupreme, executive power, and with it the power of convoking and diffolving the other two within certain periods of time

2 An affembly of hereditary nobility.

3. An affembly of reprefentatives chofen, *pro tempore,* by the people Such a form of government fuppofed, it is evident,

§ 214. *Firft,* That when fuch a fingle perfon, or prince, fets up his own arbitrary will in place of the laws, which are the will of the fociety, declared by the legiflative, then the *legiflative is changed ·* for that being in effect the legiflative, whofe rules and laws are put in execution, and required to be obeyed; when other laws are fet up, and other rules pretended, and inforced, than what the legiflative, conftituted by the fociety, have enacted, it is plain that the *legiflative is changed.* Whoever introduces new laws, not
being

being thereunto authorized by the fundamental appointment of the fociety, or fubveits the old, difowns and overturns the power by which they were made, and fo fets up a *new legiflative*.

§. 215. *Secondly*, When the prince hinders the legiflative from affembling in its due time, or from acting freely, purfuant to thofe ends for which it was conftituted, the *legiflative is altered:* for it is not a certain number of men, no, nor their meeting, unlefs they have alfo freedom of debating, and leifure of perfecting, what is for the good of the fociety, wherein the legiflative confifts when thefe are taken away or altered, fo as to deprive the fociety of the due exercife of their power, the *legiflative* is truly altered, for it is not names that conftitute governments, but the ufe and exercife of thofe powers that were intended to accompany them ; fo that he, who takes away the freedom, or hinders the acting of the legiflative in its due feafons, in effect takes *away the legiflative*, and *puts an end to the government*.

§. 216. *Thirdly*, When, by the arbitrary power of the prince, the electors, or ways of election, are altered, without the confent, and contrary to the common intereft of the people, there alfo the *legiflative is altered* for, if others than thofe whom the fociety hath authorized thereunto, do chufe, or in another way than what the fociety hath prefcribed, thofe chofen are not the legiflative appointed by the people

§ 217. *Fourthly*, The delivery alfo of the people into the fubjection of a foreign power, either by the prince, or by the legiflative, is certainly a *change of the legiflative*, and fo a *diffolution of the government* for the end why people entered into fociety being to be preferved one intire,

free,

free, independent society, to be governed by its own laws; this is lost, whenever they are given up into the power of another

§ 218 Why, in such a constitution as this, the *dissolution of the government* in these cases is to be imputed to the prince, is evident, because he, having the force, treasure and offices of the state to employ, and often persuading himself, or being flattered by others, that as supreme magistrate he is uncapable of controul, he alone is in a condition to make great advances toward such changes, under pretence of lawful authority, and has it in his hands to terrify or suppress opposers, as factious, seditious, and enemies to the government whereas no other part of the legiflative, or people, is capable by themselves to attempt any alteration of the legiflative, without open and visible rebellion, apt enough to be taken notice of, which, when it prevails, produces effects very little different from foreign conquest Besides, the prince in such a form of government, having the power of dissolving the other parts of the legiflative, and thereby rendering them private persons, they can never in opposition to him, or without his concurrence, alter the legiflative by a law, his confent being necessary to give any of their decrees that fanction But yet, so far as the other parts of the legiflative any way contribute to any attempt upon the government, and do either promote, or not, what lies in them, hinder such defigns, they are guilty, and partake in this, which is certainly the greatest crime men can be guilty of one towards another

§ 219 There is one way more whereby such a government may be diffolved, and that is, when he who has the supreme executive power, neglects and abandons that charge, so that the laws already

already made can no longer be put in execution
This is demonftratively to reduce all to anarchy,
and fo effectually *to diffolve the government* for
laws not being made for themfelves, but to be,
by their execution, the bonds of the fociety, to
keep every part of the body politic in its due
place and function; when that totally ceafes, the
government vifibly *ceafes,* and the people become
a confufed multitude, without order or connexion.
Where there is no longer the adminiftration of
juftice, for the fecuring of men's rights, nor any
remaining power within the community to direct
the force, or provide for the neceffities of the
public, there certainly is *no government left.*
Where the laws cannot be executed, it is all one
as if there were no laws, and a government
without laws, is, I fuppofe, a myftery in politics,
unconceivable to human capacity, and inconfiftent with human fociety

§ 220. In thefe and the like cafes, *when the
government is diffolved,* the people are at liberty
to provide for themfelves, by erecting a new legiflative, differing from the other, by the change
of perfons, or form, or both, as they fhall find
it moft for their fafety and good for the *fociety*
can never, by the fault of another, lofe the native and original right it has to preferve itfelf,
which can only be done by a fettled legiflative,
and a fair and impartial execution of the laws
made by it But the ftate of mankind is not fo
miferable that they are not capable of ufing this
remedy, till it be too late to look for any. To
tell the *people* they *may provide for themfelves,* by
erecting a new legiflative, when by oppreffion,
artifice, or being delivered over to a foreign power, their old one is gone, is only to tell them,
they may expect relief when it is too late, and
the

the evil is paft cure. This is in effect no more
than to bid them firft be flaves, and then to take
care of their liberty; and when their chains are
on, tell them, they may act like freemen This,
if barely fo, is rather mockery than relief; and
men can never be fecure from tyranny, if there
be no means to efcape it till they are perfectly
under it : and therefore it is, that they have not
only a right to get out of it, but to prevent it.

§ 221 There is therefore, fecondly, another
way whereby *governments are diffolved*, and that
is, when the legiflative, or the prince, either of
them, act contrary to their truft.

Firft, The *legiflative acts againft the truft* re-
pofed in them, when they endeavour to invade
the property of the fubject, and to make themfelves, or any part of the community, mafters,
or arbitrary difpofers of the lives, liberties, or
fortunes of the people

§. 222. The reafon why men enter into fociety,
is the prefervation of their property; and the
end why they chufe and authorize a legiflative,
is, that there may be laws made, and rules fet,
as guards and fences to the properties of all the
members of the fociety, to limit the power, and
moderate the dominion, of every part and member of the fociety · for fince it can never be fuppofed to be the will of the fociety, that the
legiflative fhould have a power to deftroy that
which every one defigns to fecure, by entering
into fociety, and for which the people fubmitted
themfelves to legiflators of their own making;
whenever the *legiflators endeavour to take away,
and deftroy the property of the people,* or to reduce
them to flavery under arbitrary power, they put
themfelves into a ftate of war with the people,
who are thereupon abfolved from any farther obedience,

dience, and are left to the common refuge, which God hath provided for all men, against force and violence. Whenfoever therefore the *legiflative* shall tranfgrefs this fundamental rule of fociety; and either by ambition, fear, folly or corruption, *endeavour to grasp* themfelves, *or put into the hands of any other, an absolute power* over the lives, liberties, and eftates of the people; by this breach of truft they *forfeit the power* the people had put into their hands for quite contrary ends, and it devolves to the people, who have a right to refume their original liberty, and, by the eftablifhment of a new legiflative, (fuch as they fhall think fit) provide for their own fafety and fecurity, which is the end for which they are in fociety What I have faid here, concerning the legiflative in general, holds true alfo concerning the fupreme executor, who having a double truft put in him, both to have a part in the legiflative, and the fupreme execution of the law, acts againft both, when he goes about to fet up his own arbitrary will as the law of the fociety. He *acts* alfo *contrary to his truft*, when he either employs the force, treafure, and offices of the fo-ciety, to corrupt the *reprefentatives*, and gain them to his purpofes; or openly pre-engages the *electors*, and prefcribes to their choice, fuch, whom he has, by follicitations, threats, promifes, or otherwife, won to his defigns, and employs them to bring in fuch, who have promifed before-hand what to vote, and what to enact Thus to regulate candidates and electors, and new-mo-del the ways of election, what is it but to cut up the government by the roots, and poifon the very fountain of public fecurity? for the people hav-ing referved to themfelves the choice of their *reprefentatives*, as the fence to their properties,

P   could

could do it for no other end, but that they might always be freely chosen, and so chosen, freely act, and advise, as the necessity of the commonwealth, and the public good should, upon examination, and mature debate, be judged to require. This, those who give their votes before they hear the debate, and have weighed the reasons on all sides, are not capable of doing. To prepare such an assembly as this, and endeavour to set up the declared abettors of his own will, for the true *representatives* of the people, and the law-makers of the society, is certainly as great a *breach of trust*, and as perfectly a declaration of a design to subvert the government, as is possible to be met with To which, if one shall add rewards and punishments visibly employed to the same end, and all the arts of perverted law made use of, to take off and destroy all that stand in the way of such a design, and will not comply and consent to betray the liberties of their country, it will be past doubt what is doing. What power they ought to have in the society, who thus employ it contrary to the trust went along with it in its first institution, is easy to determine ; and one cannot but see, that he, who has once attempted any such thing as this, cannot any longer be trusted

§ 223 To this perhaps it will be said, that the people being ignorant, and always discontented, to lay the foundation of government in the unsteady opinion and uncertain humour of the people, is to expose it to certain ruin ; and *no government will be able long to subsist,* if the people may set up a new legislative, whenever they take offence at the old one To this I answer, Quite the contrary People are not so easily got out of their old forms, as some are apt to suggest.

geſt. They are hardly to be prevailed with to amend the acknowledged faults in the frame they have been accuſtomed to And if there be any original defects, or adventitious ones introduced by time, or corruption, it is not an eaſy thing to get them changed, even when all the world ſees there is an opportunity for it. This ſlowneſs and averſion in the people to quit their old conſtitutions, has, in the many revolutions which have been ſeen in this kingdom, in this and former ages, ſtill kept us to, or, after ſome interval of fruitleſs attempts, ſtill brought us back again to our old legiſlative of king, lords and commons: and whatever provocations have made the crown be taken from ſome of our princes heads, they never carried the people ſo far as to place it in another line

§ 224 But it will be ſaid, this *hypotheſis* lays a *ferment for* frequent *rebellion.* To which I anſwer,

Firſt, No more than any other *hypotheſis :* for when the people are made miſerable, and find themſelves *expoſed to the ill uſage of arbitrary power,* cry up their governors, as much as you will, for ſons of *Jupiter* ; let them be ſacred and divine, deſcended, or authorized from heaven ; give them out for whom or what you pleaſe, the ſame will happen *The people generally ill treated,* and contrary to right, will be ready upon any occaſion to eaſe themſelves of a burden that ſits heavy upon them They will wiſh, and ſeek for the opportunity, which in the change, weakneſs and accidents of human affairs, ſeldom delays long to offer itſelf He muſt have lived but a little while in the world, who has not ſeen examples of this in his time ; and he muſt have

read

read very little, who cannot produce examples of it in all forts of governments in the world.

§. 225 *Secondly,* I anfwer, fuch *revolutions happen* not upon every little mifmanagement in public affairs *Great miftakes* in the ruling part, many wrong and inconvenient laws, and all the *flips* of human frailty, will be *borne by the people* without mutiny or murmur But if a long train of abufes, prevarications and artifices, all tending the fame way, make the defign vifible to the people, and they cannot but feel what they lie under, and fee whither they are going, it is not to be wondered, that they fhould then rouze themfelves, and endeavour to put the rule into fuch hands which may fecure to them the ends for which government was at firft erected, and without which, ancient names, and fpecious forms, are fo far from being better, that they are much worfe, than the ftate of nature, or pure anarchy; the inconveniencies being all as great and as near, but the remedy farther off and more difficult.

§ 226. *Thirdly,* I anfwer, that *this doctrine* of a power in the people of providing for their fafety a-new, by a new legiflative, when their legiflators have acted contrary to their truft, by invading their property, is *the beft fence againft rebellion,* and the probableft means to hinder it. for *rebellion* being an oppofition, not to perfons, but authority, which is founded only in the conftitutions and laws of the government; thofe, whoever they be, who by force break through, and by force juftify their violation of them, are truly and properly *rebels* for when men, by entering into fociety and civil-government, have excluded force, and introduced laws for the prefervation of property, peace, and unity amongft
themfelves,

themfelves, thofe who fet up force again in oppofition to the laws, do *rebellare*, that is, bring
back again the ftate of war, and are properly rebels which they who are in power, (by the
pretence they have to authority, the temptation
of force they have in their hands, and the flattery of thofe about them) being likelieft to do ;
the propereft way to prevent the evil, is to fhew
them the danger and injuftice of it, who are under the greateft temptation to run into it

§. 227 In both the fore-mentioned cafes, when
either the legiflative is changed, or the legiflators
act contrary to the end for which they were conftituted, thofe who are guilty are *guilty of rebellion* for if any one by force takes away the
eftablifhed legiflative of any fociety, and the laws
by them made, purfuant to their truft, he thereby takes away the umpirage, which every one
had confented to, for a peaceable decifion of all
their controverfies, and a bar to the ftate of war
amongft them. They, who remove, or change
the legiflative, take away this decifive power,
which no body can have, but by the appointment and confent of the people , and fo deftroying the authority which the people did, and no
body elfe can fet up, and introducing a power
which the people hath not authorized, they actually *introduce a ftate of war*, which is that of
force without authority and thus, by removing
the legiflative eftablifhed by the fociety, (in
whofe decifions the people acquiefced and united
as to that of their own will) they untie the knot,
and *expofe the people a-new to the ftate of war*.
And if thofe, who by force take away the legiflative, are *rebels*, the *legiflators* themfelves, as
has been fhewn, can be no lefs efteemed fo ;
when they, who were fet up for the protection,

and

and prefervation of the people, their liberties and properties, fhall by force invade and endeavour to take them away, and fo they putting themfelves into a ftate of war with thofe who made them the protectors and guardians of their peace, are properly, and with the greateft aggravation, *rebellantes*, rebels.

§ 228. But if they, who fay *it lays a foundation for rebellion*, mean that it may occafion civil wars, or inteftine broils, to tell the people they are abfolved from obedience when illegal attempts are made upon their liberties or properties, and may oppofe the unlawful violence of thofe who were their magiftrates, when they invade their properties contrary to the truft put in them, and that therefore this doctrine is not to be allowed, being fo deftructive to the peace of the world. they may as well fay, upon the fame ground, that honeft men may not oppofe robbers or pirates, becaufe this may occafion diforder or bloodfhed   If any *mifchief* come in fuch cafes, it is not to be charged upon him who defends his own right, but *on him that invades* his neighbours.

If the innocent honeft man muft quietly quit all he has, for peace fake, to him who will lay violent hands upon it, I defire it may be confidered, what a kind of peace there will be in the world, which confifts only in violence and rapine; and which is to be maintained only for the benefit of robbers and oppreffors.   Who would not think it an admirable peace betwixt the mighty and the mean, when the lamb, without refiftance, yielded his throat to be torn by the imperious wolf? *Polyphemus*'s den gives us a perfect pattern of fuch a peace, and fuch a government, wherein *Ulyffes* and his companions had nothing to do, but quietly to fuffer themfelves to be devoured.

voured. And no doubt *Ulysses*, who was a prudent man, preached up *passive obedience*, and exhorted them to a quiet submission, by representing to them of what concernment peace was to mankind; and by shewing the inconveniences might happen, if they should offer to resist *Polyphemus*, who had now the power over them

§. 229. The end of government is the good of mankind, and which is *best for mankind*, that the people should be always exposed to the boundless will of tyranny, or that the rulers, should be sometimes liable to be opposed, when they grow exorbitant in the use of their power, and employ it for the destruction, and not the preservation of the properties of their people?

§. 230. Nor let any one say, that mischief can arise from hence, as often as it shall please a busy head, or turbulent spirit, to desire the alteration of the government. It is true, such men may stir, whenever they please, but it will be only to their own just ruin and perdition: for till the mischief be grown general, and the ill designs of the rulers become visible, or their attempts sensible to the greater part, the people, who are more disposed to suffer than right themselves by resistance, are not apt to stir. The examples of particular injustice, or oppression of here and there an unfortunate man, moves them not But if they universally have a persuasion, grounded upon manifest evidence, that designs are carrying on against their liberties, and the general course and tendency of things cannot but give them strong suspicions of the evil intention of their governors, who is to be blamed for it? Who can help it, if they, who might avoid it, bring themselves into this suspicion? Are the people to be blamed, if they have the sense of rational crea-

P 4

tures, and can think of things no otherwise than as they find and feel them? And is it not rather *their fault,* who put things into such a posture, that they would not have them thought to be as they are? I grant, that the pride, ambition, and turbulency of private men have sometimes caused great disorders in common-wealths, and factions have been fatal to states and kingdoms. But whether *the mischief* hath *oftener* begun *in the peoples wantonnefs,* and a desire to cast off the lawful authority of their rulers, or *in the rulers infolence,* and endeavours to get and exercise an arbitrary power over their people; whether oppression, or disobedience, gave the first rise to the disorder, I leave it to impartial history to determine This I am sure, whoever, either ruler or subject, by force goes about to invade the rights of either prince or people, and lays the foundation for *overturning* the constitution and frame of *any just government,* is highly guilty of the greatest crime, I think, a man is capable of, being to answer for all those mischiefs of blood, rapine, and desolation, which the breaking to pieces of governments bring on a country And he who does it, is justly to be esteemed the common enemy and pest of mankind, and is to be treated accordingly

§ 231. That *subjects* or *foreigners,* attempting by force on the properties of any people, may be *resisted* with force, is agreed on all hands. But that *magistrates,* doing the same thing may be *resisted,* hath of late been denied as if those who had the greatest privileges and advantages by the law, had thereby a power to break those laws, by which alone they were set in a better place than their brethren whereas their offence is thereby the greater, both as being ungrateful

for

for the greater fhare they have by the law, and breaking alfo that truft, which is put into their hands by their brethren.

§. 232. Whofever ufes *force without right*, as every one does in fociety, who does it without law, puts himfelf into a *ftate of war* with thofe againft whom he fo ufes it, and in that ftate all former ties are cancelled, all other rights ceafe, and every one has a right to defend himfelf, and *to refift the aggreffor*. This is fo evident, that *Barclay* himfelf, that great affertor of the power and facrednefs of kings, is forced to confefs, That it is lawful for the people, in fome cafes, to *refift* their king; and that too in a chapter, wherein he pretends to fhew, that the divine law fhuts up the people from all manner of rebellion. Whereby it is evident, even, by his own doctrine, that, fince they may in fome cafes *refift*, all refifting of *princes* is not rebellion His words are thefe. *Quod fiquis dicat, Ergone populus tyrannicæ crudelitati & furori jugulum femper præbebit? Ergone multitudo civitates fuas fame, ferro, & flammâ vaftari, feque, conjuges, & liberos fortunæ ludibrio & tyranni libidini exponi, inque omnia vitæ pericula omnefque miferias & moleftias á rege deduci patientur? Num illis quod omni animantium generi eft á naturâ tributum, denegari debet, ut fe vim vi repellant, fefeq; ab injuriâ tueantur? Huic breviter refponfum fit, Populo univerfo negari deferfionem, quæ juris naturalis eft, neque ultionem quæ præter naturam eft adverfus regem concedi debere. Qua-propter fi rex non in fingulares tantum perfonas aliquod privatum odium exerceat, fed corpus etiam reipublicæ, cujus ipfe caput eft, i e totum populum, vel infignem aliquam ejus partem immani & intolerandâ fævitiâ feu tyrannide divexet; populo, quidem hoc cafu refiftendi*

P 5

ac

ac tuendi se ab injuriâ poteſtas competit, ſed tuendi se tantum, non enim in principem invadendi & reſtituendæ injuriæ illatæ, non recedendi à debitâ reverentia propter acceptam injuriam Præſentem denique impetum propulſandi non vim præteritam ulciſcendi jus habet. Horum enim alterum à naturâ eſt, ut vitam ſcilicet corpuſque tueamur Alterum vero contra naturam, ut inferior de ſuperiori ſuppli-cium etiam ſumat. Quod itaque populis malum, an-tequam factum ſit, impedire poteſt, ne fiat, poſtquam factum eſt, in regem authorem ſceleris vindicare non poteſt. populus igitur hoc ampliùs quam privatus quiſpiam habet : quod huic, vel ipſis adverſariis ju-dicibus, excepto Buchanano, nullum niſi in patientia remedium ſupereſt. Cùm ille ſi intolerabilis tyrannus eſt (modicum enim ferre omnino debet) reſiſtere cum reverentiâ poſſit, Barclay contra Monarchom. l. III. c. 8.

In *Engliſh* thus.

§. 233. *But if any one ſhould aſk, Muſt the peo-ple then always lay themſelves open to the cruelty and rage of tyranny? Muſt they ſee their cities pilla-ged, and laid in aſhes, their wives and children ex-poſed to the tyrant's luſt and fury, and themſelves and families reduced by their king to ruin, and all the miſeries of want and oppreſſion, and yet ſit ſtill? Muſt n en alone be debarred the common privilege of oppoſing force with force, which nature allows ſo freely to all other creatures for their preſervation from injury? I anſwer · Self-defence is a part of the law of nature ; nor can it be denied the commu-nity, even againſt the king himſelf: but to revenge themſelves upon him, muſt by no means be allowed them ; it being not agreeable to that law. Where-fore if the king ſhall ſhew an hatred, not only to*
ſome

some particular persons, but sets himself against the body of the common-wealth, whereof he is the head, and shall, with intolerable ill usage, cruelly tyrannize over the whole, or a considerable part of the people, in this case the people have a right to resist and defend themselves from injury but it must be with this caution, that they only defend themselves, but do not attack their prince they may repair the damages received, but not for any provocation exceed the bounds of due reverence and respect. They may repulse the present attempt, but must not revenge past violences for it is natural for us to defend life and limb, but that an inferior should punish a superior, is against nature The mischief which is designed them, the people may prevent before it be done; but when it is done, they must not revenge it on the king, though author of the villany This therefore is the privilege of the people in general, above what any private person hath, that particular men are allowed by our adversaries themselves (Buchanan *only excepted) to have no other remedy but patience; but the body of the people may with respect resist intolerable tyranny; for when it is but moderate, they ought to endure it.*

§ 234 Thus far that great advocate of monarchical power allows of *resistance*

§. 235 It is true, he has annexed two limitations to it, to no purpose :

First, He says, it must be with reverence

Secondly, It must be without retribution, or punishment; and the reason he gives is, *because an inferior cannot punish a superior.*

First, How to *resist force without striking again,* or how to *strike with reverence,* will need some skill to make intelligible He that shall oppose an assault only with a shield to receive the blows, or in any more respectful posture, without
a sword

a fword in his hand, to abate the confidence and force of the affailant, will quickly be at an end of his *refiftance*, and will find fuch a defence ferve only to draw on himfelf the worfe ufage. This is as ridiculous a way of *refifting*, as *Juvenal* thought it of fighting, *ubi tu pulfas, ego vapulo tantum* And the fuccefs of the combat will be unavoidably the fame he there defcribes it:

——*Libertas pauperis hæc eft.*
Pulfatus rogat, & pugnis concifus, adorat,
Ut liceat paucis cum dentibus inde reverti.

This will always be the event of fuch an imaginary *refiftance*, where men may not ftrike again. He therefore *who may refift, muft be allowed to ftrike.* And then let our author, or any body elfe, join a knock on the head, or a cut on the face, with as much *reverence* and *refpect* as he thinks fit. He that can reconcile blows and reverence, may, for ought I know, defire for his pains, a civil, refpectful cudgeling where-ever he can meet with it.

Secondly, As to his fecond, *An inferior cannot punifh a fuperior*, that is true, generally fpeaking, whilft he is his fuperior But to refift force with force, being *the ftate of war* that *levels the parties*, cancels all former relation of reverence, refpect, and *fuperiority* · and then the odds that remains, is, that he, who oppofes the unjuft aggreffor, has th s *fuperiarity* over him, that he has a right, when he prevails, to punifh the offender, both for the breach of the peace, and all the evils that followed upon it *Barclay* therefore, in another place, more coherently to himfelf, denies it to be lawful to *refift* a king in any cafe But he there affigns two cafes, whereby a king may un-king himfelf His words are,

Quid

Quid ergo, nulline casus incidere possunt quibus populo sese erigere atque in regem impotentius dominantem arma capere & invadere jure suo suâque authoritate liceat? Nulli certe quamdiu rex manet Semper enim ex divinis id obstat, Regem honorificato; & qui potestati resistit, Dei ordinationi resistit· *non aliàs igitur in eum populo potestas est quam si id committat propter quod ipso jure rex esse definat Tunc enim se ipse principatu exuit atque in privatis constituit liber· hoc modo populus & superior efficitur, reverso ad eum si jure illo quod ante regem inauguratum in interregno habuit. At sunt paucorum generum commissa ejusmodi quæ hunc effectum pariunt At ego cum plurima animo perlustrem, duo tantum invenio, duos, inquam, casus quibus rex ipso facto ex rege non regem se facit & omni honore & dignitate regali atque in subditos potestate destituit; quorum etiam meminit* Winzerus *Horum unus est, Si regnum disperdat, quemadmodum de Nerone fertur, quod is nempe senatum populumque Romanum, atque adeo urbem ipsam ferro flammaque vastare, ac novas sibi sedes quærere decrevisset. Et de Caligula, quod palam denunciarit se neque civem neque principem senatui amplius fore, inque animo habuerit interempto utriusque ordinis electissimo quoque* Alexandriam *commigrare, ac ut populum uno ictu interimeret, unam ei cervicem optavit. Talia cum rex aliquis meditatur & molitur serio, omnem regnandi curam & animum illico abjicit, ac proinde imperium in subditos amittit, ut dominus servi pro derelicto habiti dominium*

§. 236 *Alter casus est, Si rex in alicujus clientelem se contulit, ac regnum quod liberum à majoribus & populo traditum accepit, alienæ ditioni mancipavit. Nam tunc quamvis forte non eâ mente id agit populo plane ut incommodet: tamen quia quod præcipuum est regiæ dignitatis amisit, ut summus scilicet*

cet

cet in regno secundum Deum sit, & solo Deo inferior,
atque populum etiam totum ignorantem vel invitum,
cujus libertatem sartam & tectam conservare debuit, ut
alterius gentis ditionem & potestatem dedidit, hâc
velut quadam regni ab alienatione effecit, ut nec quod
ipse in regno imperium habuit retineat, nec in eum
cui collatum voluit, juris quicquam transferat, at-
que ita eo facto liberum jam & suæ potestatis popu-
lum relinquit, cujus rei exemplum unum annales
Scotici suppeditant. Barclay contra Monarchom.
l. iii. c. 16.

Which in *English* runs thus.

§. 237. *What then, can there no case happen,*
wherein the people may of right, and by their own
authority, help themselves, take arms, and set upon
their king, imperiously domineering over them? None
at all, whilst he remains a king. Honour the king,
and he that resists the power, resists the ordinance
of God, *divine oracles that will never permit it.*
The people therefore can never come by a power over
him, unless he does something that makes him cease
to be a king for then he divests himself of his crown
and dignity, and returns to the state of a private
man, and the people become free and superior, the
power which they had in the interregnum, *before*
they crowned him king, devolving to them again.
But there are but few miscarriages which bring the
matter to this state After considering it well on all
sides, I can find but two Two cases there are, I
say, whereby a king, ipso facto, *becomes no king,*
and loses all power and regal authority over his peo-
ple; which are also taken notice of by Winzerus.

The first is, If he endeavour to overturn the go-
vernment, that is, if he have a purpose and design to
ruin the kingdom and common-wealth, as it is re-
corded.

corded of Nero, *that he refolved to cut off the fenate and people of* Rome, *lay the city wafte with fire and fword, and then remove to fome other place.* And of Caligula, *that he openly declared, that he would be no longer a head to the people or fenate, and and that he had it in his thoughts to cut off the worthieft men of both ranks, and then retire to* Alexandria *and he wifht that the people had but one neck, that he might difpatch them all at a blow.* Such defigns as thefe, *when any king harbours in his thoughts, and ferioufly promotes, he immediately gives up all care and thought of the common-wealth; and confequeutly forfeits the power of governing his fubjects, as a mafter does the dominion over his flaves whom he hath abandoned*

§. 238 *The other cafe is, When a king makes himfelf the dependent of another, and fubjects his kingdom which his anceftors left him, and the people put free into his hands, to the dominion of another for however perhaps it may not be his intention to prejudice the people; yet becaufe he has hereby loft the principal part of regal dignity,* viz. *to be next and immediately under God, fupreme in his kingdom; and alfo becaufe he betrayed or forced his people, whofe liberty he ought to have carefully preferved, into the power and dominion of a foreign nation. By this, as it were, alienation of his kingdom, he himfelf lofes the power he had in it before, without transferring any the leaft right to thofe on whom he would have beftowed it; and fo by this act fets the people free, and leaves them at their own difpofal* One example of this is to be found in the Scotch *Annals*

§. 239 In thefe cafes *Barclay*, the great champion of abfolute monarchy, is forced to allow, that a king may be *refifted*, and *ceafes to be a king*. That is, in fhort, not to multiply cafes, in whatfoever he has *no authority*, there he is *no king*, and

may

may be *refisted* · for wherefoever the *authority ceafes, the king ceafes too,* and becomes like other men who have no authority And thefe two cafes he inftances in, differ little from thofe above mentioned, to be deftructive to governments, only that he has omitted the principle from which his doctrine flows, and that is, the breach of truft, in not preferving the form of government agreed on, and in rot intending the end of government itfelf, which is the public good and prefervation of property When a king has dethroned himfelf, and put himfelf in a ftate of war with his people, what fhall hinder them from profecuting him who is no king as they would any other man, who has put himfelf into a ftate of war with them; *Barclay,* and thofe of his opinion, would do well to tell us This farther I defire may be taken notice of out of *Barclay,* that he fays, *The mifchief that is defigned them, the people may prevent before it be done* whereby he allows *refiftance* when tyranny is but in defign. *Such defigns as thefe* (fays he) *when any king harbours in his thoughts and ferioufly promotes, he immediately gives up all care and thought of the common-wealth*; fo that, according to him, the neglect of the public good is to be taken as an evidence of fuch *defign,* or at leaft for a fufficient caufe of *refiftance* And the reafon of all, he gives in thefe words, *Becaufe he betrayed or forced his people, whofe liberty he ought carefully to have preferved* What he adds, *into the power and dominion of a foreign nation,* fignifies nothing, the fault and forfeiture lying in the lofs of their *liberty,* which he *ought to have preferved,* and not in any diftinction of the perfons to whofe dominion they were fubjected The peoples right is equally invaded, and their liberty loft, whether they are made flaves to any of

their

their own, or a *foreign nation* ; and in this lies the injury, and againſt this only have they the right of defence   And there are inſtances to be found in all countries, which ſhew, that it is not the change of nations in the perſons of their governors, but the change of government, that gives the offence   *Bilſon*, a biſhop of our church, and a great ſtickler for the power and prerogative of princes, does, if I miſtake not, in his treatiſe of *Chriſtian ſubjection*, acknowledge, that *princes may forfeit their power*, and their title to the obedience of their ſubjects , and if there needed authority in a caſe where reaſon is ſo plain, I I could ſend my reader to *Bracton*, *Forteſcue*, and the author of *the Mirrour*, and others, writers that cannot be ſuſpected to be ignorant of our government, or enemies to it   But I thought *Hooker* alone might be enough to ſatisfy thoſe men, who relying on him for their eccleſiaſtical polity, are by a ſtrange fate carried to deny thoſe principles upon which he builds it   Whether they are herein made the tools of cunninger workmen, to pull down their own fabric, they were beſt look. This I am ſure, their civil policy is ſo new, ſo dangerous, and ſo deſtructive to both rulers and people, that as former ages never could bear the broaching of it, ſo it may be hoped, thoſe to come, redeemed from the impoſitions of theſe *Egyptian* under-taſk-maſters, will abhor the memory of ſuch ſervile flatterers, who, whilſt it ſeemed to ſerve their turn, reſolved all government into abſolute tyranny, and would have all men born to, what their mean ſouls fitted them for, ſlavery.

§. 240 Here it is like, the common queſtion will be made, *Who ſhall be judge*, whether the prince or legiſlative act contrary to their truſt ?
This,

This, perhaps, ill-affected and factious men may spread amongst the people, when the prince only makes use of his due prerogative. To this I reply, *The people shall be judge*; for who shall be *judge* whether his trustee or deputy acts well, and according to the trust reposed in him, but he who deputes him, and must, by having deputed him, have still a power to discard him, when he fails in his trust? If this be reasonable in particular cases of private men, why should it be otherwise in that of the greatest moment, where the welfare of millions is concerned, and also where the evil, if not prevented, is greater, and the redress very difficult, dear and dangerous?

§. 141 But farther, this question, (*Who shall be judge?*) cannot mean, that there is no judge at all · for where there is no judicature on earth, to decide controversies amongst men, *God* in heaven is *judge*. He alone, it is true, is judge of the right. But *every man is judge* for himself, as in all other cases, so in this, whether another hath put himself into a state of war with him, and whether he should appeal to the Supreme Judge, as *Jeptha* did.

§ 242 If a controversy arise betwixt a prince and some of the people, in a matter where the law is silent, or doubtful, and the thing be of great consequence, I should think the proper *umpire*, in such a case, should be the body of the *people* · for in cases where the prince hath a trust reposed in him, and is dispensed from the common ordinary rules of the law ; there, if any men find themselves aggrieved, and think the prince acts contrary to, or beyond that trust, who so proper to *judge* as the body of the *people*, (who, at first, lodged that trust in him) how far they meant it should extend? But if the prince, or

whoever

whoever they be in the administration, decline that way of determination, the appeal then lies no where but to heaven; force between either persons, who have no known superior on earth, or which permits no appeal to a judge on earth, being properly a state of war, wherein the appeal lies only to heaven, and in that state the *injured party must judge* for himself, when he will think fit to make use of that appeal, and put himself upon it.

§ 243 To conclude, The *power that every individual gave the society*, when he entered into it, can never revert to the individuals again, as long as the society lasts, but will always remain in the community; because without this there can be no community, no common-wealth, which is contrary to the original agreement: so also when the society hath placed the legislative in any assembly of men, to continue in them and their successors, with direction and authority for providing such successors, *the legislative can never revert to the people* whilst that government lasts; because having provided a legislative power to continue for ever, they have given up their political power to the legislative, and cannot resume it But if they have set limits to the duration of their legislative, and made this supreme power in any person, or assembly, only temporary, or else, when by the miscarriages of those in authority, it is forfeited, upon the forfeiture, or at the determination of the time set, *it reverts to the society*, and the people have a right to act as supreme, and continue the legislative in themselves, or erect a new form, or under the old form place it in new hands, as they think good.

F I N I S

Lightning Source UK Ltd.
Milton Keynes UK
UKHW051900231022
410976UK00003B/9